Edited by
ANDREAS MARNEROS

Late-Onset Mental Disorders

The Potsdam Conference

GASKELL

© The Royal College of Psychiatrists 1999

Gaskell is an imprint and registered trade mark of the Royal College of Psychiatrists, 17 Belgrave Square, London SW1X 8PG

British Library Cataloguing-in-Publication Data
A catalogue record for this book is available from
the British Library.
ISBN 1-901242-26-9

Distributed in North America
by American Psychiatric Press, Inc.
ISBN 0-88048-596-5

Printed in Great Britain by Bell & Bain Limited, Glasgow

Contents

Contributors

J. Angst, Zurich University Psychiatric Hospital, Lenggstraße 31, PO Box 68, 8029 Zürich, Switzerland

Robert C. Baldwin, Consultant in Old Age Psychiatry, York House, Manchester Royal Infirmary, Oxford Road, Manchester M13 9BX, UK

Mathias Berger, Department of Psychiatry and Psychotherapy, Albert-Ludwigs-University Freiburg, Germany, Hauptstraße 5, 79104 Freiburg, Germany

G. E. Berrios, Department of Psychiatry, University of Cambridge, Addenbrooke's Hospital, Box 189, Hills Road, Cambridge CB2 2QQ, UK

Dan G. Blazer, J. P. Gibbons Professor of Psychiatry and Behavioral Sciences, Dean of Medical Education, Duke University Medical Center, Durham, NC 27710, USA

Alistair Burns, Professor of Old Age Psychiatry, Department of Psychiatry, University of Manchester, Withington Hospital, Manchester M20 8LR, UK

Ulrich M. Fleischmann, University of Applied Sciences, Salvator Straße 7, 97074 Würzburg, Germany

H.-J. Gertz, Psychiatrische Klinik und Poliklinik der Freien Universität Berlin, Eschenalle 3, D-14050 Berlin, Germany

H. Helmchen, Psychiatrische Klinik und Poliklinik der Freien Universität Berlin, Eschenalle 3, D-14050 Berlin, Germany

Dilip V. Jeste, Professor of Psychiatry and Neurosciences, Director, Geriatric Psychiatry Clinical Research Center, University of California, San Diego, San Diego VA Medical Center, 116A-1, 3350 La Jolla Village Drive, San Diego, CA 92161, USA

M. Linden, Psychiatrische Klinik und Poliklinik der Freien Universität Berlin, Eschenalle 3, D-14050 Berlin, Germany

Andreas Marneros, Department of Psychiatry and Psychotherapy, Martin-Luther University, Halle-Wittenberg, D-06097 Halle, Germany

H.-J. Möller, Psychiatric Hospital, Ludwig-Maximilians University, Nußbaumstraße 7, D-80336 Munich, Germany

G. D. Pearlson, Department of Psychiatry, Johns Hopkins University School of Medicine, 1915 East Medicine Street, Baltimore, MD 21205, USA

F. M. Reischies, Psychiatrische Klinik und Poliklinik der Freien Universität Berlin, Eschenalle 3, D-14050 Berlin, Germany

Laura L. Symonds, Department of Psychiatry, Michigan State University, A235-B East Fee Hall, East Lansing, MI 48824-1316, USA

Ulrich Voderholzer, Department of Psychiatry and Psychotherapy, Albert-Ludwigs-University Freiburg, Germany, Hauptstraße 5, 79104 Freiburg, Germany

T. Wernicke, Neurologische Abteilung, Krankenhaus Hennigsdorf, Marwitzer Straße 91, D–16761 Hennigsdorf, Germany

H. Wolf, Psychiatrische Klinik und Poliklinik der Freien Universität Berlin, Eschenalle 3, D-14050 Berlin, Germany

Preface

Hippocrates considered that some types of mental illness relate to the age of human beings: some were more common in youth, some only in boys and some only in girls; some of them were common in middle age and some of them in old age. Nevertheless, the study of late-onset mental disorder began only in the 19th century, as Berrios points out. As well as dementia, considered to be a late mental disorder *par excellence*, other disorders such as depression ('involutional melancholia') and paranoid states ('paraphrenia' and 'presbyophrenia' or 'late schizophrenia', *Spätschizophrenie*) came to be of interest. Kraepelin thought that the depression of old age was a distinct entity, differing essentially from melancholia of other ages. But he changed his opinion after the results of the research of his pupil Dreyfuss – and included old-age depression as a common melancholia; the wisdom of this correction was proved by the work of Angst in 1966, which showed that there are no significant clinical or prognostic differences between late-onset and early-onset depression. Delusional depression in the elderly is not uncommon but the symptoms seem to be similar to those of non-delusional depression. Is there, then, anything special about old-age depression?

After the description of M. Bleuler of a late type of schizophrenia, many authors tried to find the differences between early-onset and late-onset schizophrenia. What are these differences? Are there any atypical features of late-onset schizophrenia? How frequent are late-onset schizoaffective disorders?

Besides questions concerning depression, dementia and psychosis, this book also looks at sleep and sleep disturbances in the elderly, anxiety, special features of pharmacological treatment, and psychological processes.

The above questions were discussed during the 'Potsdam Conference on Late-Onset Mental Disorders' in September 1996, from which the contributions to this book have been drawn. We thank Bayer AG, Germany, especially Dr Uschi von der Osten, for sponsoring the conference.

Andreas Marneros
Halle-Wittenberg, Germany

1 Late-onset mental disorders: a conceptual history*

G. E. BERRIOS

The category 'late-onset mental disorder' (LOMD) names a group of psychiatric conditions whose only common feature is their (putatively) higher *incidence* in middle and old age. Because of its question-begging nature – LOMD is based on categories of ageing which themselves remain qualitative and social (i.e. are products of a particular historical period, and not rooted in stable biological notions) – LOMD per se is of little help in the diagnosis of the very conditions it purports to cluster (although it must be conceded that progress in the molecular biology of ageing may, after all, generate stable categories). The view that certain diseases are related to certain periods of life appeared only in the second half of the 19th century. Rather surprisingly, its history has not yet been told.

The historical appearance of LOMD can hence be seen as a discovery or as a construction. According to the former view, LOMD 'existed' in nature before it was 'found' by a 'discoverer', that is, noticed that some mental disorders start only after a certain age; according to the latter view, LOMD results from a change in social concepts (e.g. people's ages) and in the way diseases relate to the general category 'time'. The specific needs of psychiatry (as a medical subject) require that an intermediate position be taken, namely, one in which the final definition of disease results from an interaction between biological signals and changing concepts.

To understand this interaction, however, the clinician and the historian must pay close attention to the enunciative context in which a category first appeared. This advice is not always followed. Indeed, clinicians have the habit of *detaching* concepts from their social frames

---

*This chapter is dedicated to Professor Dr Christoph Mundt, whose scholarly comments on the lecture on which the chapter is based drew my attention to Goethe and *Sturm und Drang*.

1

and reifying them into eternal objects. Hence, younger colleagues can be forgiven for believing that such concepts (and their referents) have 'always been there'. To clinicians, it may matter little where these categories come from, for the legal framework in which they work, and the mandarins of the profession, tell them what to do. There is a widespread belief that clinical categories are discoveries (i.e. not creations) that have emerged from research programmes run by clever people, and that professions are divided into 'elite' and 'troops', and the job of the latter is to carry out the views of the former, a practice now rebaptised 'evidence-based medicine'.

The 'discovery' view is assumed in questions such as: when was LOMD (or hallucinations or delusions, etc.) actually 'noticed', by whom, and what was the first publication containing the new category? To be answered these questions need to be reformulated and context-ualised; that is, a great deal must first be learned about 'historical facts', 'documents', and the definition of LOMD. For example, should one consider that the notion of LOMD was established if documentary evidence shows that, back in 1835, some vicar (who was, say, a naturalist of some repute) stated in his Sunday sermon on 'growing older' that some diseases affected only his elderly parishioners? Or perhaps should one wait until 1868, when Charcot uttered a similar view in his lectures on 'Les maladies des vieillards' (Charcot, 1868)? In this chapter, the historical hypothesis is tested that LOMD was *constructed* to deal with specific conceptual, clinical and social problems which first appeared during the second half of the 19th century. (It follows that LOMD should not be expected to stay for good; indeed, its survival depends upon whether the 'problems' remain extant in the 21st century.)

The problems in question concerned the need to *understand* medical categories in terms of new developmental and evolutionary views of human life (Canguilhem *et al*, 1962), and to *map* specific diseases on to people in middle age or later, a group that was rapidly increasing in the second half of the 19th century. The formulation of the concept of LOMD was facilitated by evolution theory (Bowler, 1983; Nye, 1984; Kohn, 1985; Ritvo, 1990), degeneration theory (Dallemagne, 1895; Mairet & Ardin-Delteil, 1907; Genil-Perrin, 1913; Pick, 1989; Dowbiggin, 1991), developmental psychology (Baldwin, 1903; Richards, 1987) and ethology (Romanes, 1888; Morgan, 1903; Darwin, 1904), as well as by the deeper presence of a 'historicist' frame of reference (Mannheim, 1924) which relentlessly pushed into all disciplines the concept of 'time' (on the general concept and history of time see Fraisse, 1967; Toulmin & Goodfield, 1967; Fraser, 1989; Pomian, 1990; and on time in biology see Jacob, 1974). As will be shown below, alienism in general, and the concept of mental illness in particular, were very responsive to this change. This can be illustrated by comparing the concept of *mental illness* among alienists of the first half of the 19th century (e.g. Haslam, Pinel, Esquirol, Bayle, Georget, Prichard, or Feuchtersleben) with that of 'transitional' writers such as Griesinger and Flemming, and then with writers from the second half of the century (e.g. Kahlbaum, Magnan, Kraft-Ebbing, Chaslin, Freud and Kraepelin), among whom the concept of time had been fully incorporated. In order to understand how the notion of mental illness was 'temporalised' (and how this, in turn, led to the concept of LOMD), a brief analysis must be made of the Western concept of mental disorder before such changes took place. This is not a simple task for there was no European consensus. Should one follow the choice of their contemporaries, of later generations, of current historians? Is one to choose writers whose views reflected orthodoxy or fresh views? Should German views be preferred to French ones during this period or vice versa? Once again, we shall choose alienists who seemed aware of the larger ideological issues in their time.

Views on mental illness

Views on mental illness at the beginning of the 19th century roughly fell into three categories. First, there were 'medical' views of the type sponsored by, say, William Cullen (and still defended internationally by his disciples, e.g. Pinel in France, Chiarugi in Italy, Rush in the USA, and Pargeter or Haslam in England), which attempted to naturalise mental disorder by assimilating it into the general classi-fication of diseases. However odd the nosological *content* of classes such as 'neurosis' or 'vesania' may now sound, the medical 'approach' remains intelligible to the 20th-century mind. This is because for each 'condition' Cullen listed main manifestations, physiopathology and natural history (López-Piñero, 1983).

The second, 'metaphysical' category includes, for example, the views on mental disorder of Kant and Heinroth. Although superficially built upon a more botanico taxonomy, in terms of both their nosological content and aetiology, these views deviate from the medical approach. For example, Kant's ideas on mental disorder are based less on clinical observation than on a deductive system based on his own philosophy of mind (Kant, 1974, pp. 73–86). Likewise, Heinroth's (1975) definition sets him apart from Cullen:

> "madness is a disease of the reason and not of the soul, but it originates from the passions within the soul. When free of passion, we may err and be deceived, but the free spirit soon turns away

from error and deception; but madness is a truly diseased state of the spirit since it originates from a diseased state of the soul." (p. 16)

To say that Heinroth believed that "mental illness was the result of sin" (e.g. Alexander & Selesnick, 1966, p. 141) may be a distortion but nonetheless his definition contains moral overtones which set it apart from Cullen and the medical tradition (Marx, 1990; Cauwenbergh, 1991).

The third category includes 'literary' views on mental disorder, as expressed in the work of some great writers of the period (e.g. Lenz, Coleridge, Büchner) (Crighton, 1993). These views are more than 'distortions' of ongoing medical or metaphysical views and can be said to be reflections of a hidden rhetorical tradition which since the Greeks has remained culturally exiled in Western thinking (Conley, 1990; Farrell, 1993). Within this tradition, mental illness is less a 'disease' than an attack on the logos, a breaking through into rational consciousness of powerful Dionysian forces.

These three early approaches have features in common, namely, they were monolithic, atemporal, related mental illness to parts of the body in a *symbolic* sense and held on to the old belief that the 'soul' (mind) could *not* really be diseased.

Monolithic categories

The great clinical 'psychiatric' categories up to, and including, Pinel's are monolithic in that each is based on a more or less fixed form whose elements or components (these cannot yet be called 'symptoms' – see Berrios, 1996) are specific to the disease in question. In Cullen, Kant, Heinroth, Pinel or Büchner there is not yet a theory concerning symptoms – 'visions', 'rage' or 'melancholia' cannot be said to be natural kinds or units of analysis, that is, elements which remain the same regardless of the disease in which they appear. In other words, their theory of disease is not yet based on the view that conditions are but combinations of symptoms.

Atemporality

This feature is of particular importance to the theme of this chapter as the 'temporalisation' of mental disorder which was to occur after the 1850s relates precisely to the loss of this metaphysical quality. Up to the end of the 18th century, mental illness was not considered as *occurring* in real time. Becoming mentally ill entailed not so much acquiring an extra feature by accident, but changing one's essence, one's ontology (in a sense, in the current terminology, that a mental illness is a trait rather than a state). It follows that the concepts of 'acute' and 'chronic' mental disorder did not really exist; indeed, such temporal definitions appeared only after the middle of the 19th century (Lanteri-Laura, 1972, 1986). It also follows that mental disorders were not considered to be related to any age or period of life; and that the notions of remission or recovery were ambiguous, for it was not clear whether a mental illness could actually 'abandon' its host. Emphasis on the concept of 'lucid interval' suggests that it was generally assumed that madness did not go even when, for a while, the patient 'behaved normally'. Analysis of this issue is made difficult by the fact that in the medical literature of the early 19th century the 'relevant' questions are never asked; but mental disorders are often spoken of in the manner of physical disorders and this creates the impression that both were considered as anchored in body processes and hence in time.

Mental illness and the body

The history of the relationship between disease and the body is complex, for it was thought to occur at various levels. Since before the Greeks, the belief had existed that diseases somehow inhabited the body (it would be very wrong, however, to equate such beliefs with current ideas – early beliefs did not include the mediating notion of 'mechanism'). The problem becomes more intractable in relation to 'mental' disorders, where the issue concerns the relationship between *behavioural* anomalies and some 'part' of the body. These relationships were handled by the ancients by means of different models and symbols. To the 20th-century mind, the relevant 'part' is the brain. Why? The answer is likely to be 'It happens to be true', but the force of this reply is less than it sounds. A better answer might be that things 'are true' and 'make sense to us' for we share an epistemological frame and a body of knowledge. This is why it is hard to understand why the ancients chose the heart, stomach, hypochondrium or womb: all we have is their reified claim without sharing their evidential and emotional apparatus. Defining their view of 'location' and 'relationship' (as in 'melancholia resides in the heart') in terms of temporo-spatial co-ordinates or a cause–effect model (respectively) will not do. The ancients (well up to Broussais in the early 19th century, who saw a role for the stomach in the origin of mental illness) were using models of location and relationship unavailable to our minds.

What sort of models might these be? This is not the place to tackle this complex issue but it could be suggested that the type of relationship implied in earlier 'localisations' of mental illness was not temporo-spatial but *symbolic*. Cassirer (1957) called humans 'symbolic animals', that is, animals with the capacity to create symbols; the latter are but 'social signs', signs with the added capacity to be shared and under-stood by a given intellectual or emotional collective (Schlesinger, 1909). Thus, for earlier writers to say that hysterical behaviour was placed in the womb, melancholia in the heart, memory in the posterior ventricle or neurosis in the stomach, was to say that certain behaviours were related to the ongoing meaning of those parts of the body, *not* to say that those parts of the body possessed mechanisms and systems to generate those behaviours or behaviours in general. Such a 'symbolis-ing function' remains equally active in current neurobiological theories of mental illness (except that we see it as the truth). This results from the understandable mirage created by the 'scientific approach'.

Imperviousness of the soul to disease

A confusing and little-known feature of the notion of mental disease before the 19th century is how it related to the 'soul', that is, the question of whether mental illness actually affected this important human attribute. After the 1850s this question was no longer pressing to most alienists, but their earlier counterparts had to consider it. In this regard, writers agreed that the soul was beyond the reach of mental disorder. No doubt the Cartesian separation between body and mind, made on both ontological and epistemological grounds (Carter, 1983), facilitated the view that mental illness fundamentally affected the body machine.

The underlying belief that the soul is untouched by mental illness creates an important problem when comparing successive 'organic' theories of mental disease. Thus, the way in which Thomas Willis or William Battie actually described the relationship between brain changes and mental illness sounds very similar to what Meynert, Wernicke or Goldstein could have said, or for that matter what a current neuroscientist would say. There are, however, important differences, for the assumption of the unity and imperviousness of the soul was upheld up to the middle of the 19th century. For example, Falret (1864) argued against monomania and faculty psychology on the basis of the unity of the mind: "nothing could be more false and contrary to observation, both in the normal and the mentally ill patient, than a fragmentation of the human soul into separate components able to function or become ill independently" (pp. 431–432).

Changes in the historical matrix that made late-onset mental disorder possible

To summarise, up to the beginning of the 19th century, the concept of mental illness was characterised by four features: its monolithic nature, atemporality, symbolic relationship to the body, and the assumption of the unity and imperviousness of the soul. These principles shaped the way in which mental disorders were defined and classified. For example:

(a) there was no clear concept of *full* cure;
(b) the notion of 'lucid interval' became a *deus ex machina* which explained remissions and other changes in the course of the disease;
(c) the notion of 'partial insanity' could not be clarified and caused persistent problems among clinicians and philosophers;
(d) diagnosis was mostly based on cross-sectional observation (indeed, longitudinal observation would have added very little to diagnostic decision making);
(e) there was no conception of acute and chronic forms of mental disorder;
(f) no *special* mental disorders were recognised that were related to childhood or old age.

Comparison of the concepts of mental illness entertained, say, in 1800 and 1900 shows major differences. One concerns what can be called its 'temporalisation': by the end of the 19th century mental illness was considered as a 'process' occurring within a time frame. Thus, by the 1890s alienists had a clear view of acute and chronic disorders, diseases of childhood and old age, and remission. To understand these changes, three (interrelated) historical frames must be briefly explored: historicism, romanticism, and evolutionism.

Historicism

Historicism (*Historismus*) is the collective name, coined around the middle of the 19th century, for a group of ideologies whose common denominator is reflected in Dilthey's famous phrase: *Was der Mensch sei, erfährt er nur durch der Geschichte* (what man is, is what he experiences through history), that is, that history is the only fundamental frame within which man and his creations can be understood (Lee & Beck, 1953–54). Thus historicism, as an epistemological attitude, developed out of an awareness of the past, of the fact that things then were different from what they are now. This led to searching both for commonalities or continuities (the search for stability) and for differences, singularities and the uniqueness of specific events. Historicism can be said to be more akin to the latter interest. To some writers, the attribute of 'historicity' (*Geschichtlichkeit*) pertained only to human beings (e.g. Ortega's dictum that 'man has no nature but history') (i.e. anthropological historicism); to others, nature itself and the cosmos also fall under the aegis of historicism (i.e. cosmological historicism).

In a way, its breath depends upon its function: to some, historicism should have only an epistemological function, to provide a conceptual frame (or episteme) in relation to which everything should be interpreted; to others, it has a deeper function, namely, to be a creative force (in this sense, historicism has an ontological role). Of these, 'anthropological' and 'epistemological' historicism are relevant to the temporalisation of mental disease. Epistemological historicism is said to lead to cultural relativism, namely, the view that there can be no proper understanding of the past as each period operates according to a logic which is now gone forever. This was the problem that Troeltsch, the great Heidelberg theologian, tried to solve by saying that historicism only causes epistemological problems when the past is broken up into fragments or artificial periods (centuries, epochs, epistemes, etc.) (Rand, 1964). But if the past is allowed to flow unbroken then human beings will share general values and categories which allow them to understand other historical contexts. Troeltsch's approach belongs to the group of solutions that appeal to principles which exist *sub specie æternitatis*. These invariants or constants would remain the same even if real epistemological breaks do take place in the flow of history. This problem also underlies the debate on whether definitions of mental illness are dependent on the period in which they were created, and the claims that they are only sociopolitical constructs, that there is no progress or improvement from one period to the next, and hence current views are no better than any from the past. To deal with this argument recent writers have resorted to using transhistorical and transcultural invariants that might underlie the notion of disease (e.g. neurobiology) (Berrios, 1994a).

The 19th century can be said to be the century of historicism *par excellence*, and its view that all events are transfixed by the arrows of time (Jacob, 1974), that all things have a beginning, a development, and an end, and that there is 'progress' (Gruner, 1981), either intermittently or in a sort of 'chain of being' (Lovejoy, 1960), have affected all disciplines, including the natural sciences, biology and medicine.

Romanticism

Romanticism is the name for a broad and elusive intellectual orientation that blossomed in Western culture in the late 18th to the mid-19th century, and which first and foremost was based on a rejection of the enlightenment principles of order, calm, harmony, balance, idealisation, rationality, and physical materialism. Romanticism emphasised the individual, the subjective, the irrational, the imaginative, the spontaneous, the emotional, the visionary and the transcendental, and its influence was felt in the arts, medicine, and historiography. Its sources of knowledge were the beauty of nature and the deep exploration of the self and personality.

This interest in individuality was reflected in an undue curiosity in the genius, the hero, the weird, the diseased and the exceptional, and a preference for emotions over reason, senses over intellect. The imagination was considered the entry point to a new transcendent experience and spiritual truth. In the event, it was inevitable that the artist (and to a certain extent the mentally ill) was to become the romantic prototype of the human being, and that romanticism was to develop an exaggerated interest in medieval tales, folklore and national culture (see Lovejoy, 1924). The tenets and literary products of the German movement generically called *Sturm und Drang* (storm and stress) are a good example of romanticism, in that its exaltation of nature, feeling, and human individualism sought to overthrow the enlightenment cult of rationalism.

Romanticism had a marked effect on European science, including neurosciences in England (Jacyna, 1984).

Evolutionism

Mannheim (1924) once stated that "*evolutionism* was the first manifestation of modern *historicism*". Both terms, however, have changed in meaning since the 18th century (Bowler, 1975). *Ab initio*, evolution did not necessarily imply development in 'time', as for example was the case with pre-formationists, who employed the term to describe the "unfolding or unrolling of pre-existing parts of the embryo" (already created by God) (Roger, 1963). During the first half of the 19th century, Lyell (1832) first linked 'evolutionism' to 'time' when commenting upon Lamarck's (1984) theory of 'variation and progression'; indeed, Lyell (1863) believed that the French naturalist had "introduced the element of time into the definition of a species". Although tempting, it is historically inaccurate to postulate a neat progression of evolutionary ideas from geology to biology, and then to sociology, psychology and history:

"The *simultaneous* emergence of evolutionary theories in biology and sociology in the nineteenth century presents an interesting problem in historical interpretation. How were these two types of evolutionary theory related to each other?" (Greene, 1962, p. 419, my emphasis)

Although not the first to suggest that organisms could 'change' (evolve) from generation to generation (Glass *et al*, 1968), Wallace and Darwin were the first to propose a mechanism by means of which such changes accumulated (Kottler, 1985). They suggested that heritable variations occurred in conjunction with a never-ending competition for survival, and that variations favouring survival were automatically preserved. The continued accumulation of variations then resulted in the emergence of new forms. Because the variations that are preserved relate to survival, the survivors are highly adapted to their environment. To this process Wallace and Darwin gave the name 'natural selection'. Earlier writers, such as Lamarck (1988), had been willing to accept the idea of species variation, even though to do so meant denying the doctrine of special creation. But Lamarck believed that at the basis of variation there was an idealised perfecting principle, expressed through the habits and 'willingness' of organisms (Burckhardt, 1977; Jordanova, 1984). The contrast between the romanticism of Lamarck and the objective analysis of Wallace and Darwin highlights the revolutionary change brought about by the concept of natural selection. Interestingly, Darwin (1883) went on to apply similar principles to the development of the mind and behaviour.

Soon enough, ideas of *social change* (Schoenwald, 1965) were also recast in a Darwinian framework. This led to the excesses of the so-called social Darwinists (Burrow, 1970). However, the concept of social change is important in itself. Already fully adopted during the 18th century, it included the idea of: decline, or *degeneration*; *cyclical* change – a pattern of subsequent and recurring phases of growth and decline; and continuous *progress*. All three ideas included a temporal parameter and became fashionable in different historical periods. For example, degeneration was fashionable after the work of Morel (1857); indeed, its final effect on European thought (Pick, 1989; Soloway, 1990; Liégeois, 1991) and on the notion of mental illness (Genil-Perrin, 1913) has not yet been fully estimated.

The idea of progress

The idea of progress, a key to understand 19th-century theories of social evolution, also implied a form of inevitable evolutionism along one line of development (directional change with time) and governed by natural laws. Herbert Spencer's theory of social evolution linked social and biological evolution, and required a strong concept of progress (Burrow, 1970). According to Spencer, biological organisms and human societies followed the same universal, natural evolutionary law (1890, p. 380): "a change from a state of relatively indefinite, incoherent, homogeneity to a state of relatively definite, coherent, heterogeneity". In other words, like biological entities or the cosmos itself, societies grew in size, became more complex, saw their parts specialised into different functions, becoming, in the end, more interdependent. A similar view was taken of the functions of the mind, and such models were to be the frameworks within which the new concept of mental illness in its association with periods of life and evolution was to develop. For example, there is little doubt that J. H. Jackson was influenced by evolutionary ideas. The question remains, however, whether these came from H. Spencer (Denton, 1921) (as he himself and others since have claimed) (e.g. Smith, 1982) or from other writers such as J. Fisk and W. K. Clifford (Berrios, 1985). Be that as it may, and for reasons which remain to be studied, Jackson had little influence on ideas of mental illness in Britain (Berrios, 1977). Things are further complicated by the fact that Jackson was also influenced by Richard Owen (e.g. Jackson, 1863) whose idealist and religious approach to the issue of anatomical specialisation led him to reject natural selection and evolutionary theory (Owen, 1894). It was otherwise in the Continent, particularly France, where Jackson instigated the work of Th. Ribot (Delay, 1957) and P. Janet (Rouart, 1950); in Italy, C. Lombroso was also inspired by Jacksonian ideas (Nicasi, 1989).

Evolution and psychological theory

To explore the origin of LOMD, this section will briefly explore the way in which *time* was introduced into definitions of behaviour and psychological development in general and mental illness in particular, in other words, the 'temporalisation' (Lovejoy, 1960) of psychiatry.

In fact, far more attention has been given to the effect of evolutionary theory on psychology (Richards, 1987) than on psychiatry, particularly on the concept of mental illness. Darwin started this trend with his influential book on the expression of emotions in man and animals (Darwin, 1904; Browne, 1985a,b). (Darwin actually quotes the work of clinicians such as Gratiolet, Holland, Crichton Brown and Maudsley, but these references mainly concern their ideas on psychology or the occasional case report, such as the case of anger in an 'insane lady', transcribed on p. 253.) Soon enough his ideas were generalised to all aspects of psychology, and as Gruber (1974) has written:

> "[Darwin's] concern for the adaptive significance of all biological functions helped in the construction of a functional psychology focused on the interplay and utility of psychological processes, as compared with a structural psychology preoccupied with the discovery of the static elements of experience." (p. 219)

Concerning the significance of evolutionary psychology for psychology, Mackenzie (1976) has rightly distinguished *methodological* from *substantive* or theoretical aspects. To gather evidence, Darwin and his followers used *methods* and a logic of demonstration that differed from what other natural sciences, such as physics, were using at the time. After Darwin, psychology became thus more observational and naturalistic. But in doing so, as Hodos & Campbell (1969) suggested, psychology risked what they called the '*scala naturae* fallacy', namely that:

> "comparative psychologists failed to distinguish between data obtained from living representatives of a common evolutionary lineage and data from animals which represent diverse lineages ... only the former can provide a foundation for inference about the phylogenetic development of behavioural patterns." (p. 337)

The *substantial* significance of evolutionism for psychology has been beautifully summarised by Canguilhem (1975):

> "It is certainly right that Darwin has the merit of having substituted the idea that animals are faulty men with the idea that man is an animal that has evolved towards perfection. Thus, animality became valued in itself for it was important to explain humanity; and studying animals became a positive act, something valuable in itself." (p. 125)

And it is certainly true that during the last quarter of the 19th century animal behaviour became an important area of research, particularly in so-called comparative and developmental psychology, where the predominant issues were the behavioural *continuity* between animals and man (Romanes, 1888), the need of some sort of teleological or *purposive* dimension to behavioural adaptation (Baldwin, 1903), and the 'emergence' of *consciousness* in the *scala naturae* (Morgan, 1903). Thus, influenced by Darwin's *Descent of Man* (1883), Romanes (1888) attacked the compromise expressed by the French Quatrefages that "no valid distinction between man and brute can be drawn in respect of rationality or intellect", except in "the faculties of conscience and religion" (p. 17). Baldwin, the great American developmental psychologist, wrote thus on the issue of 'utility' in the process of behavioural adaptation: "passages, indeed, might be quoted abundantly from Darwin , which show what his doctrine of organic adaptation probably would have been if he had developed it" (1903, p. 247, footnote 1). Morgan is usually credited with rejecting "the view that teleology is operative throughout the living world" (Goudge, 1967, p. 392); however, as Costall (1993, p. 113) suggests, "Morgan was convinced that the behaviour of animals and humans could only be treated in intentionalist terms". Morgan's concept of 'emergent' has undergone a revival in the current concept of 'supervenience' (Kim, 1993).

Time, evolution and mental illness

How did evolutionary theory influence the concept of mental illness in Europe during the second half of the 19th century? This question, not yet answered by historians, is crucial to understand the origins of LOMD. For unless it is known how mental illness was 'temporalised' (i.e. considered to be a process which occurred in time), and how its relationship to behaviours already present in lower species was envisaged (e.g. were mental disorders perhaps vestigial or atavistic conducts which had reappeared in human beings?), it would be difficult to explain why, sometime towards the end of the 19th century, alienists began to believe that some of these disorders were more likely to occur in certain periods of life (indeed, the concept of 'period of life' itself can be understood in biological terms only against a temporal dimension).

France

Next to nothing has been written on either of these questions. One possible reason for this dearth of research may be that Darwinian ideas were being resisted in the very country where the most important work on the new models of mental illness was being carried out, namely, France (Conry, 1974):

> "by the mid-nineteenth century a thoroughly French tradition of evolutionary *transformisme* existed which accounted for the nature of species across a broad spectrum of biological disciplines. This tradition, based on the hereditary theories of the eighteenth-century naturalist Jean-Baptiste Lamarck, was so well rooted in the life sciences that Darwinian evolution, first introduced in the 1860s,

failed to gain a firm foothold in French scientific thought." (Nye, 1984, p. 119).

Dowbiggin (1991) also agrees with this view: "Darwin's theory of natural selection made little headway in French science because of the fierce chauvinistic allegiance to the transformist ideas of the eighteenth century naturalist Jean Baptiste Lamarck" (p. 148).

There is also little doubt that Lamarckism was rampant in French medicine and alienism:

> "I would suggest that one reason anthropologists, criminologists, psychiatrists and other human scientists so readily and contentedly incorporated a Lamarckian construction of transformism into their vision of both research and therapeutic possibilities was that the tradition of anthropological medicine had nurtured and carried within it language and concepts that had intimate affinities with Lamarck's thought." (Williams, 1994, p. 270)

According to Dowbiggin (1991, p. 148), it can also be found built into Morelian degeneration theory: "Degeneracy theory was the medical counterpart to Lamarckian biology. It explained how physical and mental disorders could result over several generations from accommodation to a pathogenic environment".

For years after the publication of *Origins*, Darwin was not mentioned in the psychiatric literature. Indeed, the first, and indirect, mention of Darwinian evolutionism I have found in the *Annales Médico-Psychologiques*, the most important psychiatric periodical of the period, is one by Achilles Foville (1869), who in his section on 'Anthropology' asked the question (which many in France thought was central to Darwinism) "is it possible that man descends from the apes?" A few years earlier, and in the same journal, Professor Chauvet (1863) had published his lecture on comparative psychology. He quoted Pardies, Buillier, Daniel and Bonjeaut on *l'âme des bêtes* and Leroy on *la perfectibilité des animaux*, and even Flourens on *l'intelligence des animaux*, but in vain will the reader look for any reference to evolutionary theory.

It is less clear whether the same hidden temporal dimension of Lamarckian transformism also inspired Charcot (1868) to deliver his famous lectures on the diseases of old age. (Although it must be added that, surprisingly, important monographs on Charcot have neglected to study this early book – see, for example, Bannour, 1992; Thuillier, 1993; Goetz *et al*, 1995; Gasser, 1995.) Lamarck does not appear in the list of conceptual antecedents that the great man thought important to his doctrine. In addition to the classics, Charcot mentions Hourmann and Dechambre, Prus, Canstatt, Durand-Fardel, Mettenheimer, and so on. On the strength of this list, his approach would seem to be purely observational and empirical. However, as Charcot (1868) himself recognised, Canstatt had written his book under the spell of romanticism and *Naturphilosophie* (Canstatt's interest in the diseases of the elderly may have been influenced by the 'historicist' dimension of *Naturphilosophie*):

> "Unfortunately this work, dated 1839, was composed under the influence of Schelling's teaching which reigned so long at the other side of the Rhine, and which bears the ambitious name of the philosophy of Nature. Imagination holds an immense place in it at the expense of impartial and positive observation." (p. 26)

For a study of the role of Charcot in the science of geriatrics see Lellouch (1992).

Germany

It has been suggested that Kraepelin borrowed his views on a 'longitudinal' model of mental illness from Kahlbaum (Bumke, 1928; Boor, 1954; Berrios & Hauser, 1988; Hoff, 1994), and the idea of using 'outcome' as a classificatory criterion from:

> "Hagen in Erlangen [who] had already pointed out the necessity to clarify the final course of illness in the cases observed. He pointed out that one should collect cases with the same final state, as far as the mental disease was concerned, and then investigate what developments had led to this particular final state." (Kraepelin, 1987, p.60)

Kahlbaum

What were Kahlbaum's views in relation to the incorporation of time into the concept of mental illness? There is agreement in the literature that in addition to the traditional criteria of symptoms, cause and pathological anatomy, Kahlbaum sought to investigate the course (*Verlauf*) of the disease (Katzenstein, 1963, p. 35; see also Boor, 1954). Indeed, in his classical book on *Die Gruppirung der psychischen Krankheiten*, Kahlbaum (1863) touched both upon the issues of course and time.

Karl Ludwig Kahlbaum (1828–99) remains one of the great figures of 19th-century psychiatry (Leibbrand & Wettley, 1969). Jaspers (1948) dated the change in Kraepelin's intellectual fortune to the time when he "engaged in the fruitful use of Kahlbaum's ideas" (p. 474). In his *Memoirs*, Kraepelin (1987) wrote that as a young man he always kept "Kahlbaum's and Hecker's ideas in mind" (p. 59 – Kraepelin was referring here to Ewald Hecker (1843–1909), a collaborator of Kahlbaum whose 1871 paper on hebephrenia, a putative variety of early-onset schizophrenia, was to become one of the classic publications of the late 19th century). Recent historians have also considered Kahlbaum's ideas as essential to the development of the Kraepelinian system (e.g. Bercherie, 1980, pp. 106–112; Pichot, 1984, pp. 36–37; Hoff, 1995, pp. 262–263; Berrios & Hauser, 1995, pp. 261–279), and as the origins of an important psychiatric school in Germany (Harms, 1962; Lanczik & Elliger, 1988). In spite of this work, much research yet needs to be done to understand the intellectual and social origins of Kahlbaum's ideas.

Kahlbaum was both a practical clinician and a great thinker. From the perspective of the 20th century, his views on the definition of mental disorder may prove to be his most lasting contribution. Influenced by the French nosologists of the first half of the 19th century (Lanczik, 1992), he came to believe early in his career that cross-sectional presentations of disease were misleading and that the variable 'time' needed to be incorporated into the definition of mental disease. This meant that the 'course' of the disease, as identified in longitudinal observation of patient cohorts, was the key to defining its boundaries. Kraepelin (1918) put this well:

> "[he was] the first to remark upon the need to combine the condition of the patient, his temporary symptoms, and the basic pattern of the disease. Disease in one and the same patient may change often and in various ways and confound treatment. Identical or similar symptoms may accompany different diseases. Hence their nature may only be revealed in their course and termination and, in some instances, at post-mortem. On the basis of these, Kahlbaum outlined a *second pattern* of illness similar to that of general paralysis which also included mental and physical features: an example of this was catatonia, where 'muscular tension' provided [Kahlbaum] with a basis to compare it with general paralysis. Although this view is open to criticism, Kahlbaum should be credited for suggesting a new approach. Attention to the progress and termination of mental disorders, information obtained from autopsies, and extra knowledge into causes have made possible the combination of clinical evidence and diagnosis, on the basis of symptom pattern."

To argue for the concept of 'course', Kahlbaum (1863) starts with the crucial point that, in psychiatry, diseases have a *longer* tempo than in the rest of medicine:

> "Influenced by the fact that in general medicine diseases tend to have a short course, [it has been] neglected to observe that the processes of psychical life take longer to evolve, and hence that in the long term mental disorders change their presentation. This

means that reducing the number of diseases or even resisting their fractionation in the face of multiple presentations, may not help to produce stable classifications. [The only solution, therefore, is to] differentiate between 'habitual form' and 'course' of a disease.... The habitual forms included in the classifications analysed earlier were based on averages of clinical phenomena tending to occur simultaneously. The ones I have proposed are based upon elements occurring *successively*, and where the diagnosis is based on the course of the disease." (pp. 137–182)

The use of the 'time' criterion is well illustrated in Kahlbaum's proposal for a classification which included four categories: *neophrenia, paraphrenia, vecordia* and *vesania*. The neophrenias are acquired before (*innata*) or soon after birth (*morbosa*) (*Seelenstörung, vor, mit oder nach der Geburt in den ersten Jahren erworben*); and the paraphrenias are conditions occurring in the transition between biological stages of development (*im Anschluss an eine Uebergangsperiode der biologischen Entwicklung entstehend*): *paraphrenia hebetica* will thus occur during puberty, and *paraphrenia senilis* in old age (Kahlbaum, 1863, pp. 133–136). *Paraphrenia senilis* can thus be considered as the first clear-cut LOMD to be described in the medical literature. This is *not* because it concerned the claim that a disease may be associated with a particular age of life for, as Charcot (1868) once remarked, Hippocrates, following a particular theory of climates, had already "considered different ages as the seasons of life, and consequently attributed to them special maladies" (pp. 8–9). It is because the *rationale* provided by Kahlbaum included the concept of biological stage of development. (On the question of the conceptual basis of earlier approaches to geriatric medicine, see Berrios, 1991, 1994b).

Kraepelin

Darwinism, degenerationism, positivism, the 19th-century theory of natural kinds and the developing eugenic ideology uncomfortably converge in the work of Emil Kraepelin. Much work needs to be done on the intellectual biography of this giant of psychiatry to ascertain the extent to which he was fully aware of his role in bringing into psychiatry a number of (not always compatible) 19th-century ideologies. His sources are varied. On the one hand, and throughout his life, Kraepelin was under the influence of his elder brother Karl, a famous botanist and zoologist:

"With his distinct talent for scientific matters, my brother Karl had a considerable influence over me during my entire youth. He introduced me to botany at an early age and later encouraged my

enthusiasm for zoology, the doctrine of evolution and chemistry....
I even made a childish attempt to write a presentation on the history
of evolution according to the Kant–Laplace theory." (Kraepelin,
1987, p. 2)

In the various international trips they made together to collect
specimens, Emil seems to have acted as Karl's assistant. It is highly
likely that he was thus introduced to 19th-century models of taxonomy
and to the crucial concepts of natural selection, species and natural
kind.

On the other hand, as Hoff (1995) has indicated, while at
Leipzig and Würzburg, Kraepelin read the British empiricists,
and also de la Mettrie, Kant, Schopenhauer, Avenarius, and so on.
Hoff (1995) also makes the point that, although Kraepelin rarely
wrote on matters philosophical, three trends – realism, psychophysical
parallelism and experimentalism – are readily identifiable in his
work. As Genil-Perrin (1913) had already noticed, criteria based on
degeneration theory are also central to some of the clinical
categories included in Kraepelin's classification, such as constitutional
depression, obsessions, impulsive insanity and sexual perversions.
His views on the degeneration of the human race were also important
to his strong stance against alcoholism and crime, and in favour
of eugenics (Engstrom, 1991).

In the work of Kraepelin, the concept of LOMD reaches a mature
form. He seemed to have been interested in the relationship of certain
conditions to old age:

> "As the 25-year jubilee of the [Heidelberg] clinic was to be
> celebrated in 1903, I planned a large clinical investigation on
> psychoses in the elderly for this occasion. We intended to use
> the observations made on patients over 45 years of age and try
> to put them into groups. I hoped to be able to clarify the question
> of melancholia, late catatonia and paranoid diseases during
> the involution years. I also expected to be able to classify some
> smaller groups of psychoses typical for old age." (Kraepelin,
> 1987, p. 107)

One of these groups was the 'involutional melancholia' group to which
Kraepelin had applied the old observation that "quite a few depressions during old age did not lead to recovery but to dementia and did
not have the generally favourable prognosis of the manic–depressive
diseases" (p. 66). (For a study of Kraepelin's change of mind with
regard to involutional melancholia, and the role of Dreyfus and
Thalbitzer in this affair, see Berrios, 1991.)

Conclusions

The view that certain diseases seem to be related to particular stages of life was already familiar to the Greeks, for example Hippocrates. Based on metaphors borrowed from the concept of 'constitution', and on the cyclical changes of the seasons, this view did not include any reference to a linear, evolutionary or temporalised model of life. The concept of linear time was introduced into biology only during the late 18th century, and was carried into the 19th by a *Zeitgeist* in which romanticism, historicism and eventually evolutionary theory played an important role. Up to this period, the concept of mental illness had been monolithic and atemporal and its relationship to the body conceived in symbolic terms. This meant that concepts such as full remission, cure, and acute and chronic disease had a *different* meaning; indeed, often enough it was believed that there could not really be full recovery, but only 'lucid intervals'. From the point of view of diagnosis, it also meant that a cross-sectional assessment sufficed (on this see Lain-Entralgo, 1961, 1982, on the history of anamnesis, case taking and diagnosis).

The 19th century, particularly after the 1860s, *temporalised* the concept of mental illness. The latter became a state, a *process* stretching in time whose definition, from then on, would require information on *course* and *outcome*. This change started with Kahlbaum and culminated in Kraepelin. The temporalisation of disease also led to the redefinition of the concept of 'period of life' in terms of ontogeny, anatomy and physiology. This meant that the relationship of certain diseases to biological stages of life was to be interpreted not as a *metaphor* but as the result of specific pathological changes. Kahlbaum and Charcot were pioneers in this field, but once again the idea achieved its full development in Kraepelin. However, the concept of period of life (so-called 'climacteric years') has changed since Chéreau's (1875) first classification, and seems to be governed by hidden social variables. If so, these factors will threaten the conceptual and scientific stability of the concept of LOMD for a long time to come.

References

ALEXANDER, F. G. & SELESNICK, S. T. (1966) *The History of Psychiatry.* New York: Harper & Row.

BALDWIN, J. M. (1903) *Mental Development in the Child and the Race* (2nd edn). New York: Macmillan (1st edn, 1894).

BANNOUR, W. (1992) *Jean-Martin Charcot et l'hystérie.* Paris: Métailié.

BERCHERIE, P. (1980) *Les Fondements de la Clinique.* Paris: La Bibliothèque d'Ornicar.

BERRIOS, G. E. (1977) Henri Ey, Jackson et les idées obsédantes. *L'Evolution Psychiatrique,* **42**, 685–699.

—— (1985) Positive and negative symptoms and Jackson: a conceptual history. *Archives of General Psychiatry,* **42**, 95–97.

—— (1991) Affective disorders in old age: a conceptual history. *International Journal of Geriatric Psychiatry,* **6**, 337–346.

—— (1994a) Historiography of mental symptoms and diseases. *History of Psychiatry,* **5**, 175–190.

—— (1994b) A conceptual history in the nineteenth century. In *Principles and Practice of Geriatric Psychiatry* (eds J. M. R. Copeland, M. T. Abou-Saleh & D. G. Blazer), pp. 11–16. Chichester: Wiley.

—— (1996) *The History of Mental Symptoms. Descriptive Psychopathology since the 19th century.* Cambridge: Cambridge University Press.

—— & HAUSER, R. (1988) The early development of Kraepelin's ideas on classification. A conceptual history. *Psychological Medicine,* **18**, 813–821.

—— & —— (1995) Kraepelin. In *History of Clinical Psychiatry* (eds G. E. Berrios & R. Porter), pp. 280–291. London: Athlone Press.

BOOR, W. DE (1954) *Psychiatrische Systematik. Ihre Entwicklung in Deutchland seit Kahlbaum.* Berlin: Springer.

BOWLER, P. J. (1975) The changing meaning of evolution. *Journal of the History of Ideas,* **36**, 95–114.

—— (1983) *Evolution. The History of an Idea.* Revised 1989. Berkeley: University of California Press.

BROWNE, J. (1985a) Darwin and the face of madness. In *The Anatomy of Madness. Vol. I. People and Ideas* (eds W. F. Bynum, R. Porter & M. Shepherd), pp. 151–165. London: Tavistock Publications.

—— (1985b) Darwin and the expression of the emotions. In *The Darwinian Heritage* (ed. D. Kohn), pp. 307–326. Princeton: Princeton University Press.

BUMKE, O. (1928) *Die gegenwärtigen Strömungen in der Psychiatrie* (5th edition). Berlin: Springer.

BURCKHARDT, R. W. (1977) *The Spirit of System: Lamarck and Evolutionary Biology.* Cambridge: MIT Press.

BURROW, J. W. (1970) *Evolution and Society. A Study of Victorian Social Theory.* Cambridge: Cambridge University Press.

CANGUILHEM, G. (1975) *Études d'histoire et de philosophie des sciences.* Paris: Vrin.

——, Lapassade, G., Piquemal, J. & Ulmann, J. (1962) *Du Développement à l'évolution au XIXe siècle.* Paris: Presses Universitaires de France.

CARTER, R. B. (1983) *Descartes' Medical Philosophy. The Organic Solution to the Mind–Body Problem.* Baltimore: Johns Hopkins University Press.

CASSIRER, E. (1957) *The Philosophy of Symbolic Forms. Vol. 3: The Phenomenology of Knowledge.* New Haven: Yale University Press.

CAUWENBERGH, L. (1991) J.C. Heinroth (1773–1843): psychiatrist of the German Romantic era. *History of Psychiatry,* **2**, 365–384.

CHARCOT, J. M. (1868) *Clinical Lectures on Senile and Chronic Diseases* (trans. W. S. Tuke, 1881). London: New Sydenham Society.

CHAUVET, E. (1863) Première leçon d'un course de psychologie comparée. *Annales Médico Psychologiques,* **22**, 157–173.

CHÉREAU, A. (1875) Climatériques ou climactériques (années). In *Dictionnaire Encyclopédique des Sciences Médicales, Vol. 18* (eds A. Dechambre & L. Lereboullet), pp. 122–125. Paris: Masson.

CONLEY, T. M. (1990) *Rhetoric in the European Tradition.* Chicago: University of Chicago Press.

CONRY, I. (1974) *L'Introduction du Darwinisme en France au XIXe siècle.* Paris: Vrin.

COSTALL, A. (1993) How Lloyd Morgan's canon backfired. *Journal of the History of the Behavioral Sciences,* **29**, 113–122.

CRIGHTON, J. L. (1993) *The Portrayal of Madness in Georg Büchner's Lenz and Woyzeck and Some Possible Sources.* PhD Dissertation, University of Leicester.

DALLEMAGNE, J. (1895) *Dégénérés et Déséquilibrés.* Paris: Alcan.

DARWIN, C. (1883) *The Descent of Man* (2nd edn). London: John Murray (1st edn 1874).

——— (1904) *The Expression of the Emotions in Man and Animals* (2nd edn). London: John Murray (1st edn 1872).

DELAY, J. (1957) Jacksonism and the works of Ribot. *Archives of Neurology and Psychiatry,* **78**, 505–515.

DENTON G. B. (1921) Early psychological theories of Herbert Spencer. *American Journal of Psychology,* **32**, 5–15.

DOWBIGGIN, I. (1991) *Inheriting Madness.* Berkeley: University of California Press.

ENGSTROM, E. J. (1991) Emil Kraepelin: psychiatry and public affairs in Wilhelmine Germany. *History of Psychiatry,* **2**, 111–132.

FALRET, J. P. (1864) *Des maladies mentales et des asiles d'aliénés.* Paris: J. P. Baillière.

FARRELL, T. B. (1993) *Norms of Rhetorical Culture.* New Haven: Yale University Press.

FOVILLE, A. (1869) Revue anthropologique. *Annales Médico-Psychologiques,* **27**, 89–103.

FRAISSE, P. (1967) *Psychologie du Temps.* Paris: Presses Universitaires de France.

FRASER, J. T. (ed.) (1989) *Time and Mind. Interdisciplinary Issues.* Madison: International Universities Press.

GASSER, J. (1995) *Aux origines du cerveau moderne. Localisations, langage et mémoire dans l'œuvre de Charcot.* Paris: Fayard.

GENIL-PERRIN, G. (1913) *Histoire des origines et de l'évolution de l'idée de dégénérescence en médicine mentale.* Paris: A. Leclerc.

GLASS, B., TEMKIN, O. & STRAUS, W. L. (1968) *Forerunners of Darwin: 1745–1859.* Baltimore: Johns Hopkins University Press.

GOETZ, C. G., BONDUELLE, M. & GELFAND, T. (1995) *Charcot. Constructing Neurology.* Oxford: Oxford University Press.

GOUDGE, T. A. (1967) Morgan, C Lloyd. In *The Encyclopaedia of Philosophy, Vol. 5* (ed. P. Edwards), pp. 392–393. London: Collier Macmillan.

GREENE, J. C. (1962) Biology and social theory in the nineteenth century. Auguste Comte and Herbert Spencer. In *Critical Problems in the History of Science* (ed. M. Claggett), pp. 419–446. Madison: University of Wisconsin Press.

GRUBER, H. E. (1974) *Darwin on Man.* Revised 1981. Chicago: University of Chicago Press.

GRUNER, R. (1981) Progressivism and historicism. *Clio,* **10**, 279–290.

HARMS, E. (1962) *Origins of Modern Psychiatry.* Springfield: Thomas.

HECKER, E. (1871) Die Hebephrenie. *Virchows Archiv,* **52**, 394–429.

HEINROTH, J. C. (1975) *Textbook of Disturbances of Mental Life* (trans. J. Schmorak). Baltimore: Johns Hopkins University Press (1st German edn 1818).

HODOS, W. & CAMPBELL, C. B. G. (1969) Scala naturae: why there is no theory of comparative psychology. *Psychological Review,* **76**, 337–350.

HOFF, P. (1994) *Emil Kraepelin und die Psychiatrie als klinische Wissenschaft.* Heidelberg: Springer.

——— (1995) Kraepelin. In *History of Clinical Psychiatry* (eds G. E. Berrios & R. Porter), pp. 261–279. London: Athlone Press.

JACKSON, J. H. (1863) *Suggestions for Studying Diseases of the Nervous System on Professor Owen's Vertebrate Theory.* London: Lewis.

JACOB, F. (1974) *The Logic of Living Systems. A History of Heredity.* London: Allen Lane.

JACYNA, L. S. (1984) Principles of general physiology: the comparative dimension to British neuroscience in the 1830s and 1840s. In *Studies in the History of Biology, Vol. 7* (eds W. Coleman & C. Limoges), pp. 47–92. Baltimore: Johns Hopkins University Press.

JASPERS, K. (1948) *Allgemeine Psychopathologie* (5th edn). Berlin: Springer.

JORDANOVA, L. J. (1984) *Lamarck*. Oxford: Oxford University Press.

KAHLBAUM, K. (1863) *Die Gruppirung der psychischen Krankheiten und die Eintheilung der Seelenstörungen. Entwurf einer historische-kritischen Darstellung der bisherigen Eintheilungen und Versuch zur Anbahnung einer empirisch-wissenschaftlichen Grundlage der Psychiatrie als klinischer Disciplin.* Danzig: A.W. Kafemann.

KANT, I. (1974) *Anthropology from a Pragmatic Point of View* (trans. M. J. Gregor). The Hague: Martinus Nijhoff (1st edn 1798).

KATZENSTEIN, R. (1963) *Karl Ludwig Kahlbaum*. Zürich: Juris.

KIM, J. (1993) *Supervenience and Mind*. Cambridge: Cambridge University Press.

KOHN, D. (ed.) (1985) *The Darwinian Heritage*. Princeton: Princeton University Press.

KOTTLER, M. J. (1985) Charles Darwin and Alfred Russel Wallace: two decades of debate over natural selection. In *The Darwinian Heritage* (ed. D. Kohn), pp. 367–432. Princeton: Princeton University Press.

KRAEPELIN, K. (1918) Hundert Jahre Psychiatrie. Ein Beitrag zur Geschichte menschlicher Gesittung. *Zeitschrift der Neurologie*, **38**, 161–275.

—— (1987) *Memoirs*. Heidelberg: Springer.

LAÍN-ENTRALGO, P. (1961) *La Historia Clínica. Historia y Teoría del Relato Patográfico.* Barcelona: Salvat.

—— (1982) *El Diagnóstico Médico. Historia y Teoría*. Barcelona: Salvat.

LAMARCK, J. B. (1984) *Zoological Philosophy*. Chicago: University of Chicago Press.

—— (1988) *Système analytique des connaissances positives de l'homme*. Paris: Presses Universitaires de France (1st edn 1820).

LANCZIK, M. (1992) Karl Ludwig Kahlbaum (1828–1899) and the emergence of psychopathological and nosological research in German psychiatry. *History of Psychiatry*, **3**, 53–58.

—— & ELLIGER, T. (1988) Die Görlitzer Psychiatrische Schule: Von Kahlbaum zu Ziehen. Zur Entwicklung einer systematischen Nosologie in der Kinder- und Jugendpsychiatrie. In *Depression in Kindheit und Jugend* (eds H. J. Friese & G. E. Trott), pp. 40–49. Bern: Huber.

LANTERI-LAURA, G. (1972) La chronicité dans la psychiatrie moderne française. *Annales*, May–June, 548–568.

—— (1986) Acuité et pathologie mentale. *L'Evolution Psychiatrique*, **51**, 403–416.

LEE, D. E. & BECK, R. N. (1953–54) The meaning of historicism. *American Historical Review*, **59**, 568–577.

LEIBBRAND, W. & WETTLEY, A. (1969) *Der Wahnsinn. Geschichte der abendländischen Psychopathologie.* Freiburg: Karl Aber.

LELLOUCH, A. (1992) *Jean Martin Charcot et les Origins de la Gériatrie*. Paris: Payot.

LIÉGEOIS, A. (1991) Hidden philosophy and theology in Morel's theory of degeneration and nosology. *History of Psychiatry*, **2**, 419–428.

LÓPEZ-PIÑERO, J. M. (1983) *Historical Origins of the Concept of Neurosis* (trans. D. Berrios). Cambridge: Cambridge University Press.

LOVEJOY, A. O. (1924) On the discrimination of romanticisms. *Proceedings of the Modern Language Association of America*, **39**, 229–253.

—— (1960) *The Great Chain of Being*. New York: Harper Torchbooks (1st edn 1936).

LYELL, Ch. (1832) *Principles of Geology, Vol. 2*. London: Murray.

—— (1863) *The Antiquity of Man*. 4th edn 1873. London: Murray.

MACKENZIE, B. (1976) Darwinism and positivism as methodological influences on the development of psychology. *Journal of the History of the Behavioral Sciences*, **12**, 330–337.

MAIRET, A. & ARDIN-DELTEIL, P. (1907) *Hérédité et Prédisposition*. Montpellier: Coulet & Fils.

MANNHEIM, K. (1924) Historismus. *Archiv für Socialwissenschaft und Socialpolitik*, **52**, 1–60.

MARX, O. M. (1990) German romantic psychiatry: Part I. *History of Psychiatry*, **1**, 351–382.

MOREL, B. A. (1857) *Traité des dégénérescences physiques intellectuelles et morales de l'espèce humaine.* Paris: Baillière.

MORGAN C. L. (1903) *An Introduction to Comparative Psychology* (2nd edn). London: Walter Scott Publishing.

NICASI, S. (1989) Atavismo: patologia di un ritorno. In *Passioni della mente e della storia* (ed. F. M. Ferro), pp. 363–371. Milano: Pubblicazioni della Università Cattolica del Sacro Cuore.

NYE, R. A. (1984) *Crime, Madness and Politics in Modern France: The Medical Concept of National Decline.* Princeton: Princeton University Press.

OWEN, R. (1894) *The Life of Richard Owen.* Reprinted (1970). Farnborough: Gregg.

PICHOT, P. (1984) *A Century of Psychiatry.* Paris: Dacosta.

PICK, D. (1989) *Faces of Degeneration: A European Disorder, c1848–1918.* Cambridge: Cambridge University Press.

POMIAN, K. (1990) *El Orden del Tiempo.* Madrid: Júcar.

RAND, C. G. (1964) Two meanings of historicism in the writings of Dilthey, Troeltsch and Meinecke. *Journal of the History of Ideas,* **25**, 503–518.

RICHARDS, R. J. (1987) *Darwin and the Emergence of Evolutionary Theories of Mind and Behaviours.* Chicago: University of Chicago Press.

RITVO, L. B. (1990) *Darwin's Influence on Freud. A Tale of Two Sciences.* New Haven, CT: Yale University Press.

ROGER, J. (1963) *Les Sciences de la vie dans la pensée Française du XVIII siècle.* New edn 1993. Paris: Albin Michel.

ROMANES, G. J. (1888) *Mental Evolution in Man. Origin of Human Faculty.* London: Kegan Paul, Trench & Co.

ROUART, J. (1950) Janet et Jackson. *L'Evolution Psychiatrique,* **26**, 484–501.

SCHLESINGER, M. (1909) Die Geschichte des Symbolbegriffs in der Philosophie. *Archiv für Geschichte der Philosophie,* **22**, 49–79.

SCHOENWALD, R. L. (ed.) (1965) *Nineteenth-Century Thought: The Discovery of Change.* Upper Saddle River, Prentice-Hall.

SMITH, C. U. M. (1982) Evolution and the problem of mind: Part I. Herbert Spencer; Part II. John Hughlings Jackson. *Journal of the History of Biology,* **15**, 55–88; 241–262.

SOLOWAY, R. A. (1990) *Demography and Degeneration. Eugenics and the Decline of the Birth rate in Twentieth-Century Britain.* Chapel Hill: University of North Carolina Press.

SPENCER, H. (1890) *First Principles* (5th edn). London: Williams & Northgate.

THUILLIER, J. (1993) *Monsieur Charcot de la Salpêtrière.* Paris: Laffont.

TOULMIN, S. & GOODFIELD, J. (1967) *The Discovery of Time.* London: Penguin.

WILLIAMS, E. A. (1994) *The Physical and the Moral. Anthropology, Physiology and Philosophical Medicine in France 1750–1850.* Cambridge: Cambridge University Press.

2 Epidemiology of mental disorders in old age

H. HELMCHEN, M. LINDEN, F. M. REISCHIES and T. WERNICKE

Life expectancy has steadily increased over the decades – at least in the developed countries. This is due to the decreased mortality rates among not only the newborn but also elderly people. In particular, the life expectancy of people aged over 60 years is increasing steadily (Dinkel, 1992). The consequence is that persons above the age of 80 or even 90 years are no longer rare exceptions but form a growing group in society.

From the psychiatric point of view it is predominantly dementia that impairs the everyday life of old persons (Crimmins et al, 1989; Krämer, 1992). For the entire population above 65 years most estimations yield a prevalence rate of dementia of at least 5% (Kay et al, 1985; Henderson, 1986; Jorm et al, 1988). Differentiated according to age, this rate amounts to 1% in persons of 65 years, then doubles about every five years, to more than 30% in persons above 90 years (Copeland et al, 1976, 1992; Jorm et al, 1987; Hofman et al, 1991; Skoog et al, 1993; Wernicke & Reischies, 1994).

In contrast, reports of the frequency of other psychiatric disorders among those aged over 65 years show much variance. Prevalence rates of moderate and severe depressions vary between 0.7% and 5.4% (Weissman & Myers, 1978; Regier et al, 1988; Blazer, 1989), and of all forms and degrees of clinically relevant depressive disturbances between 11.5% and 26.2% (Kay et al, 1964; Copeland et al, 1987). No definite age trend is reported. The same is reported for schizophrenia, the much lower prevalence rates of which vary between 0.1% (Cooper & Sosna, 1983) and 1.7% in this age group (Kay et al, 1970; Lauter, 1974; Häfner et al, 1991). The prevalence rate of alcohol dependence, at 0.5% for men and 0.05% for women, is considerably lower than in younger age groups (Grant, 1993).

Because many epidemiological investigations are restricted to selected disorders only, or report only either syndromal or nosological distributions, or are related to different degrees of severity, reported total prevalence rates of psychiatric morbidity in old age vary widely, from 12.3% to 54.1% (Parson, 1965; Myers *et al*, 1984; Dilling *et al*, 1989; Häfner, 1992; Skoog *et al*, 1993). Prevalence rates of severe psychiatric morbidity stay at 20% to 25% (Weyerer & Dilling, 1984; Cooper, 1986; Dilling *et al*, 1989; Welz *et al*, 1989). Except for dementia, it cannot be stated definitely at present whether there are age-dependent changes in the frequencies or in the spectrum of psychiatric disorders after the age of 65 years. Nevertheless, it seems worth recalling that the years after this age average nearly one-third of the human life span.

Uncertainty in assessment

Uncertainty over the type and extent of psychiatric morbidity in old age can be explained by some specifics of its assessment (Helmchen & Linden, 1993).

The border between mental health and disorder can be defined much less certainly in old age than at younger ages, partly because of the normative expectations with regard to age. For example, in younger persons decreasing interest in events or an abatement of memory may provoke the suspicion of a mental disorder, whereas in old persons the same signs will be interpreted as normal changes due to ageing.

Diagnostic orientation solely in terms of absolute thresholds or fixed cut-offs of dimensional criteria may blur the decisive diagnostic significance of individual changes. Thus, premorbid intelligence plays an important role for reaching the threshold for the diagnosis of dementia. For example, less educated persons with a level of cognitive performance just above this dementia threshold will surpass it in the course of benign ageing without suffering from a dementive disease. Persons with a high premorbid intelligence may compensate for mild cognitive deficits and, thus, will not fulfill the criteria of the diagnosis of dementia (Crum *et al*, 1993) although with regard to their individual decline of cognitive efficacy a dementive disease must be assumed.

The use of modern *operationalised psychiatric diagnoses* such as ICD–10 or DSM–IV may cause additional misperceptions if these diagnostic conventions are taken for granted. This is particularly valid for the investigation of the elderly because these instruments were not developed for this age group. These systems aim at a high specificity at the expense of sensitivity. The result is the danger of false negatives – diagnoses that do not fulfil the operational criteria but nevertheless, according to clinical experience, may have the quality of a disease, may demand the use of medical services, and may impair quality of life. These conditions are termed 'sub-diagnostic', 'sub-syndromal', 'sub-clinical', 'sub-threshold', or fall under the rubric of disorders 'not otherwise specified' (Blazer, 1989; Goldberg & Sartorius, 1990; Henderson *et al*, 1993).

The age-specific increase in *comorbidity* must be taken into account. Many non-specific but frequent somatic complaints, such as insomnia, loss of appetite, weakness, muscle pain, or disorders of the chest or stomach may be a sign of a somatic as well as of a psychic disorder (Linden & Borchelt, 1995). Furthermore, the comorbidity within the psychiatric disorders should be considered. This may arise by chance, or two syndromes may be pathogenetically interdependent, as with dementia and depression, described by the term 'depressive pseudo-dementia' (Helmchen & Linden, 1993).

Epidemiological estimations of prevalence rates

Epidemiological samples are mainly drawn according to the demographic age distribution (Cooper & Sosna, 1983; Dilling *et al*, 1984; Weyerer & Dilling, 1984; Weissman *et al*, 1985; Copeland *et al*, 1987, 1992; Welz *et al*, 1989; Fratiglioni *et al*, 1991; Fuhrer *et al*, 1992). Consequently the old old, that is, persons above the age of 85 years, are represented so rarely that reliable statements on this age group are not possible in most studies. Thus, to investigate the age dependence of a disorder the old old and particularly men must be over-represented in the study sample.

Prevalence rates of distinct psychiatric disorders such as dementia of the Alzheimer type and vascular dementia may be different in different age cohorts; for example, some studies report a negative age correlation of the prevalence of vascular dementia (Bickel, 1995). The same may be valid for risk factors such as the Apo E4 allele (Corder *et al*, 1993; Saunders *et al*, 1993). On the other hand, chronic diseases may accumulate with increasing age. Therefore, cross-sectional assessments of prevalence rates must be supplemented by longitudinal studies in order to yield statements on the actual relationship between age(ing) and mental disorders.

Differential prevalence rates of different types of mental disorders, particularly of Alzheimer's dementia versus vascular dementia, should be treated cautiously because brain imaging is necessary for the differential diagnosis *in vivo*, and yet the systematic application of these methods is almost impossible in field studies. The same is true of the neuropathological confirmation of the diagnosis, because this method yields the highest degree of diagnostic certainty but the least representativeness.

Selection biases may be created by a selective lack of access to probands – for example, demented persons because of their frailty or their incapacity to consent, or by exclusion of special groups such as institutionalised persons.

Further difficulties with regard to comparability between studies are created by differences between instruments, diagnostic criteria, and gradings of severity.

Finally, description of mental disorders in old age must consider aspects beyond psychopathological symptoms. Even in the case of an unequivocal biological aetiology, as in the dementias, additional biographical factors as such somatic diseases, lifestyle, or educational level may have pathogenetic, pathoplastic, or predictive significance. There is a significant negative association between the premorbid level of intelligence and education and the probability of odd values in the Mini Mental State Examination, an internationally accepted screening instrument for dementia (Folstein *et al*, 1975; Crum *et al*, 1993). This is true even more if psychiatric disorders are assessed not only psychopathologically but also by their consequences on everyday behaviour, quality of life, or the use of medical services. Therefore, the study of psychiatric disorders in old age has to take into consideration the simultaneous assessment of somatic, psychic and social variables, which involves an interdisciplinary approach. Such an approach should correct discipline-specific narrows such as a negative stereotype of age by physicians, as opposed to the tendency of gerontological psychologists to concentrate their attention mainly on the potentials of age.

The Berlin Aging Study

Overcoming or at least reducing some of these methodological problems was the objective in designing the Berlin Aging Study (BASE). For the theoretical background, organisational details and specific results of this study, see Baltes *et al* (1993) and Baltes & Mayer (1998). The study is outlined below.

Sample heterogeneity was assured by random selection of a population-based sample stratified by age and gender and including institutionalised people. The focus was on the very old (70–105 years of age), and the sample was selected with a view to ensuring the statistical significance of findings for age groups above 90 years. An interdisciplinary approach was adopted, and the study involved scientists from sociology, psychology, internal medicine and psychiatry.

Further strengths of BASE included: DSM–III–R diagnoses, with the whole spectrum of psychiatric disorders and all levels of severity, including mild and sub-threshold cases; standardised examinations, scales and tests; a sleep study; a drug and complaint interview; a consensus conference with psychiatrists and internists to evaluate all the individual findings in each case with regard to diagnosis and medication.

The BASE study is discussed below in terms of three of the facets of epidemiological studies of the elderly mentioned above: the dependence of prevalence rates on different thresholds of caseness; prevalence rates of all psychiatric DSM–III–R diagnoses; and differential age relationships, particularly of dementia and depression.

Sample and methods

In 1990–93 a sample of 1908 persons was randomly drawn from the West Berlin central residents' registration office from a source population of 281 675 old people above 70 years of age. Due to the age- and gender-stratified sample selection, each of six five-year age groups (70–74, 75–79, etc. to 95+) of the final IP (see below) sample ($n = 516$) consisted of 86 persons – 43 men and 43 women in each age group.

Where there was any doubt over a subject's capacity to consent ($n = 89$), this was assessed by a psychiatrist. Persons lacking capacity to consent, mainly with severe dementia, were excluded ($n = 54$) and treated separately in the estimation of prevalence of dementia. If there was any doubt as to whether the patient could stand the examination due to severe physical illness ($n = 8$) this was assessed by an internist.

A three-phase design was used to measure study variables. Out of the 1908 persons in the source sample, 1264 persons could be contacted for the first phase, which comprised a short interdisciplinary examination with regard to basic information on somatic and mental health, education and competence in daily living. In the second phase an interdisciplinary 'intake assessment' (IA) could be performed with 928 persons, and in the third phase 516 persons agreed to participate in an 'intensive protocol' (IP), which included a further 13 sessions (three sessions of each of the four research units psychology, sociology, internal medicine and psychiatry, and an investigation by a dentist). All sessions took place at the home of the participants, with the exception of a part of the internal investigation and the dental assessment.

This stepwise procedure offered the possibility of comparing the frequency of important variables at different levels of selection, and with Berlin census data. Analyses of the representativeness of the sample showed that the IP sample was somewhat positively selected with regard to some variables, but never by more than a half standard deviation (Lindenberger *et al*, 1996).

All subjects were examined and diagnosed by psychiatrists using the Geriatric Mental State Examination (GMS–A) and the History and Aetiology Schedule (HAS). The latter takes into account the case history and information from family members or others close to the participants. (Not described here are the many instruments used in BASE for specific questions – see Helmchen *et al*, 1996.) The neurological and physical investigations were carried out by physicians of the BASE internal medicine unit. In a consensus conference of internists and psychiatrists the data for each participant were jointly evaluated for psychiatric symptoms and diagnoses concerning drug effects and those of somatic morbidity. This was the basis for the clinical diagnoses according to the diagnostic criteria and grading of DSM–III–R.

TABLE 2.1
Thresholds of psychiatric caseness

Case definition	Criteria
No case	No or at the most single psychopathological symptoms
Threshold 1	—
Syndrome case	At least one psychopathological core symptom, and additionally at least one cognitive or two depressive symptoms according to GMS–A scores; symptoms continuously or recurring during the last four weeks
Threshold 2	—
Illness case	Criteria of syndrome case given clinical diagnosis of disorder (by case history, subjective suffering, objective handicaps), and need of therapeutic intervention only NOS (not otherwise specified), but no specified DSM–III–R diagnosis possible
Threshold 3	—
Diagnostic case	Criteria of illness case given, and specified DSM–III–R diagnosis possible

Syndrome cases and illness cases below threshold 3 are called sub-diagnostic or sub-threshold cases

TABLE 2.2
Grading of severity of psychiatric morbidity

Grades	Criteria
Mild	GAF score 70–61 General functioning pretty well Therapeutic intervention questionable
Moderate	GAF score 60–41 Moderate social impairment Therapeutic intervention indicated
Severe	GAF score below 40 Considerable impairment in several areas Therapeutic intervention by admission to hospital indicated

GAF, Global Assessment of Functioning Scale (according to DSM–III–R).

A hierarchical procedure was applied to establish 'caseness' (Table 2.1). A first threshold between mental health and questionable psychiatric morbidity was defined as *no case* versus *syndrome case*, the latter of which was characterised as clear psychopathological symptoms in the GMS–A. A second threshold between a syndrome case and an *illness case* was defined by a score on the Global Assessment of Functioning Scale (GAF) below 70, which indicates impairment and suffering of pathological degree. If the frequency, spectrum or intensity of symptoms did not reach the criteria of a specified DSM–III–R diagnosis, the disorder was categorised as 'not otherwise specified' (NOS). The third threshold was defined as between these NOS illness cases and specified DSM–III–R *diagnostic cases*.

The severity of disorders was graded on the GAF, according to DSM–III–R criteria (Jones *et al*, 1995; Patterson & Lee, 1995) and the indication for therapeutic intervention (Table 2.2). Threshold 2 described above is of course a grey zone between an intensive syndrome case without the need of therapeutic intervention and a mild illness case with an only questionable need for such a therapeutic intervention.

The interrater reliability for the GMS–A ratings among the three psychiatrists (kappa values) varied between 0.70 and 0.83. Prevalence rates, standard errors and confidence intervals were calculated by weighting factors for age and gender for each subject, for age groups and for the total sample. Chi-squared tests were used to compare degrees of severity of psychiatric illness, and to compare sexes. Analysis of variance was applied to compare the prevalence in age groups.

TABLE 2.3

Psychiatric morbidity in the elderly according to different caseness thresholds: results from the Berlin Aging Study (BASE)

	Weighted prevalence (%)
All participants (*n*=516)	100.0
Threshold 1 (between no case and syndrome case)	
Subjects with psychopathological symptoms	72.7
Threshold 2 (between syndrome case and illness case)	
Subjects with clinical diagnoses	
(DSM–III–R, including insomnia and NOS)	49.4
Threshold 3 (between illness case and diagnostic case)	
Subjects with specified DSM–III–R diagnoses	35.6
Subjects with specified DSM–III–R diagnoses without insomnia	23.5
Subjects with specified DSM–III–R diagnoses without insomnia and dementia	11.3
Hierarchical prevalence rates of mental disorders (mutually exclusive categories)	
Diagnostic cases (specified DSM–III–R diagnosis, except insomnia)	23.5
DSM–III–R diagnosis of insomnia	12.1
Illness only cases	13.8
Syndrome only cases	23.3
No cases	27.3

Results

Dependence of prevalence rates on different thresholds of caseness

Table 2.3 shows that the prevalence rates of psychiatric morbidity vary by a factor of eight or at least of four according to the different thresholds of caseness. Only 27.3% of the IP sample was without any psychopathological symptoms (no cases). At least a further 23.3% had unequivocal psychopathological symptoms but had been diagnosed by the psychiatrists as not ill (syndrome cases). Another 13.8% had been diagnosed as having only a psychiatric illness (illness cases) not otherwise specified (NOS) but below the threshold of a specified psychiatric DSM–III–R diagnosis. Excluding from the residual group of specified DSM–III–R diagnoses (diagnostic cases) those cases with the sole diagnosis of insomnia (DSM–III–R 307.42) (12.1%) yields a final group of 23.5% of diagnostic cases.

TABLE 2.4
Grading of severity of psychiatric morbidity (illness cases and diagnostic cases)

Grades	Prevalence rates (%)
Mild	16.4
Moderate	19.8
Severe	4.2

Cases above threshold 1 but below threshold 3, that is, syndrome cases plus illness cases, are called sub-diagnostic or sub-threshold cases. It was mentioned above that the exact definition and establishment of the border between these two different types of sub-diagnostic cases, that is, the border between health and morbidity, is difficult and a source of uncertainty and variation of prevalence rates of total psychiatric morbidity. However, more important is the fact that evidently this group with sub-diagnostic morbidity is a large one and, moreover, its meaning in terms of individual suffering, burdens for next of kin and costs for the health-care system is quite unknown and a concern for future research (Henderson *et al*, 1993).

A major reason why threshold 2 is not a sharp border but a more or less wide grey zone lies in the fact that the large majority of illness cases show only mild or at most moderate grades of severity (Table 2.4).

Prevalence rates of all psychiatric DSM–III–R diagnoses

Table 2.5 gives an overview on the prevalence rates of all (NOS and specified) DSM–III–R diagnoses in all 516 persons of the IP sample. The spectrum of psychiatric disorders is characterised by the predominance of the relatively non-specific disorders such as insomnia (18.8%) and NOS depressive states (17.8%) followed by dementia (13.8%) and specified depressive disorders (9.1%). (These figures are higher than in Table 3 because here they also include those cases with additional other specified diagnoses (comorbidity).) All anxiety disorders together amount to 4.4%. All other psychiatric disorders, including dependence disorders, show prevalence rates below 1%. The rates of specified disorders correspond to the rates reported from most other epidemiological studies, whereas the rate of insomnia specifically established in BASE has not been reported by others, and the rate of NOS depressions was not a specific focus in other studies. Thus, the main features of psychiatric morbidity in old age are depression, dementia, insomnia and anxiety.

TABLE 2.5

Prevalence of DSM–III–R diagnoses (n=516, prevalence rates weighted according to age and gender)

DSM–III–R diagnoses	Prevalence (%)
290.00 Dementia (primary degenerative; NOS)	12.5
290.20 Dementia (primary degenerative; NOS) with delusions	0.3
290.21 Dementia (primary degenerative; NOS) with depression	1.0
293.81 Organic delusional disorder	0.0
293.82 Organic hallucinosis	0.6
294.80 Organic mental disorder NOS	1.6
295.62 Schizophrenia, residual type, chronic	0.2
297.10 Delusional (paranoid) disorder	0.5
296.22 Major depression, single epidose, moderate	4.2
296.23 Major depression, single episode, severe	0.5
296.24 Major depression, single episode, with psychotic features	0.1
296.25 Major depression, single episode, in partial remission	0.2
296.35 Major depression, recurrent, in partial remission	0.4
300.00 Anxiety disorder NOS	2.5
300.01 Panic disorder without agoraphobia	0.0
300.02 Generalised anxiety disorder	0.9
300.22 Agoraphobia without panic disorder	0.8
300.30 Obsessive–compulsive disorder	0.2
300.40 Dysthymic disorder	2.0
303.90 Alcohol dependence	0.5
304.10 Sedative, hypnotic dependence	0.5
305.00 Alcohol abuse	0.7
305.40 Sedative, hypnotic intoxication	0.2
307.42 Insomnia	18.8
309.00 Adjustment disorder with depressed mood	0.7
309.24 Adjustment disorder with anxious mood	0.0
310.10 Organic personality disorder	0.6
311.00 Depressive disorder NOS	17.8
Main groups of diagnoses:	
Dementia and other organic mental disorders	16.8
Major depression and other depressive disorders	26.9
Insomnias	18.8
Anxiety disorders	4.4

Differential age relationship, particularly of dementia and depression

In agreement with the internationally most important epidemiological studies (Jorm *et al*, 1987; Hofman *et al*, 1991; Copeland *et al*, 1992; Skoog *et al*, 1993), BASE found a steep increase in the age-related prevalence rates of dementia, from 1% in the age group 70–74 up to

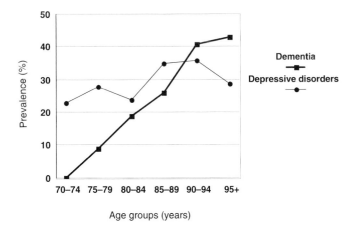

Fig. 2.1. Prevalence (%) of dementia and depressive disorders (DSM–III–R specified and NOS) by age.

43% in those aged over 90 years (Fig. 2.1). From a theoretical point of view it is remarkable that the data show a flattening of this increase above the age of 90 years, which, however, presumably cannot be validated by estimated rates corrected with regard to selectivity (Lindenberger *et al*, 1996).

The prevalence rates of depressive disorders, on the other hand, show no significant age-related increase. However, the impression of a slight age-related increase of depression in Fig. 2.1 can be clarified by using the potential of BASE for more in-depth analyses. Table 2.6 reveals that this insignificant increase is valid for major depression alone and for males alone, whereas females show a slight but significant age-related increase in depressive disorders. More remarkable was the finding that on the level of depressive symptoms, no significant increase could be found with regard to observer ratings on the Hamilton Rating Scale for Depression, but there was a clear and significant age-related increase in depressive symptoms with regard to self-ratings by the Center for Epidemiologic Studies – Depression Scale (CES–D), again more in females than in males (Table 2.7). (On both scales, females also have more depressive symptoms in younger age groups.) For interpretation it should be remembered that symptom scales, particularly self-rating scales, can be used as screening instruments for depression. This means that they have a higher sensitivity at the cost of specificity. Thus, in addition, they partially represent non-depressive complaints and feelings of burden (Wallace & O'Hara,

TABLE 2.6
Relationship to age of depressive disorders: prevalence rates (%)

Age (years)	Depressive disorders (DSM–III–R and NOS)			Major depression (DSM–III–R)		
	Males	*Females*	*All*	*Males*	*Females*	*All*
70–74	16	26	23	2.3	4.7	3.9
75–79	16	33	28	2.3	4.7	4.4
80–84	19	26	24	4.7	7.0	3.9
85–89	33	35	33	7.0	7.0	7.0
90–94	19	40	36	4.7	9.3	8.5
95+	19	30	29	2.3	4.7	4.4
F/χ^2	2.3	3.7	5.1	1.0	1.3	2.3
P	NS	0.02	NS	NS	NS	NS
Gender differences						
All	19	30	27	3.5	5.9	5.3
t-test *P* = (two-tailed)		0.02			NS	

1992). This may be especially valid for females (Fuhrer & Rouillon, 1989) and in persons with age-related comorbidity (Berkman *et al*, 1986; Gatz & Hurwics, 1990; Helmchen *et al*, 1996).

In summary it can be stated that there is a steep age-related increase in the prevalence of dementia, up to almost 50% above the age of 90 years (with the possibility of a plateau beyond this age), whereas depressive disorders show no such age-related increase. An age-related

TABLE 2.7
Relationship to age of depressive syndromes (means)

Age (years)	CES–D (self-rating)			Hamilton scale (observer rating)		
	Males	*Females*	*All*	*Males*	*Females*	*All*
70–74	10.2	11.7	10.9	3.7	5.1	4.4
75–79	11.3	15.5	13.3	3.8	7.9	5.9
80–84	10.8	14.8	12.8	5.3	6.7	6.0
85–89	13.5	16.8	15.1	5.3	7.0	6.1
90–95	14.8	19.4	17.0	5.2	6.9	6.1
95+	13.6	16.8	15.1	4.5	6.8	5.7
F/χ^2	2.3	3.0	4.9	0.8	0.9	1.0
P	0.05	0.012	0.0002	NS	NS	NS
Gender differences						
All	12.3	15.8	14.0	4.6	6.7	5.7
t-test *P* = (two-tailed)		0.001			0.001	

increase of depression – at a low level – only in self-ratings and in females may indicate the influence of non-specific factors, the meaning of which is not clearly understood, revealing the need for research on sub-threshold morbidity.

Conclusions

Methodological problems with epidemiological research in the elderly population was one focus of BASE. Some results of this study are presented here with regard to the following:

(a) Different thresholds of caseness reveal a large group (approximately 15% of cases) with pure so-called sub-diagnostic or sub-threshold morbidity, mainly with affective disturbances.

(b) Prevalence rates of specified DSM–III–R diagnoses amount to a total of approximately 35%, or 23.5% not including insomnia, and are comparable to prevalence rates reported from other studies and probably also to those in younger ages (with the exception of dementia).

(c) The differential age-relationship is shown by a steep age-related increase in the prevalence rates of dementia but there is no such increase in depressive disorders; concerning the latter, another differential age relationship became evident insofar as on the level of depressive symptoms, an age relationship was not found in observer ratings by the Hamilton Rating Scale for Depression, but solely in self-ratings by the CES–D.

References

BALTES, P. B., MAYER, K. U., HELMCHEN, H., *et al* (1993) The Berlin Aging Study (BASE): overview and design. *Ageing and Society*, **13**, 483–515.

—— & MAYER, K. U. (eds) (1998) *The Berlin Aging Study. Aging from 70 to 100.* Cambridge: Cambridge University Press.

BERKMAN, L. F., BERKMAN, C. S., KASL, S., *et al* (1986) Depressive symptoms in relation to physical health and function in the elderly. *American Journal of Epidemiology*, **124**, 372–388.

BICKEL, H. (1995) A retrospective population-based study of dementia. *Seventh Congress of the International Psychogeriatric Association.* Sydney, Australia.

BLAZER, D. G. (1989) Depression in late life. *Current Opinion in Psychiatry*, **2**, 515–519.

——, KESSLER, R. C., McGONAGE, K. A., *et al* (1994) Prevalence and distribution of major depression in a national community sample: The National Comorbidity Survey. *American Journal of Psychiatry*, **151**, 979–986.

COOPER, B. (1986) Mental illness, disability and social conditions among old people in Mannheim. In *Mental Health in the Elderly* (eds H. Häfner, G. Moschel & N. Sartorius), pp. 35–45. Berlin: Springer.

—— & Sosna, V. (1983) Psychische Erkrankungen in der Altenbevölkerung. *Der Nervenarzt*, **54**, 239–257.

Copeland, J. R. M., Kelleher, M. J., Kellet, J. M., *et al* (1976) A semi-structured clinical interview for the assessment of diagnosis and mental state in the elderly. The Geriatric Mental State Schedule. 1. Development and reliability. *Psychological Medicine*, **6**, 439–457.

——, Dewey, M. E., Wood, N., *et al* (1987) Range of mental illness among the elderly in the community. *British Journal of Psychiatry*, **150**, 815–823.

——, Davidson, I. A., Dewey, M. E., *et al* (1992) Alzheimer's disease, other dementias, depression and pseudodementia: prevalence, incidence and three-year outcome in Liverpool. *British Journal of Psychiatry*, **161**, 230–239.

Corder, E. H., Saunders, A. M., Strittmatter, W. J., *et al* (1993) Gene dose of apolipoprotein E type 4 allele and the risk of Alzheimer's disease in late-onset families. *Science*, **261**, 921–923.

Crimmins, E. M., Saito, Y. & Ingegneri, D. (1989) Changes in life expectancy and disability free life expectancy in the United States. *Population Development Review*, **15**, 235–267.

Crum, R. M., Anthony, J. C., Bassett, S. S., *et al* (1993) Population based norms for the Mini Mental State Examination by age and educational level. *Journal of the American Medical Association*, **269**, 2386–2391.

Dilling, H., Weyerer, S. & Castell, R. (1984) *Psychische Erkrankungen in der Bevölkerung*. Stuttgart: Enke.

——, Weyerer, S. & Fichter, M. (1989) The Upper Bavarian Studies. *Acta Psychiatrica Scandinavica*, **79** (suppl. 348), 113–140.

Dinkel, R. H. (1992) Demographische Alterung: Ein Überblick unter besonderer Berücksichtigung der Mortalitätsentwicklungen. *Zukunft des Alterns und gesellschaftliche Entwicklung* (eds P. B. Baltes & J. Mittelstraß), pp. 62–94. Berlin: De Gruyter.

Folstein, M. F., Folstein, S. E. & McHugh, P. R. (1975) Mini-Mental State. A practical method of grading the cognitive state of patients for the clinician. *Journal of Psychiatric Research*, **12**, 189–198.

Fratiglioni, L., Grut, M., Forsell, Y., *et al* (1991) Prevalence of Alzheimer's disease and other dementias in an elderly urban population. *Neurology*, **41**, 1886–1892.

Fuhrer, R. & Rouillon, F. (1989) La version française de l'échelle CES-D (Center for Epidemiologic Studies – Depression Scale): Description et traduction de l'échelle d'autoévaluation. *Psychiatrie et Psychobiologie*, **4**, 163–166.

——, Antonucci, T. C., Gagnon, M., *et al* (1992) Depressive symptomatology and cognitive functioning: an epidemiological survey in an elderly community sample in France. *Psychological Medicine*, **22**, 159–172.

Gatz, M. & Hurwics, M. L. (1990) Are old people more depressed? Cross-sectional data on Center for Epidemiologic Studies – Depression Scale factors. *Psychology and Aging*, **5**, 284–290.

Goldberg, D. P. & Sartorius, N. (1990) Introduction. *Psychological Disorders in General Medical Settings* (eds N. Sartorius, D. P. Goldberg, G. De Girolamo, *et al*), pp. 1–5. Göttingen: Hogrefe & Huber.

Grant, B. F. (1993) Comparison of DSM–III–R and draft DSM–IV alcohol abuse and dependence in a general population sample. *Addiction*, **88**, 1709–1716.

Häfner, H. (1992) Psychiatrie des höheren Lebensalters. In *Zukunft des Alterns und gesellschaftliche Entwicklung* (eds P. B. Baltes & J. Mittelstraß), pp. 151–179. Berlin: De Gruyter.

——, Maurer, K., Löffler, W., *et al* (1991) Schizophrenie und Lebensalter. *Der Nervenarzt*, **62**, 536–548.

Helmchen, H. & Linden, M. (1993) The differentiation between depression and dementia in the very old. *Ageing and Society*, **13**, 589–617.

—— & Baltes, M. M. (1996) Die Berliner Altersstudie (BASE): Psychiatrische Ziele. *150 Jahre Psychiatrie, Vol. 2* (eds U. H. Peters, M. Schifferdecker & A. Krahl), pp. 933–942. Cologne: Martini Verlag.

——, ——, GEISELMANN, B., *et al* (1996) Psychische Erkrankungen im Alter. In *Die Berliner Altersstudie (BASE)* (eds K. U. Mayer & P. B. Baltes), pp. 185–219. Berlin: Akademie Verlag.

HENDERSON, A. S. (1986) Epidemiology in mental illness. *Mental Health in the Elderly* (eds G. Häfner, G. Moschel & N. Sartorius), pp. 29–34. Berlin: Springer.

——, JORM, A. F., MACKINNON, A., *et al* (1993) The prevalence of depressive disorders and the distribution of depressive symptoms in later life: a survey using draft ICD–10 and DSM–III–R. *Psychological Medicine*, **23**, 719–729.

HOFMAN, A., ROCCA, W. A., BRAYNE, C., *et al* (1991) The prevalence of dementia in Europe: a collaborative study of 1980–1990 findings. *International Journal of Epidemiology*, **20**, 736–748.

JONES, S. H., THORNICOFT, G., COFFEY, M., *et al* (1995) A brief mental health outcome scale. *British Journal of Psychiatry*, **166**, 654–659.

JORM, A. F., KORTEN, A. E. & HENDERSON, A. S. (1987) The prevalence of dementia: a quantitative integration of the literature. *Acta Psychiatrica Scandinavica*, **76**, 465–479.

——, —— & JACOMB, P. A. (1988) Projected increase in the number of dementia cases for 29 developed countries: application of a new method for making projections. *Acta Psychiatrica Scandinavica*, **78**, 493–500.

KAY, D. W. K., BEAMISH, P. & ROTH, M. (1964) Old age mental disorders in Newcastle upon Tyne. *British Journal of Psychiatry*, **110**, 146–158.

——, BERGMANN, K., FORSTER, E., *et al* (1970) Mental illness and hospital usage in the elderly: a random sample followed up. *Comparative Psychiatry*, **11**, 26–35.

——, HENDERSON, A. S., SCOTT, R., *et al* (1985) Dementia and depression among the elderly living in Hobart community: the effect of diagnostic criteria on the prevalence rates. *Psychological Medicine*, **15**, 771–788.

KRÄMER, W. (1992) Altern und Gesundheitswesen. Probleme und Lösungen aus der Sicht der Gesundheitsökonomie. In *Zukunft des Alterns und gesellschaftliche Entwicklung* (eds P. B. Baltes & J. Mittelstraß), pp. 563–580. Berlin: De Gruyter.

LAUTER, H. (1974) Epidemiologische Aspekte alterspsychiatrischer Erkrankungen. *Der Nervenarzt*, **45**, 277–288.

LINDEN, M. & BORCHELT, M. (1995) The impact of somatic morbidity on the Hamilton Depression Scale in the very old. In *Aging, Health and Healing* (eds M. Bergener, J. C. Brocklehurst & S. I. Finkel), pp. 420–426. Berlin: Springer.

LINDENBERGER, U., GILBERG, R., PÖTTER, U., *et al* (1996) Die Berliner Altersstudie (BASE): Stichprobenselektivität und Generalisierbarkeit der Ergebnisse. In *Die Berliner Altersstudie: Von 70–100* (eds K. U. Mayer & P. B. Baltes), pp. 85–108. Berlin: Akademie Verlag.

MYERS, J. K., WEISSMAN, M. M., TISCHLER, G. L., *et al* (1984) Six month prevalence of psychiatric disorders in three communities. *Archives of General Psychiatry*, **41**, 959–967.

PARSON, P. L. (1965) Mental health of Swansea's folk. *British Journal of Preventive and Social Medicine*, **19**, 43–47.

PATTERSON, D. A. & LEE, M. S. (1995) Field trial of the Global Assessment of Functioning Scale – Modified. *American Journal of Psychiatry*, **152**, 1386–1388.

REGIER, D. A., BOYD, J. H., BURKE, Jr, J. D., *et al* (1988) One-month prevalence of mental disorders in the United States. *Archives of General Psychiatry*, **45**, 977–986.

SAUNDERS, A. M., STRITTMATTER, W. J., SCHMECHEL, D., *et al* (1993) Association of apolipoprotein E allele E4 with late-onset familial and sporadic Alzheimer's disease. *Neurology*, **43**, 1467–1472.

SKOOG, I., NILSSON, I., PALMERTZ, B., *et al* (1993) A population-based study of dementia in 85-year-olds. *New England Journal of Medicine*, **328**, 153–158.

WALLACE, J. & O'HARA, M. W. (1992) Increases in depressive symptomatology in the rural elderly: results from a cross-sectional and longitudinal study. *Journal of Abnormal Psychology*, **101**, 398–404.

WEISSMAN, M. M. & MYERS, J. K. (1978) Rates and risks of depressive symptoms in a US urban community. *Acta Psychiatrica Scandinavica*, **57**, 219–231.

WEISSMAN, M. M., MYERS, J. K., TISCHLER, G. L., *et al* (1985) Psychiatric disorders (DSM–III) and cognitive impairment among the elderly in a U.S. urban community. *Acta Psychiatrica Scandinavica*, **71**, 366–379.

WELZ, R., LINDNER, M., KLOSE, M., *et al* (1989) Psychische Störungen und körperliche Erkrankungen im Alter. *Fundamental Psychiatry*, **3**, 223–229.

WERNICKE, T. F. & REISCHIES, F. M. (1994) Prevalence of dementia in old age: clinical diagnoses in subjects aged 95 years and older. *Neurology*, **44**, 250–253.

WEYERER, S. & DILLING, H. (1984) Prävalenz und Behandlung psychischer Erkrankungen in der Allgemeinbevölkerung. *Der Nervenarzt*, **55**, 30–42.

3 Psychodiagnostic aspects of late-onset mental disorders: cognitive speed and the diagnosis of dementia

ULRICH M. FLEISCHMANN

Mental disorder is a broad term, still lacking a consistent definition, which covers the complete spectrum of diagnostic situations. Consistent definitions, however, are required for assessing, classifying and analysing the variety of clinically or behaviourally relevant symptoms that occur in an individual.

Reviewing ICD–10 or DSM–III–R/DSM–IV, we find conceptual frameworks that define mental disorders as behavioural, psychological or biological dysfunction, designated as statistical deviation, disability, distress or dyscontrol. These diagnostic concepts are then refined into operational definitions and assessment procedures that:

(a) are clearly in accordance with the underlying constructs of mental disorders;
(b) are in line with independent empirical data from clinical and experimental research;
(c) are valid indicators over a wide range of diagnostic settings;
(d) comply with psychometric criteria and deliver apt tools for clinical practice.

This chapter outlines the research into the basic diagnostic dimensions of dementia. A rather neglected cognitive function, namely cognitive speed, will be discussed as an apposite operational criterion for diagnosing dementia.

Diagnostic guidelines for dementia and experimental ageing research

According to the guidelines set out in ICD–10 and DSM–III–R/DSM–IV, deficits in memory functioning are the primary criterion for the diagnosis of dementia. Deficits in attention, language, motor activities, object identification and executive functions, such as planning or sequencing, should be examined additionally. This diagnostic scheme is specified as age independent. Its clinical acceptance, practicality and face validity are beyond dispute.

A different picture of dementia in old age emerges from the results of experimental ageing research (e.g. Kausler, 1982; Poon, 1986). As shown below, experimental ageing research outlines memory as a complex cognitive unit that encompasses separate functions, and these have to be considered in a systematic way. Cognitive speed is the most important measure of cognitive performance in normal as well as in pathological ageing, as it influences a broad range of other cognitive functions (e.g. Salthouse, 1985; Cerella, 1990).

Basic results from memory research

In terms of psychogerontological memory research, declining memory in old age is seen as the result of changes in basic cognitive processes. It has been shown that the amount of information which can simultaneously be kept over a short time diminishes with age. Elderly patients suffer problems in encoding information as well as in retrieving stored information. Furthermore, memory processes slow down and formerly independent memory functions merge. These alterations are confirmed as critical changes in normal as well as in pathological ageing (e.g. Kausler, 1982).

Factor analyses of psychometric investigations (Fleischmann *et al*, 1995) result in three memory dimensions, which may be characterised as:

(a) short-term retention of information (primary memory);
(b) effortful processes of organising information in memory (secondary memory);
(c) speed-demanding cognitive operations (cognitive speed).

The clearly age-correlated dimension of cognitive speed (Fig. 3.1) should be part of any exhaustive memory assessment.

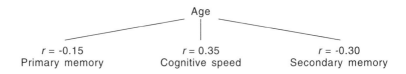

Fig. 3.1. Basic memory functions derived from factor analyses.

Diagnosing dementia by 'cognitive speed'

There is little doubt that the most frequent forms of dementia (senile dementia of the Alzheimer type and multi-infarct dementia) affect secondary memory, that is, tasks which require active information processing (e.g. Wilson *et al*, 1983). Surprisingly, our data show that cognitive speed is actually more sensitive than secondary memory in the detection of early dementia processes (Fleischmann *et al*, 1995).

To illustrate this, the discriminative power of two age-adjusted and highly reliable tests of cognitive speed, the Digit Symbol Substitution Test (DSS, a modified version of the DSS sub-test of the Wechsler Adult Intelligence Scale; Wechsler, 1958) and the Zahlen-Verbindungs Test (ZVT–G, a modified version of Raitan's Trail Making Test A; Raitan, 1958), are shown in Tables 3.1 and 3.2, respectively.

Table 3.1 shows the distribution of the DSS test scores for the age groups 62–79 years and 80–89 years based on 41 healthy elderly and 41 age-matched patients with senile dementia of the Alzheimer type.

TABLE 3.1

Distributions of DSS scores in patients with senile dementia of the Alzheimer type and age-matched normals

DSS test score	No. of normals aged: (n=41)		No. of patients aged: (n=41)	
	62–79	80–89	62–79	80–89
51–55	1	–	–	–
46–50	1	1	–	–
41–45	3	–	–	–
36–40	4	1	–	–
31–35	–	3	–	–
26–30	6	2	1	1
21–25	3	5	4	2
16–20	2	3	7	3
11–15	1	4	6	2
6–10	–	1	4	6
0–5	–	–	2	3

TABLE 3.2
The differentiation of normal and pathological cognitive ageing using cognitive speed assessed by the ZVT–G

ZVT-G score	55–69 years		70–79 years		80–95 years	
	Sensitivity	Specificity	Sensitivity	Specificity	Sensitivity	Specificity
29	0.73	0.88				
30	0.75	0.88				
31	0.79	0.88				
32	**0.80**	**0.88**	0.70	0.88		
33	0.81	0.75	0.72	0.81		
34	0.82	0.75	0.73	0.81		
35	0.85	0.75	0.75	0.75		
36	0.86	0.75	0.75	0.75		
37	0.87	0.75	0.79	0.75		
38	0.88	0.75	**0.81**	**0.69**		
39	0.90	0.75	0.82	0.69		
40			0.84	0.69		
41			0.86	0.69		
42			0.87	0.69		
43			0.87	0.69	0.73	0.67
44			0.88	0.69	0.75	0.56
45			0.89	0.69	0.75	0.56
46			0.90	0.62	0.77	0.56
47			0.90	0.62	0.78	0.56
48					0.78	0.56
49					0.79	0.50
50					0.79	0.50
51					**0.80**	**0.44**
52					0.80	0.44
53					0.81	0.44

Bold indicates the cut-off score used for each age group.

Dementia was diagnosed on the basis of comprehensive psychiatric and neurological examinations, including DSM–III criteria, the Hachinski scale (Hachinski *et al*, 1975), electroencephalography (EEG) and computerised tomography scan. Patients with clear depressive symptoms were excluded from this analysis. There is only a small overlap in the DSS distributions between the two diagnostic groups.

Using the DSS for diagnostic classification, for the younger age group (62–79 years) both the sensitivity and the specificity were 0.85 at a threshold of 22/23 DSS points (receiver operating characteristic (ROC) performance $W = 92$; $P < 0.001$; see Hanley & McNeil, 1982). Corresponding values in the older age group (80–89 years) were significantly lower ($z = 3.37$, $P > 0.01$), with 0.60 for sensitivity and 0.80

TABLE 3.3
Dementia classification using the ZVT–G (with MMSE scores for comparison)
(questionable: ZVT–G with limits +/- SD/4 at the age-specific cut-off scores)

| Cognitive status | Age | | | | | |
| | < 70 years | | 70–79 years | | > 80 years | |
	ZVT–G	MMSE	ZVT–G	MMSE	ZVT–G	MMSE
Normal ageing	<29	–	<33	24	<45	23
Questionable	29–36	21	33–43	21	45–59	23
Pathological ageing	>36	19	>43	20	>59	21

for specificity at a DSS cut-off of 19/20 (ROC performance $W = 0.72$, $P < 0.001$).

Comparisons with commonly used tests assessing primary memory (e.g. Digit Span) and secondary memory (e.g. word lists, Benton test; Benton, 1974) show that the DSS is better able to discriminate between patients with Alzheimer-type dementia and age-matched normal subjects of equal age.

Table 3.2 shows the ZVT–G scores of a composite sample of 522 healthy subjects, and people with diagnoses of Alzheimer-type and multi-infarct dementia. The table lists the rate of correctly identified dementia patients in the sensitivity column as well as the rate of correctly classified healthy subjects in the specificity column, for three age groups. As with the DSS, the proportion of subjects correctly classified by the ZVT–G measure of cognitive speed diminishes with increasing age, with $W = 0.88$, 0.82 and 0.72 for the age groups 55–69, 70–79 and 80–95 years, respectively (overall classification rate W, equivalent to Wilcoxon's statistic, W). In other words, normal and pathological ageing processes in old age are less clearly separated by cognitive speed.

As an additional step, Table 3.3 proposes a classification of cognitive status based on the ZVT–G (scores on the Mini Mental State Examination (MMSE) are given for comparison). Again, it can be seen that with advancing age, the range of what is 'questionable' increases. That is, normal and pathological ageing merge in very old age.

Discussion

This chapter aims at an empirically based extension of the well established schemes for diagnosing dementia in old age. It has been argued that results from experimental ageing research may be used in a constructive way, as exemplified by the use of cognitive speed as a measure of pathological ageing

Focusing on the clinical diagnosis of dementia in the elderly, empirical findings from cognitive ageing research may be summarised as follows:

(a) Cognitive speed is a basic component of memory, as well as a basic cognitive function.
(b) There are highly reliable methods of quantifying cognitive speed. The DSS and the ZVT–G are prominent examples.
(c) As a fluid cognitive function (see Cattell, 1963), cognitive speed is clearly correlated with age in healthy subjects.
(d) Using tests of cognitive speed, normal and pathological ageing can be described on the basis of a single cognitive dimension. Results from structure analyses confirm the age-independent validity of measures cognitive speed (e.g. Fleischmann, 1989).
(e) The discriminative diagnostic power of cognitive speed is especially high in subjects up to the seventh decade, with a sensitivity and specificity over 0.80. Traditional memory tests are weaker in this age range.
(f) As a complement to other cognitive measures, cognitive speed can be used to diagnose dementia emerging in the eighth decade.

It is desirable for diagnostic guidelines to be strictly empirical. Cognitive speed should therefore be analysed as a basic mechanism in the dynamics of dementia. Studies have shown that there are strong correlations between cognitive speed and biological markers, such as EEG investigations. Significant correlations between cognitive speed and activities of daily living are another important reason to include this dimension in the diagnosis of dementia.

References

BENTON, A. L. (1974) *Manual: Revised Retention Test. Clinical and Experimental Applications.* New York: Psychological Cooperation.

CATTELL, R. B. (1963) Theory of fluid and crystallized intelligence. *Psychological Bulletin*, **40**, 153–193.

CERELLA, J. (1990) Aging and information-processing rate. In *Handbook of the Psychology of Aging* (eds J. E. Birren & K. W. Schaie), pp. 201–221. San Diego: Academic Press.

FLEISCHMANN, U. M. (1989) *Gedächtnis und Alter.* Bern: Huber.

——, OSWALD, W. D., OSWALD, B., *et al* (1995) *Neuropsychological Ageing Inventory (NAI)* Seattle: Hogrefe & Huber Publishers.

HACHINSKI, V. C., ILIFF, L. D., ZILHKA, E., *et al* (1975) Cerebral blood flow in dementia. *Archives of Neurology*, **32**, 632–637.

HANLEY, J. A. & McNEIL, B. (1982) The meaning and use of the area under a receiver operating characteristic (ROC) curve. *Radiology*, **143**, 29–36.

KAUSLER, D. H. (1982) *Experimental Psychology and Human Aging.* New York: Wiley.

POON, L. W. (1986) *Handbook for Clinical Memory Assessment of Older Adults.* Washington, DC: American Psychological Association.

RAITAN, R. M. (1958) Validity of the trail making test as an indicator or organic brain damage. *Perceptual and Motor Skills,* **8,** 271–276.

SALTHOUSE, T. A. (1985) *A Theory of Cognitive Aging.* Amsterdam: North-Holland.

WECHSLER, D. (1958) *Measurement of Adult Intelligence.* Baltimore: Williams & Wilkins.

WILSON, R. S., BACON, L. D., FOX, J. H., *et al* (1983) Primary memory and secondary memory in dementia of the Alzheimer type. *Journal of Clinical Neuropsychology,* **5,** 337–344.

4 Late-onset depression: long-term course and outcome

J. ANGST

The endogenous psychoses, that is, schizophrenia, schizoaffective disorder and bipolar manic–depression, mostly start early in life. In contrast, unipolar depression can develop at any age, from adolescence to old age. Risk does not decrease with age. Both bipolar and unipolar affective disorders show a two-peak distribution in their age of onset, with a first peak between 20 and 30 years, and a second between 40 and 60 (Angst, 1966; Marneros *et al*, 1991; Angst & Preisig, 1995a). In 1938, Slater showed a bimodal distribution of the total group of manic–depressive psychoses. Certain contradictory findings (Loranger & Levine, 1978; Taylor & Abrams, 1981) for bipolar disorder and for unipolar depression (Peselow *et al*, 1982) may derive from the selection of younger, non-representative samples.

Attempts to prove the heterogeneity of unipolar depressive disorder by distinguishing between early- and late-onset depression have not been very successful (Mendlewicz & Baron, 1981). Winokur *et al*'s (1971) early attempt to characterise early-onset depression in females and late-onset depression in males (the latter manifesting alcoholism and sociopathy among first-degree relatives) has not been confirmed, nor has the trichotomy of Winokur (1972) and Winokur *et al* (1978) of 'depressive spectrum disease', 'pure depressive disease' and 'sporadic depressive disease'. The thorough investigations conducted by Perris *et al* (1982, 1983) failed to corroborate the suggested differences between subgroups.

Nevertheless, a bimodal distribution of the onset of a disorder always suggests heterogeneity. Late-onset (versus early-onset) depression clearly correlates with higher recurrence rates (Swift, 1907; Kraepelin, 1921; Malzberg 1929; Paskind, 1930; Pollock, 1931; Steen, 1933; Lundquist, 1945; Grof *et al*, 1974; Taschev & Roglev, 1973; Angst *et al*, 1980; Zis *et al*, 1980). Another good reason to study late-onset

47

depression is the high suicide rate among elderly people with depression; yet another is the correlation between age and chronic outcome.

There is controversy, however, as to whether age at onset also predicts poor recovery. Murphy (1983) was unable to establish any difference in outcome between early- and late-onset depression. Post (1972) reported high recovery rates in almost two-thirds of late-onset cases, and Winokur & Morrison (1973) failed to find any correlation between age at onset of unipolar depression and a chronic outcome. It has therefore to be assumed that it is not age at onset but rather age itself that worsens the prognosis.

There is no generally agreed definition of early-onset and late-onset depression; the distinction itself appears somewhat artificial as long as unipolar depression has not been shown to be truly heterogeneous. In this context, it is of interest to note that the distinction between neurotic depression with an early onset and endogenous depression with a later onset has been found not to be valid. Scott *et al*'s (1996) long-term follow-up of the Newcastle sample originally described by Roth *et al* (1972, 1981) does not support the distinction between neurotic and endogenous depression.

Community studies have shown depression in the elderly to be very frequent and a major health-care problem; furthermore, depressive illness shortens life expectancy (Weeke, 1979; Baldwin, 1980; Weeke & Vaeth, 1986). In the elderly, somatic disorders in the presence of depression worsen the prognosis of both and shorten life expectancy still further. For all these reasons an investigation of the course and outcome of depression with an onset during the second half of life is a matter of great interest.

For this purpose some longitudinal data from a patient study recently reported by Angst & Preisig (1995a,b) were reanalysed and will be presented in this chapter. The general question to be addressed is whether age of onset modifies or specifically worsens the course and outcome of depression.

Sample of subject with unipolar depression

The sample consisted of the 137 patients with unipolar depression mentioned in the report of Angst & Preisig (1995a,b), a subsample of a larger study of 406 hospitalised patients with unipolar, bipolar and schizoaffective disorders admitted to the Zurich University Psychiatric Hospital between 1959 and 1964. The patients represent all admissions over these years. The patients suffered severe depression, illustrated by a 30% rate of psychotic cases. All subjects met diagnostic criteria for major depression. These patients were followed prospectively at least every five years until 1985. Further methodological details are given in the papers mentioned above. At the last follow-up, 43% of the total sample were interviewed personally. For the others, it was possible to obtain a telephone interview or to gather important information from interviewed relatives and doctors' reports. A lifelong history of the disorder could usually be established and the final outcome was estimated by the Global Assessment Schedule (GAS; Endicott *et al*, 1976). In 1985 and 1991, the latest mortality data were collected from the Swiss Federal Office of Statistics.

Age at onset was determined at first admission to hospital; previous out-patient records were frequently available. The clinical data were collected personally between 1959 and 1963 by Angst through interviews of patients and, in many cases, their relatives. The importance of dating age at onset at the beginning of the disorder and not later in life has been shown, for instance, by the World Health Organization, which found that elderly people usually dated the onset of their disorders no more than five years before the interview (Simon *et al*, 1995).

For the purposes of our analysis, the 137 probands were classified by age at onset into five subgroups as shown in Table 4.1: <30, 30–39, 40–49, 50–59, 60+. Instead of dichotomising early- and late-onset cases, it seemed more informative to make no assumptions about a cut-off. The five decade-based classes of age at onset should in some validations be expected to show a systematic trend; for instance, if the suicide risk increased with age at onset, this risk should increase steadily from one decade to the next.

TABLE 4.1
Sample of patients with unipolar depression

	Age at onset (years)					P
	<30	30–39	40–49	50–59	60+	
Gender						
Males	3	7	6	10	10	
Females	24	12	23	21	21	
Total	27	19	29	31	31	NS
Median age at onset (years)	22	35	46	54	65	–
Median age at first hospitalisation (years)	26	36	47	55	66	–
Median age at last observation (years)	54	64	73	75	78	0.0001
Dead (%)	29.6	42.1	89.6	80.4	96.8	0.0001

P, Kruskal–Wallis χ^2 test.

The sample consisted mainly of females (73.4%). The preponderance was more marked in the youngest group, with an onset before the age of 30. It decreased slightly with age at onset, but in the late-onset group (60+) there was still a 2:1 gender ratio in favour of females. The difference between the median age at onset and the median age at first hospitalisation showed that for the severe cases in our study, hospitalisation usually occurred about one year after the onset of the disorder; the exception was the youngest group, where the interval was four years. The five groups differed not only – by definition – in the age at onset but also in their age at last observation. However, the latter difference between the three later-onset subgroups (40–49, 50–59, 60+) was relatively small (73 versus 75 versus 78 years). This fact is very important for the interpretation of some findings, for instance death rates or the prevalence of organic brain syndromes. A further significant fact is that about 90% of subjects with a later onset (at age 40 or more) had died. In most cases, therefore, lifelong histories of the course were obtained.

We shall now present the data on course, outcome and certain other clinical characteristics occurring in the five subgroups of depression defined by age of onset.

TABLE 4.2
Details of course

	Age at onset (years)					P
	<30	30 – 39	40 – 49	50 – 59	60+	
Median length of observation (years)	31.9	29.7	26.4	19.1	10.0	0.0001
Median length of illness (years)	23.4	20.8	19.3	14.4	4.9	0.0001
Median number of episodes	6	5	3	4	2	0.0002
Mean number of episodes	7.1	6.5	5.6	4.9	2.6	0.0002
Median length of episodes (months)	4.5	6.3	7	5.4	6	NS
Percentage time spent in episodes	15	20	24	21	32	NS
Mean number of episodes per year	0.23	0.25	0.31	0.34	0.38	NS
Median length of cycles (years)	5.4	5.8	4.4	4.3	4.1	NS

P, Kruskal–Wallis χ^2 test.

The course of unipolar depression by age at onset

As a result of definition and life expectancy, the five onset groups showed marked differences in the length of observation (Table 4.2). The two early-onset subgroups (up to age 39) were observed for 30 years, whereas those in the oldest group, with an onset of 60+, were followed for only 10 years. The length of illness, defined as the period between the onset of the first episode and the termination of the last episode, decreased systematically over the five onset groups, from a maximum of 23 to a minimum of five years. The same applies to the number of episodes observed, which were also a function of the length of observation and illness. The number of episodes declined systematically from six in the youngest group to two in the oldest group. Somewhat unexpectedly, there was no clear tendency for the length of episodes to be influenced by the age at onset (Fig. 4.1). As a basis for the computations, the mean of episode length for each patient was first computed and then the median for all individuals. The length of episode is log-normally distributed and the median is about 5.6 months, a figure which has not changed over the past 100 years (Ziehen, 1896, Wertham, 1929) in spite of modern psychopharmacological treatments.

Assuming poorer prognosis in the late-onset than in the early-onset group, one would expect the lifetime percentage of time spent in episodes to increase with age at onset. There was a clear systematic trend in the expected direction (Fig. 4.2), but it was not statistically significant. The early-onset group spent only half as much time (15%) of their life in episodes as the latest-onset group (60+), for whom the figure was 32%. Episode frequency per year was 0.23 versus 0.38 in the

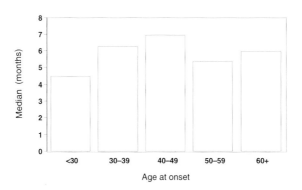

Fig. 4.1. Median length of episodes.

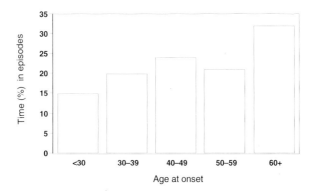

Fig. 4.2. Percentage time spent in depressive episodes.

two extreme groups (Fig. 4.3). The mean length of cycles describes the same finding in a different way. The average interval between onset of episodes was lower in the latest-onset group (4.1 years) than in the earliest onset group (5.4 years), reflecting a higher risk of recurrence in elderly depressives.

Overall, clear differences between the five subgroups can be demonstrated statistically only in variables which are dependent on life expectancy. But there is also a non-significant tendency in the direction of a more severe course of the later-onset subgroups.

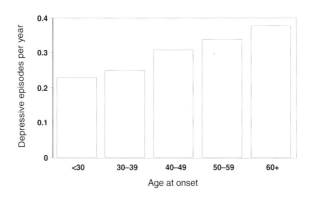

Fig. 4.3. Mean number of depressive episodes per year.

TABLE 4.3
Details of outcome

	Age at onset (years)					P1	P2
	<30	*30–39*	*40–49*	*50–59*	*60+*		
Sample size	29	19	29	31	31	–	–
Age at last observation (years)	54	64	73	75	78	0.0001	
Recovery[1] (%)	25.9	42.1	20.7	19.4	29.0	NS	NS
Chronic (>2 years) (%)	3.7	10.5	17.2	12.9	22.6	NS	0.08
Suicides (%)	22.2	5.3	20.7	19.4	6.5	NS	NS
Organic brain syndrome (%)	–	15.8	18.5	22.6	41.9	0.01	0.0001

P_1, over all 5 columns.
P_2, age at onset <40 *v*. 40+ years.
1. GAS score >60 for over 5 years.

Outcome of unipolar depression by age at onset

As it proved impossible to find any significant differences in course as a function of age at onset, the crucial question is whether outcome is dependent on age at onset. Outcome was assessed by three variables: recovery, chronicity and suicide. Recovery was defined as a remission lasting over five years without any further episodes over lifetime and a GAS score of over 60. The data in Table 4.3 show clearly that there is no correlation between recovery and age at onset, not even a slight trend in the direction of less frequent recovery in the oldest subgroup. On the other hand chronicity (defined by a depressive episode lasting two years or more without recovery) shows a tendency to develop more frequently in cases with an onset at age 40 or later (Fig. 4.4). Chronicity developed in only 3.7% of the youngest onset group, as against 22.6% of subjects in the oldest onset group. Again, however, there is no statistically significant difference between the five subgroups. If we dichotomise between early-onset cases (up to age 39) and late-onset cases (from 40+) the *P* value is 0.08, showing a trend in the expected direction.

Surprisingly, the suicide rates also did not differ over the five subgroups. They were low in the 60+ group, who were observed on average over the last ten years of life. The suicide risk of this group deserves further analysis using larger samples.

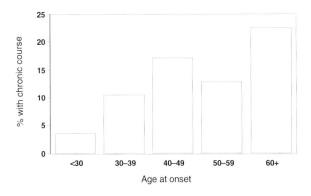

Fig. 4.4. Percentage of patients with a chronic course of depression (episode lasting two years or more without remission).

The only outcome variable which clearly showed a dependence on age at onset was the prevalence of organic brain syndromes (Fig. 4.5). This is a trivial finding, and the differences can probably be explained by age differences at last observation.

In summary, then, age at onset does not correlate with outcome.

Other clinical characteristics

Disappointed by these findings, we also looked for other clinical characteristics in the patients classified by age at onset (Table 4.4). Again, the expectations were not met: a family history of affective

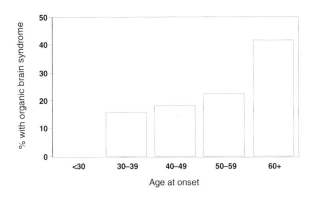

Fig. 4.5. The association of age at onset of depression and organic brain syndromes.

TABLE 4.4
Details of other clinical characteristics

	Age at onset (years)					P_1	P_2
	<30	30–39	40–49	50–59	60+		
Family history of affective disorder	33.3	36.8	20.7	22.6	25.8	NS	NS
Psychotic features	29.6	31.6	24.1	35.5	45.2	NS	NS
Mood-incongruent psychotic features	18.5	10.5	6.9	16.1	9.7	NS	NS

P_1, over all five columns.
P_2, age at onset <40 $v.$ 40+ years.

disorders among first-degree relatives did not decrease significantly with age at onset, nor did the presence of psychotic features increase significantly with age at onset (Fig. 4.6). Nevertheless, the latest onset group presented more psychotic features, which is predictable as an effect of age itself.

Discussion

Starting with the assumption that late age at onset might correlate with a more severe course and poorer outcome of depression, the findings are disappointing and largely disprove the hypothesis. The sample sizes of the five subgroups were large enough to demonstrate any clinically significant findings. Analyses of much larger samples might yield statistically significant differences, but these would be of questionable clinical relevance.

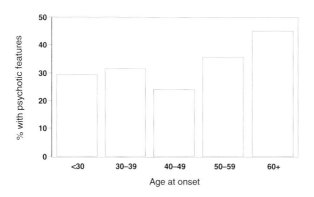

Fig. 4.6. Percentage with psychotic features of depression.

The good news is that the prognosis of late-onset depression is little worse than that of early-onset depression. These findings are in line with the literature (Post, 1972; Winokur & Morrison, 1973; Murphy, 1983; Baldwin & Jolley, 1986; Robinson, 1989). People with late-onset depression should be treated with the same optimism and thoroughness as those with early-onset depression; they deserve equal if not more attention, because the disorder has frequently not been diagnosed in time.

The finding that suicides do not increase with age at onset is consistent with an earlier finding of Angst & Stassen (1987) and Angst *et al* (1990), based on survival analysis, that in affective disorders the suicide risk is linear and therefore constant over the lifetime. It neither increases nor decreases with age nor age at onset. The only suspect positive finding of our study relates to the development of chronicity. This does indeed seem to be slightly more prevalent among later-onset cases; again, this would be a reason for treating elderly patients more intensively and for longer than early-onset patients.

From a theoretical point of view, the data demonstrate the artificiality of a dichotomy between early- and late-onset depression. All the data indicate the homogeneity of severe unipolar depression, and that it should be considered as a single disorder and part of the broad depressive spectrum consisting of double depression, combined depression, major depression, recurrent brief depression, dysthymia, minor depression and bereavement.

References

ANGST, J. (1966) *Zur Ätiologie und Nosologie endogener depressiver Psychosen. Eine genetische, soziologische und klinische Studie.* Berlin: Springer.
—— (1980) Clinical typology of bipolar illness. In: *Mania – An Evolving Concept* (eds R. H. Belmaker & H. M. van Praag), pp. 61–76. Jamaica: Spectrum.
—— & STASSEN, H. H. (1987) Verlaufsaspekte affektiver Psychosen: Suizide, Rückfallrisiko im Alter. In *Fortschritte in der Psychosen – Forschung? 7. 'Weissenauer' Schizophrenie-Symposion, Bonn 1986* (ed. G. Huber), pp. 145–165. Stuttgart: Schattauer.
—— & PREISIG, M. (1995a) Course of a clinical cohort of unipolar, bipolar and schizoaffective patients. Results of a prospective study from 1959 to 1985. *Schweizer Archiv für Neurologie und Psychiatrie*, **146**, 5–16.
—— &—— (1995b) Outcome of a clinical cohort of unipolar, bipolar and schizoaffective patients. Results of a prospective study from 1959 to 1985. *Schweizer Archiv für Neurologie und Psychiatrie*, **146**, 17–23.
——, ——, GROSS, G., *et al* (1990) Suicide in affective and schizoaffective disorders. In *Affective and Schizoaffective Disorders* (eds A. Marneros & M. T. Tsuang), pp. 168–185. Berlin: Springer.
BALDWIN, J. A. (1980) Schizophrenia and physical disease: a preliminary analysis of the data from the Oxford Record Linkage Study. In *Biochemistry of Schizophrenia and Addiction. In Search of a Common Factor* (ed. G. Hemmings), pp. 197–318. Lancaster: MTP Press.

—— & JOLLEY, D. J. (1986) The prognosis of depression on old age. *British Journal of Psychiatry*, **149**, 574–583.

ENDICOTT, J., SPITZER, R. L., FLEISS, J. L. & COHEN, J. (1976) The Global Assessment Scale. A procedure for measuring overall severity of psychiatric disturbances. *Archives of General Psychiatry*, **33**, 766–771.

GROF, P., ANGST, J. & HAINES, T. (1974) The clinical course of depression: practical issues. In *Classification and Prediction of Outcome of Depression. Symposium, Schloss Reinhartshausen/Rhein 1973* (ed. J. Angst), pp. 141–148. Stuttgart: Schattauer.

KRAEPELIN, E. (1921) Manic–depressive insanity. In *Manic–Depressive Illness. History of a Syndrome* (ed. E. A. Wolpert), pp. 33–111. New York: International Universities Press.

LORANGER, A. W. & LEVINE, P. M. (1978) Age at onset of bipolar affective illness. *Archives of General Psychiatry*, **35**, 1345–1348.

LUNDQUIST, G. (1945) Prognosis and course in manic–depressive psychoses: a follow-up study of 319 first admissions. *Acta Psychiatrica Scandinavica* (suppl. 35), 1–96.

MALZBERG, B. (1929) A statistical study of the factor of age in the manic–depressive psychoses. *Psychiatric Quarterly*, **3**, 509–604.

MARNEROS, A., DEISTER, A. & ROHDE, A. (1991) *Affektive, schizoaffektive und schizophrene Psychosen.* Berlin: Springer.

MENDLEWICZ, J. & BARON, M. (1981) Morbidity risks in subtypes of unipolar depressive illness: differences between early and late onset forms. *British Journal of Psychiatry*, **139**, 463–466.

MURPHY, E. (1983) The prognosis of depression in old age. *British Journal of Psychiatry*, **142**, 111–119.

PASKIND, H. A. (1930) Manic–depressive psychosis as seen in private praxis. Sex distribution and age incidence of first attacks. *Archives of Neurology and Psychiatry*, **23**, 152–158.

PERRIS, C., PERRIS, H., ERICSSON, U. & VON KNORRING, L. (1982) The genetics of depression. A family study of unipolar and neurotic-reactive depressed patients. *Archiv für Psychiatrie und Nervenkrankheiten*, **232**, 137–155.

——, EISEMANN, M., ERICSSON, U., *et al* (1983) Attempts to validate a classification of unipolar depression based on family data. Symptomatological aspects. *Neuropsychobiology*, **9**, 103–107.

PESELOW, E. D., DUNNER, D. L., FIEVE, R. R., *et al* (1982) Age of onset of affective illness. *Psychiatria Clinica (Basel)*, **15**, 124–132.

POLLOCK, H. M. (1931) Recurrence of attacks in manic–depressive psychoses. *American Journal of Psychiatry*, **11**, 567–574.

POST, F. (1972) The management and nature of depressive illness in late life: a follow-through study. *British Journal of Psychiatry*, **121**, 393–404.

ROBINSON, J. R. (1989) The natural history of mental disorder in old age. A long-term study. *British Journal of Psychiatry*, **154**, 783–789.

ROTH, M., GURNEY, C., GARSIDE, R. F. & KERR, T. A. (1972) Studies in the classification of affective disorders. The relationship between anxiety states and depressive illness – I. *British Journal of Psychiatry*, **121**, 147–161.

——, GARSIDE, R. F., GURNEY, C. & KERR, T. A. (1981) Depressive illness: clinically diverse? *British Journal of Psychiatry*, **138**, 162–163.

SCOTT, J., TACCHI, M. J. & KERR, A. (1996) A thirty year follow-up of the Newcastle affective disorders cohort (abstract). *8th Congress of the Association of European Psychiatrists. Annual Meeting of the Royal College of Psychiatrists.* London: Royal College of Psychiatrists.

SIMON, G. E., VON KORFF, M., ÜSTÜN, T. B , *et al* (1995) Is the lifetime risk of depression actually increasing? *Journal of Clinical Epidemiology*, **48**, 1109–1118.

SLATER, E. (1938) Zur Periodik des manisch–depressiven Irreseins. Die Eltern und Kinder von Manisch–Depressiven. *Zeitschrift für die Gesamte Neurologie und Psychiatrie*, **162**, 794–801.

STEEN, R. R. (1933) Prognosis in manic–depressive psychoses. *Psychiatric Quarterly*, **7**, 419–429.

SWIFT, H. M. (1907) The prognosis of recurrent insanity of the manic–depressive type. *American Journal of Insanity*, **64**, 311–326.

TASCHEW, T. & ROGLEV, M. (1973) Das Schicksal der Melancholiker im fortgeschrittenen Alter. *Archiv für Psychiatrie und Nervenkrankheiten*, **217**, 377–386.

TAYLOR, M. A. & ABRAMS, R. (1981) Early- and late-onset bipolar illness. *Archives of General Psychiatry*, **38**, 58–61.

WEEKE, A. (1979) Causes of death in manic–depressives. In *Origin, Prevention and Treatment of Affective Disorders* (eds M. Schou & E. Strömgren), pp. 289–299. London: Academic Press.

—— & VAETH, M. (1986) Excess mortality of bipolar and unipolar manic–depressive patients. *Journal of Affective Disorders*, **11**, 227–234.

WERTHAM, F. I. (1929) A group of benign chronic psychoses: prolonged manic excitements. With a statistical study of age, duration and frequency in 2000 manic attacks. *American Journal of Psychiatry*, **9**, 17–78.

WINOKUR, G. (1972) Depression spectrum disease: description and family study. *Comprehensive Psychiatry*, **13**, 3–8.

—— & MORRISON, J. (1973) The Iowa 500: follow-up of 225 depressives. *British Journal of Psychiatry*, **123**, 543–548.

——, CADORET, R., DORZAB, J. & BAKER, M. (1971) Depressive disease. A genetic study. *Archives of General Psychiatry*, **24**, 135–144.

——, BEHAR, D., VAN VALKENBURG, C. & LOWRY, M. (1978) Is a familial definition of depression both feasible and valid? *Journal of Nervous and Mental Disorders*, **166**, 764–768.

ZIEHEN, T. (1896) *Die Erkennung und Behandlung der Melancholie in der Praxis*. Halle: Karl Marhold.

ZIS, A. P., GROF, P., WEBSTER, M. & GOODWIN, F. K. (1980) Prediction of relapse in recurrent affective disorder. *Psychopharmacological Bulletin*, **16**, 47–49.

5 Delusional (psychotic) depression in the elderly

ROBERT C. BALDWIN

What has happened to psychosis in later life? Those who treat older patients have recently witnessed the demise of the unique psychosis of later life, paraphrenia (now termed either delusional disorder or schizophrenia) and have seen the failure (Schatzberg & Rothschild, 1992) of attempts to delineate psychotic depression as a particular subtype within DSM–IV (American Psychiatric Association, 1994). Are these major battles lost or minor skirmishes of no real significance?

In attempting to answer this point we will consider delusional depression (psychotic depression). This chapter will use the format of the paper by Schatzberg & Rothschild (1992), in which they argue the case for a distinct subgroup. Schatzberg & Rothschild do not present data specific to elderly people, even though elderly patients, particularly those with late-onset depression, may be more likely to develop delusions as part of a severe depressive episode (Hordern *et al*, 1963; Meyers & Greenberg, 1986). The main headings used by Schatzberg & Rothschild are: clinical characteristics; findings from biological studies; course and outcome; and treatment. I shall also include some data on frequency in clinical practice.

Before discussing these, a little historical background will help set the scene.

A landmark study is that of Hoch & McCurdy (1922), who studied 67 cases (mean age 55 years) of 'involutional melancholia', as was the term for severe depression. Their category of malignant (i.e. poor-outcome) cases included those patients with 'absurd ideas' and 'ridiculous hypochondriac delusions'. However, although these may have been depressive delusions, the terms used are unlike current terminology. These earlier cases may well have included patients nowadays regarded as suffering from schizophrenia, 'schizoaffective psychosis' or delusional disorder. Even so, Hoch & McCurdy high-lighted the fact that 'severe hypochondria' appeared to be associated with a bad prognosis.

In an important review Kantor & Glassman (1977) suggested that before the introduction of electroconvulsive therapy (ECT), the small percentage of people with depression who failed to recover had delusional depression. This was in keeping with the findings of authors such as Hoch & McCurdy. With the arrival of ECT, all types of severe depression were equally responsive, so that the delusional/non-delusional distinction lost its significance. With the advent of the modern pharmacological era, delusional depression seemed less responsive to tricyclic treatment. This gave rise to two modern notions: first that ECT might be the treatment of choice for delusional depression; second that delusional depression might be a distinct clinical subtype.

The frequency of delusional depression in later life

In the only community-based prevalence study of delusional depression in later life, Kivela & Pahkala (1989) found an overall prevalence of delusional depression in the over 60s of 10 per 1000 (12 per 1000 women and 6 per 1000 men). There were no hospitalised cases at the time to lower this figure artificially. Delusional cases comprised only 3.6% of all elderly community cases with depression. The prevalence of major depression in later-life community residents is approximately 3% (Baldwin & Jolley, 1986).

In specialised psychogeriatric services the figures are, not surprisingly, much higher (Table 5.1). Murphy (1983) found that 24% of patients with depression referred to two psychogeriatric services were delusional. In two further UK studies, of in-patients only, the figures were 53% (Post, 1972) and 44% (Baldwin & Jolley, 1986). In Australia,

TABLE 5.1
Reported prevalence rates of delusional depression

Study	Setting	Prevalence (%)
Post (1972)	In-patients	53
Murphy (1983)	In- and out-patients	24
Meyers & Greenberg (1986)	In-patients	45
Baldwin & Jolley (1986)	In-patients	44
Nelson *et al* (1989)	In-patients	36
Burvill *et al* (1991)	Mainly in-patients	35
Baldwin (1995)	In- and out-patients	25

Burvill *et al* (1991) calculated that 35% of their group with depression, who were mainly in-patients, were delusional. In the USA, Meyers & Greenberg (1986) reported that 45% of 161 patients with depression consecutively admitted to several psychogeriatric wards were deluded, and Nelson *et al* (1989) reported a figure of 36% for consecutive admissions of patients with depression over aged 60 years.

In a recent study (Baldwin, 1995) I ascertained the prevalence of psychosis in patients over the age of 65 with major depression referred to me over a five-year period. This study will be described in more detail in the next section. The figure of 25% (34 of 134 – see below) for delusional depression is comparable to that of Murphy (1983), who also studied both in-patients and out-patients, rather than in-patients only, where the rate is somewhat higher (Table 5.1). Seven patients per year were identified in this study. An old-age psychiatrist with a catchment population of 20 000 over-65s (reasonably typical in the United Kingdom) or about 2.5 times the study population herein, might therefore expect to see between 17 and 18 patients with psychotic depression per annum. This amounts to about one patient every three weeks. However, the author's referral rate is the second highest in the North West Region of the English National Health Service, so a figure of one patient every three to four weeks seems a reasonable estimate for the clinician with a substantial elderly practice. Psychotic depression is therefore not a rare condition.

Characteristics of delusional depression

The data presented here are part of a published study (Baldwin, 1995).

Major depressive disorder, in DSM–III–R (American Psychiatric Association, 1987), was the defined disease state. The following information was collected prospectively over five years: DSM–III–R major depression item checklist; age at onset of depression; score on the 17-item Hamilton Rating Scale for Depression (HRSD; Hamilton, 1960); and the presence of delusions at presentation, the definition being that of the Present State Examination (PSE; Wing *et al*, 1974). A number of patients had more than one type of delusion. They were categorised according to which one dominated the clinical picture. Patients were included if they had mood-incongruent delusions, provided that they also met criteria for major depression.

A cognitive screening test was administered. The Blessed and Roth scale (Blessed *et al*, 1968) was used in the first two years and the Mini-Mental State Examination (MMSE; Folstein *et al*, 1975) in later years. This change came about because of the increasing popularity of the MMSE. As a result, the scores were converted from the number of

TABLE 5.2
Comparison of deluded and control patients

	Deluded (n = 34)	Controls (n = 30)
Median age at onset (years)	71	72
Percentage with age at onset over 65 years	82	77
Median HRSD score at onset[1]	23	20**
Gender ratio (male:female)	1:1.13	1:3.34
Mean rank Hamilton guilt score	38.1	22.9***
Mean rank Hamilton anxiety score	34.6	26.5*
Mean rank Hamilton insight score	37.6	23.4***
Marital status (married:single:widowed:divorced)	7:15:11:1	12:6:11:1

1. Excludes four patients too ill to be rated.
*$P < 0.05$,**$P < 0.01$,***$P < 0.001$ (Mann–Whitney U test).

correct responses to a percentage correct. Lastly, a physical health rating scale was administered (Baldwin & Jolley, 1986).

Patients with dementia (meeting DSM–III–R criteria) and those with a history of mania were excluded.

The total number of referrals, excluding those with dementia, was 134, and they had a mean age at referral of 75.4 years. Of these, 34 were deluded and 100 were not.

To control for the effects of age and sex, 30 (of 34) deluded patients for whom an HRSD score was available were compared with 30 age- and gender-matched control subjects (drawn from the original 100 and matched to within two years of actual age) (Table 5.2).

There were no significant differences in age at referral, age at first onset of depression, cognitive score or physical health rating. Deluded patients were more likely to have had a history of depression, particularly after the age of 65 (35.3% of those with delusions compared with 10% of non-deluded patients). They were more likely to be male and to be single (44% of deluded patients compared with 20% of non-deluded patients were single). Deluded patients had more severe depression.

As already mentioned, 34 of 134 (25%) had delusions.

General characteristics

Some of the demographic findings were surprising. For the cohort as a whole the gender ratio was as one would expect, in favour of women. There were more men in the deluded group than would be expected. Secondly, single people were highly significantly over-represented in the deluded group. Kivela & Pahkala (1989) found that 58% of their deluded sample were unmarried compared with only 8% of their controls, a figure which was not commented upon because, given their small numbers, it was not statistically significant. It seems that the larger sample here has confirmed this result. Kay *et al* (1976) and Post (1967) emphasised the association between never having been married and schizophrenia in later life. Possibly, being single is also a risk factor for other psychoses, including delusional depression, in later life.

Delusion type

The main delusion types for the 34 deluded patients are shown in Table 5.3. Persecutory delusions in four patients were mood incongruent. Delusions of guilt were the most common *second* type of delusion in those patients with more than one type of delusion (guilt, 6; persecution, 3 (including mood-incongruent type, 2); hypochondriasis, 3; and delusions of reference, 2). Only five patients had more than two types of delusion. In men the most frequent delusion (main type only) was hypochondriasis (7/16) and in women it was persecution (7/18).

Kivela & Pahkala (1989) also found that hypochondriacal delusions predominated in men and guilt and paranoid delusions in women, and Meyers & Greenberg (1986) also found that delusions of persecution and hypochondriasis were the most common types, followed by delusions of guilt. There is evidence that older adults with depression, especially men, express less guilt than their younger counterparts (Small *et al*, 1986). The prominence of hypochondriacal and persecutory delusions rather than guilty ones in older people with depression might lead to inexperienced clinicians missing the diagnosis, given the prominent position which is traditionally accorded to ideas of guilt in the diagnosis of depression. Perhaps this should be highlighted more in teaching.

Both DSM–IV and ICD–10 (World Health Organization, 1992) permit non-congruent delusions in major depression/depressive

TABLE 5.3
Main type of delusion among 34 patients at presentation

Type	No. of patients
Persecutory[1]	12
Hypochondriacal	11
Nihilistic	4
Guilt	3
Poverty	3
Other	1

1. Includes four mood-incongruent delusions.

episode. However, one possible effect of this homogeneous approach to diagnosis is to underestimate the prevalence of schizoaffective disorder. One way to settle this is to conduct longitudinal follow-up studies, separating mood-congruent from non-congruent delusions. Patients reported in my 1995 study were not systematically followed up, but it is interesting to note that over 24 months two patients developed alternative diagnoses, in one case delusional disorder and in the other a vascular dementia. Both had presented initially with non-congruent delusions.

Differences in symptoms

In their review of delusional depression in younger adults, Schatzberg & Rothschild (1992) found that psychomotor change (particularly agitation) and guilt were more pronounced in deluded patients. They do not state what mechanism might underlie such differences, although psychomotor change is regarded as a significant biological correlate of depression (Rogers *et al*, 1987).

When deluded cases were compared with the 30 age- and gender-matched controls, there were no significant differences in the median ages at onset (71 years deluded; 72 controls) or proportions with an age at onset above 65 years (82% deluded; 77% controls). The total HRSD score remained significantly higher in the group with delusions (see Table 5.2). The only differences on individual HRSD score items were for guilt, anxiety and insight (see Table 5.2). There were no differences in ratings for agitation or retardation.

Overall then, there were few clinical differences between groups. As Schatzberg & Rothschild (1992) found, guilt was more marked in those with delusions but this may merely reflect severity rather than the presence of a distinct subtype. The latter view would be supported more if there had been differences in retardation and/or agitation. This may of course merely reflect the limitations of the measures and the small numbers, in other words a type II error.

The Epidemiologic Catchment Area (ECA) studies did not report differences in symptom profile, but they did find higher one-year mortality, including suicide (Johnson *et al*, 1991). Outcome will be discussed later.

Symptomatic differences, especially psychomotor change, may differentiate psychotic from non-psychotic depression. Alternatively, psychomotor disturbance may merely reflect differences in 'endo-geneity', or may simply be a marker which differentiates melancholic from non-melancholic forms of depression. Against this, Parker *et al* (1991), in a study of mixed-aged patients with melancholic depression, adjusted for the presence or otherwise of 'endogeneity' and still found that patients with endogenous psychotic depression had significantly more psychomotor change than patients with endogenous non-psychotic forms. This does support psychotic depression as a distinct subtype. Unfortunately, there have been no studies of older patients which have addressed this, although it would not be a difficult undertaking in a clinical setting.

Thus, the admittedly small number of studies of delusional depression in older people have not replicated the findings of different symptom profiles in younger patients.

Cognitive impairment

Schatzberg & Rothschild (1992) cite evidence for poorer cognitive function in younger and middle-aged patients with delusional depression than non-psychotic depression. Notably, Rothschild *et al* (1989) found worse function on frontal and temporal lobe tasks in 15 younger psychotically depressed patients than in 15 controls without psychosis. In elderly patients, Lesser *et al* (1991) compared late-onset depression with normal older controls and also found that those with psychotic depression had significantly lower full-scale IQ scores. Pearlson *et al* (1989) had also noted, in a computerised tomography (CT) study, that depressed subjects with what they termed 'dementia of depression', defined by an MMSE score of less than 24, were more often found to be delusional than those with higher scores (40% compared with 9% of those above the cut-off of 24), although the difference was not statistically significant, perhaps because of very small numbers. Lastly, psychotic symptoms in dementia are associated with greater cognitive impairment and a poorer prognosis (Zubenko *et al*, 1991; Rosen & Zubenko, 1992).

In a study of 14 elderly patients (mean age 71, range 62–81 years) Kunik *et al* (1994) compared the cognitive function of eight patients who had delusional depression with six who did not, using a comprehensive neuropsychological test battery (WAIS; Controlled Oral Association Test; Boston Naming test; an aphasia test; and the trail-making tests). They found significant deficits in the group with psychosis on: performance IQ (markedly) but also verbal IQ sub-tests, word fluency and memory. The groups were matched for severity and, in the authors' view, were not impaired by their delusions in the completion of test results.

In my own study (Baldwin, 1995) there were no differences regarding cognitive function, but only a single screening instrument (for dementia) was used and most patients scored almost full marks. So a combination of low sensitivity and a ceiling effect could easily have obscured any true differences.

It is unclear whether cognitive change in delusional depression is a specific or non-specific finding in psychoses generally. The literature on cognitive deficits in schizophrenia, typically with an early onset, is too vast to review, but there have been some studies of psychoses of later life. For example, Miller *et al* (1991) described 24 patients, all aged over 45, with late-onset delusional disorder (i.e. not delusional depressive illness) and found significant deficits compared with controls regarding IQ and tests of frontal lobe function and verbal memory. In a group with mild delusional disorder ($n = 33$), Herlitz & Forsell (1996) demonstrated a reduced performance compared with controls ($n = 66$) on tasks of recall but not of recognition or primary memory.

In Manchester, we have completed a study of treatment response in late-life depression (Simpson *et al*, 1997). From an original cohort of 99, 66 (51 with psychosis and 15 without) received a neuropsychological battery (described in Baldwin & Simpson, 1997). Overall, in keeping with other studies, the group with psychosis were more severely depressed at the outset. However, we also found that this group performed significantly worse on tests of frontal function and visuo-spatial constructional praxis (Simpson *et al*, 1999).

Schatzberg & Rothschild postulate that cognitive deficits in psychotic-ally (and some non-psychotically) depressed patients reflect increased cortisol activity. In many respects though these neuropsychological findings seen in late-onset delusional disorder are similar to the deficits seen in depression (Weingartner *et al*, 1982). The possible relevance of this is discussed below, under the heading 'Neuro-imaging'.

Biological correlates

Activity of the hypothalamic–pituitary–adrenal (HPA) axis

It is worth pointing out that the basis for delusions themselves is not truly known but that Sapolsky *et al* (1986) proposed a model based on increased HPA activity. Glucocorticoids may enhance dopaminergic activity. Human models are the psychiatric sequelae of Cushing's disease and of steroid-induced psychosis.

Schatzberg & Rothschild (1992) report that the "vast majority" of studies point to increased HPA activity in delusional depressions compared with non-delusional ones. However, in a study of elderly patients with depression this was not found to be so (O'Brien *et al*, 1997). Sixty-one patients aged over 55 years were assessed; 22 had delusional (psychotic) depression. A dexamethasone suppression test (DST) was performed on 52 subjects. There was a trend for deluded subjects with depression to be non-suppressors more frequently than non-delusional subjects (68% versus 45%) but this difference was not significant. An analysis of co-variance examining differences in post-test dexamethasone concentrations and HRSD scores also failed to find differences.

Studies of dopaminergic activity and enzyme studies

Meltzer *et al* (1976) found lower serum dopamine-beta-hydroxylase (DβH) in younger patients with psychotic depression but not in controls or patients with schizophrenia, mania or 'neurotic' depression, and Sweeney *et al* (1978) found an imbalance in the ratio of dopamine to noradrenaline metabolites in deluded patients but not in non-deluded patients with depression under the age of 65. Coryell *et al* (1982) have suggested that familial subtypes of primary unipolar depression are significantly associated with the presence of delusions, which also suggests a genetic influence towards delusionality.

These findings relate to younger groups of people with depression and suggest that for younger patients there may be a genetic component involved in the expression of delusions within depressive illnesses, acting via the dopaminergic system. Given what we know about the reduced influence of genetic factors in the aetiology of late-life depressions (e.g. Mendelwicz, 1976, but see also Angst in this volume), a genetic component toward delusionality in late-life depression seems less likely.

There are no studies of dopaminergic activity in delusional depression in later life.

Neuro-imaging

Schatzberg & Rothschild (1992) report a body of evidence concerning younger patients with psychotic depression suggestive of increased ventricle–brain ratios (VBR). A much-quoted representative study is that of Targum *et al* (1983). They studied 38 melancholic depressed patients, none elderly, with both unipolar and bipolar disorder. Their findings were that the mean VBR of the (deluded) group with psychosis was greater, although not significantly so, than that of the group with non-psychotic depression and a comparison group with neurological disorder. Five of the 20 patients with psychosis had VBRs greater than two standard deviations from the mean of patients with neurological disorder, whereas none of the 18 depressed patients without psychosis did.

In the study of O'Brien *et al* (1997), magnetic resonance imaging (MRI) scans were performed. They used a simple (blinded) clinical rating of temporal and cortical atrophy. They also rated deep white-matter lesions and periventricular hyperintensities. There were no group differences in the latter, but there was a trend for more deep white-matter change in the deluded compared with the non-deluded patients (95% versus 79%, $P = 0.08$). Obviously, there may have been a ceiling effect here and, in any case, these changes are widely reported in depression in later life (Baldwin, 1993). O'Brien *et al* (1997) found no differences in measures of atrophy.

In our recent study (Simpson *et al*, 1999), a sub-sample of 44 from an original cohort of 99 consecutive referrals with DSM–III–R major depression had an MRI brain scan. Of these, 34 were non-psychotic (using DSM–III–R criteria) and 10 were not. We analysed the scans using a multispectral technique. The brain measures most strongly associated with delusions were: diencephalic atrophy, lesions in the pontine reticular formation and left-sided frontotemporal atrophy. We found no association with white-matter change. Our findings that brain atrophy is more strongly associated with delusions than white-matter change is of aetiological relevance, which will be discussed at the end of this section.

As Schatzberg & Rothschild (1992) point out, findings such as these are in the opposite direction to those from schizophrenia research, where positive symptoms (delusions and hallucinations) are associated with smaller ventricles, and with the finding in Alzheimer's disease that delusions are associated with relative preservation of ventricular size (Burns *et al*, 1990).

Electroencephalographic (EEG) sleep profiles

Schatzberg & Rothschild (1992) cite evidence that patients with delusional major depression exhibit significantly diminished slow-wave sleep, poorer sleep efficiency, and a reduced percentage of rapid eye movement (REM) sleep and, using spectral EEG, more 'micro-arousals' in comparison with non-deluded depressed patients.

These findings have not been replicated in an elderly patient sample. Furthermore, EEG variables measured during sleep show similar changes in both depression and normal ageing (Veith & Raskind, 1988). These include similarities in night-time wakefulness, decreased slow-wave sleep, total REM sleep and REM latency, which may well obscure any differences.

Measures of serotonergic function

According to Schatzberg & Rothschild (1992) the findings are inconclusive and difficult to disentangle from changes in dopaminergic transmission. There are no data on elderly delusionally depressed subjects.

Other factors

One factor not considered by Schatzberg & Rothschild (1992), because it is really of relevance to late-life depression, is age at onset of depression. Meyers & Greenberg (1986) found an increase in delusional forms of depression with increasing age at onset. In an elderly sample of 161 patients, the average age at onset was 62.4 years for those with delusions compared with 51.5 years for those without delusions – a highly significant difference. They suggested that age at onset of depression may influence its presentation, and therefore that cerebral ageing and/or age-related pathology in the brain may modify the presentation of depression. Nelson *et al* (1989) were unable to replicate the findings of Meyers & Greenberg. Differences in the selection of cases may have influenced this.

In my 1995 study I tried to replicate the findings of Meyers & Greenberg. Age at onset for the group with delusions was 68.8 years compared with 70.5 for those without delusions. These findings and those of Meyers & Greenberg and Nelson *et al* are shown in Table 5.4. In this study a cut-off of 65 years for early versus late was chosen, this being the age criterion for admission to the service. The finding, of no significant difference, is not altered by adopting an age cut-off of 60. The proportions were 27% delusional for those with onset of depression over the age of 60 and 33% for those under it – clearly very similar. A similar calculation was carried out using the median age at onset for my own cohort, which was 72. The findings are little different: 23% delusional for onset above the median value and 30% for those below it.

This study then did not support an association between an increased age at onset of depression in older patients and the likelihood of

TABLE 5.4
Association between age at onset of depression and delusions in three studies

Study	No. of subjects	Age at referral		Age at onset		Onset
		Deluded	*Non-deluded*	*Deluded*	*Non-deluded*	
Meyers & Greenberg (1986)	161	72.6	70.9	62.4	51.5*	>60
Nelson *et al* (1989)	109	68.5	69.9	51.1	55.2	>60
Baldwin (1995)	134	75.5	75.4	68.8	70.5	>65

*$P < 0.001$ (deluded *v.* non-deluded).

that depression being delusional in form. It does not support cerebral 'ageing' as a factor predisposing to psychotic depression.

Towards a model of delusion formation in late-life psychotic depression

In our recent study of psychotic depression (Simpson *et al*, 1999) we found that brain atrophy rather than white-matter change correlated with delusion formation, and that the psychosis was associated with poor frontal lobe and visuospatial performance. Additionally, my earlier naturalistic study (Baldwin, 1995) indicated that hypochondriacal delusions were common. Interestingly, in our recent study the patients were *actually* more physically ill. These pieces of the jigsaw can be tentatively placed together to produce a hypothesis of delusion formation. Deluded patients with depression have more intense lowering of mood and therefore a greater morbid quality of mood. Coupled with the stressor of poor actual health, this may lead to intense morbid ideation. However, not all physically ill depressed patients develop psychosis. In patients with normal paralimbic function, self-rationalisation of morbid ideation usually occurs, leaving no reality distortion. In our patients we speculate that paralimbic abnormalities caused distortion of the processing of somatic information. Coupled with abnormal frontal regulation and disinhibition, also apparent in our patients on testing, this may have been the catalyst for delusion formation. Activation of the diencephalon is dependent on afferent input from the reticular activating system, which is also involved in regulating cyclical levels of arousal and concentration. Therefore our patients may have been more vulnerable to misperceptions and hence delusion formation from this source too. Lesions of the pontine reticular system were significantly predictive of delusions, independent of brain atrophy. No one area of the brain is likely to be responsible for delusion formation. Rather, an abnormal interaction of several brain areas with respect to perception, ideation and affective processing may explain why some depressed patients develop delusions.

Course and outcome

The evidence from younger adults with depression is conflicting. Robinson & Spiker (1985) showed higher chronicity in patients with psychosis over 12 months. The ECA studies (Johnson *et al*, 1991) reported more admissions and more economic impairment. However, in the IOWA 500 study there was a poorer two- to five-year outcome for patients with psychosis but no difference at 40 years when compared with patients without psychosis (Coryell & Tsuang, 1982). Lastly, Coryell *et al* (1987) found clinical outcomes to be good at two years, and although psychosocial impairment was greater at six months in the group with psychosis, this difference disappeared with longer follow-up.

Murphy (1983) found that delusional depressed patients had an especially dire prognosis. Of the 30 such patients in her cohort only 10% had recovered by the end of one year and almost a quarter had died. Using data from a previous study (Baldwin & Jolley, 1986) I set out to replicate Murphy's findings.

The study is reported in detail elsewhere (Baldwin, 1988). It was retrospective. Entry criteria for the original study were: age over 65 years; in-patient status; Feighner's (1972) criteria for primary unipolar depressive illness could be met; first admission to the psychogeriatric unit. Twenty-four patients were identified from the original 100 who were deluded at admission and without previous psychiatric history. The criterion for a delusion was that of the PSE. Simple ideas of hopelessness, self-depreciation or guilt arising out of depressed mood were not accepted but both mood-congruent and mood-incongruent delusions were, provided that the latter had occurred in the setting of severely depressed mood.

These 24 were matched to a further 24 new patients with depression, also from the original study (Baldwin & Jolley, 1986), to serve as controls. Matching was in terms of age, gender and the length of follow-up, this varying between 42 and 104 months for surviving patients.

Relapse rates were assessed by recording the number of readmissions for depression. Additional information from the case-notes enabled calculation of these rates over 48 months. The cumulative proportion of patients in the deluded group readmitted at 12, 24, 36 and 48 months were (with control group in parentheses), respectively: 12.5% (12.5%); 33% (17%); 33% (21%); and 46% (25%) (Fig. 5.1a). The figures for the deluded group are nearly double those of the controls after 12 months. Furthermore, 20 readmissions occurred in the deluded group but only eight in the controls. Out-patient relapses had also been recorded. When these are added, the cumulative relapse rates are very similar: for the deluded group (with controls in parentheses): 17% (21%); 38% (29%); 38% (42%); 50% (50%) (Fig. 5.1b). Also, the total number of relapses becomes similar (21 deluded; 18 controls).

Survival analysis. A more sound method for ascertaining whether there were real differences in the liability to relapse is the use of survival analysis. For this analysis the *total follow-up* period of 104 months, not 48 months as above, was used. The difference in the slopes in Fig. 5.2 is not statistically significant.

These findings do not signify an especially poor overall prognosis for patients with delusional forms of depression in the medium to

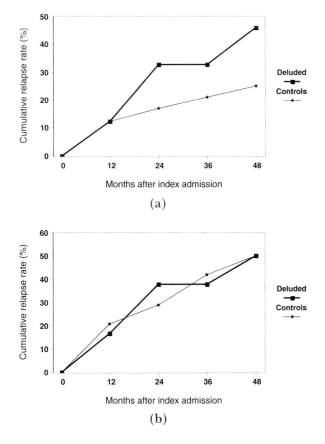

Fig. 5.1. (a) Relapses among deluded and non-deluded patients with depression, leading to in-patient treatment. (b) Relapses leading to in- or out-patient treatment.

long term. However, more of those in the deluded group had at least one relapse requiring in-patient care (54%) than had controls (38%) and, interestingly, of seven patients with unremitting depression, six were initially deluded.

Unfortunately, not many outcome studies have indicated the status of patients during the index episode in terms of psychotic symptoms or not. The few that have (e.g. Burvill *et al*, 1991; Brodaty *et al*, 1993) have not found delusions to predict poorer outcome.

The finding of Murphy (1983) that delusional depression is associated with a particularly poor prognosis is not supported. The reason for the difference from this study is not clear. It is doubtful that

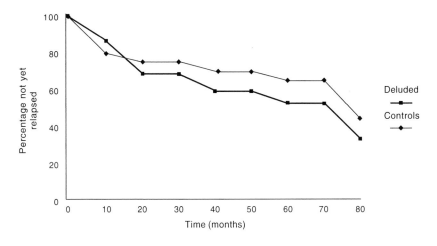

Fig. 5.2. Survival analysis, in-patient relapses.

the two cohorts differed in any important respects. One possible explanation is that the patients studied by Murphy were not adequately treated. This is supported by the observation that in this study ECT was given to 65% of patients with delusional depression and only 48% in the study of Murphy. It is doubtful whether a 12-month study such as that of Murphy (1983) can provide reliable data concerning prognosis since the natural history of severe depression exceeds a year (Hoch & McCurdy, 1922).

Findings from younger and mixed-aged populations of patients suggest a higher morbidity for delusional depression in the short to medium term, say the first two years, but more similar outcomes in the longer term. The evidence regarding suicide is inconsistent, but psychotic depression has been associated with greater suicidal ideation (Schatzberg & Rothschild, 1992). Therefore the aftercare of such patients, of whatever age, should be planned and not left to chance.

Stability of diagnosis

Leutcher & Spar (1985) questioned the stability of late-onset psychoses. Of 25 patients eventually diagnosed as suffering major affective disorder, a third had 'crossed over' from another category, compared with 17% of organic psychoses and 7% of psychiatric controls wothout psychosis (overall mean age 75 years). From this they argue that psychotic symptoms in later life, including those arising in depression, are non-specific. However, although most naturalistic studies of depression report some change in diagnosis over time, for example to paranoid psychosis, this is generally of the order of only a few per cent (Baldwin & Jolley, 1986). Probably what Leutcher & Spar have highlighted is a natural uncertainty in the early stages of making a diagnosis rather than an inherent long-term instability. For example, it is not uncommon for delusions in depression to be concealed either directly by the patients or as a result of profound psychomotor retardation. Sometimes, though, delusional depression, as with its non-delusional counterpart, will be a prodrome of another disorder, such as dementia.

Does delusional depression presage dementia? Rabins *et al* (1984) compared 18 patients with co-morbid depression and dementia with 18 who had dementia alone and a group of patients with major depression alone (all aged over 60 years). Fifteen of the group of patients with dementia/depression had delusions compared with three of those with dementia alone – a highly significant difference. At follow-up, only three patients did not recover cognitively in the group with dementia/depression. The authors emphasise that, in most cases, the dementia of depression does not progress to irreversible dementia. Since most of their sample had delusions, it seems reasonable to generalise this to delusional depression.

Continuity of symptoms

If delusional depression is due to an inherent vulnerability to psychotic symptoms then one might expect future episodes to 'run true'. Such was the finding of Charney & Nelson (1981) in a retrospective study of mixed-age patients. Thus, of 54 patients with delusional depression, 95% had had at least one previous episode characterised by delusions, whereas this was true only of 8% of the 66 non-deluded patients. Maj *et al* (1990), in a younger sample, likewise found continuity of symptoms at seven-year follow-up.

I therefore carried out a blinded analysis of subsequent relapses. At first relapse, seven out of 11 of patients from the original deluded group had delusional relapses whereas this did not occur in any of the patients who relapsed from the control group; this difference was significant at the 2% level (Fisher's exact test). If one takes the second relapse the figures are similar: five out of 10 relapses from the deluded group were delusional but none out of the seven relapses from the controls. So delusional depressions in late life do indeed seem to 'run true', supporting the view that delusional depression is a distinct subtype.

Treatments

The evidence that delusional depression is a distinct subtype derives mainly from studies of treatment which demonstrate that delusional depression has a poorer response to tricyclic antidepressants than non-delusional depression (Hordern *et al*, 1963; Glassman *et al*, 1975; Charney & Nelson, 1981; Frances *et al*, 1981; Glassman & Roose, 1981; Perry *et al*, 1982; Spiker *et al*, 1985). Further evidence for a difference between the two types of depression comes from studies comparing real and simulated ECT. These have demonstrated particular benefit (Brandon *et al*, 1984), or benefit only (Clinical Research Centre, 1984) for deluded people with depression.

These studies have been on mixed-age patients or those under the age of 65. It may therefore be unwise to extrapolate data from younger patients with depression to older ones, especially given current notions suggesting that brain changes may be a factor in later-life depressions (Baldwin, 1993). Returning to my earlier study (Baldwin, 1988) referred to above, I examined the question of treatment response of delusional people with depression in an older patient group. One patient from the deluded group was found to have a pancreatic cyst soon after admission and was transferred for surgery, leaving 23 in the deluded group. It can be seen (Table 5.5) that deluded patients responded less often to antidepressant drugs alone, were more often given ECT and required significantly more major tranquilliser usage to improve them. Secondly, more patients in the deluded group required combinations of antipsychotic drugs and antidepressants.

TABLE 5.5
Treatments required during the index illness to produce recovery or improvement

	Deluded patients (n= 23)	Controls (n=24)	Fisher's exact test
No. (%) of patients receiving antidepressants alone	4 (18)	10 (45)	$P = 0.05$
Total no. (%) of patients receiving antidepressants	13 (59)	14 (64)	NS
No. (%) of patients receiving ECT only	3 (14)	5 (23)	NS
Total no. (%) of patients receiving ECT	15 (68)	7 (32)	$P < 0.02$
Total no. (%) of patients receiving major tranquillisers	11 (50)	4 (18)	$P < 0.05$
Total no. (%) of patients receiving antidepressant plus neuroleptic	14 (64)	5 (23)	$P < 0.01$

Lastly, the period of hospitalisation of the deluded group was significantly longer (not shown in table).

Because the patients with delusion showed significantly more symptoms of depression than the controls on the HRSD, a matched-pair analysis was conducted on 11 patients with identical HRSD scores. All the differences in Table 5.5 disappeared; however, length of stay remained significantly longer for delusional depressives (9.9 weeks) compared with the controls (6.6 weeks) (Wilcoxon signed rank test, $0.025 < P < 0.05$).

Glassman & Roose (1981) proposed two hypotheses for understanding delusional depression. The one argues that delusional depression is merely a more severe form of depression. This is a state model. Thus, given a severe enough illness any patient with depression might develop delusions. The second suggests that delusions arise in a depressive illness because of a distinct vulnerability. This is a trait model. However, many severe depressions are not delusional and Glassman & Roose (1981) did not demonstrate a severity effect – deluded patients were still poor responders to antidepressants after controlling for severity. Glassman & Roose therefore opted for the vulnerability model.

My findings are somewhat at odds with those of Glassman & Roose (1981) because the matched-pair comparison which controlled for severity suggested that the treatment differences might be explained by the effect of severity of depression. More recently, Maj *et al* (1990), studying a younger group of individuals with psychotic depression, also found that symptomatic differences disappeared after controlling for severity.

Does this mean that the vulnerability theory does not apply to elderly subjects? Not necessarily. First, the differences in hospitalisation, which was longer for the deluded group, were not explained by severity of depression. Although this might reflect natural caution in discharging patients who have been deluded, it equally may point to an inherent property of delusional depression, namely slower recovery. This accords with Howarth & Grace (1985), who found that psychotic major depression responded more slowly. Second, two of the controls but none of the deluded patients recovered spontaneously, in keeping with literature from younger subjects (Charney & Nelson, 1981).

Is delusional depression in the elderly a distinct subtype?

The practical relevance of the two hypotheses of Glassman & Roose (1981), a state-severity model or a trait-vulnerability one, is summarised by Maj *et al* (1990). There are four treatment options: to treat with an antidepressant drug at similar dosage to non-deluded patients with depression; to use higher doses; to use combination therapy routinely; last, to use ECT routinely.

Only 18% of those deluded in my 1988 study responded to an antidepressant alone, which is even lower than the average figure of 34% quoted by Spiker *et al* (1985) from a number of studies. There was weak support for the hypothesis that elderly deluded patients respond less often to an antidepressant alone than those not deluded: 45% of the latter showed such a response, a difference which is of borderline significance statistically. The latter is considerably lower than the figure of 80% quoted by Hordern *et al* (1963) and Charney & Nelson (1981) for non-deluded cases. Most likely this is due to the increased physical frailty of these older patients who were, therefore, more susceptible to drug side-effects than younger patients with depression. Only a third of the two groups were free from physical pathology and a change in treatment arising directly from the complications of antidepressants occurred in about 15%. Electroconvulsive therapy is a safe procedure in the elderly and perhaps safer than antidepressants for the frail elderly, who may therefore be more likely to receive it.

This limited tolerance of antidepressants will distort treatment responses and highlights an important methodological problem when studying the elderly compared with studies of younger, fit subjects.

Controlling for severity removed the difference in antidepressant response. Glassman *et al* (1975), after controlling for this variable, still found differences in response rates to antidepressants alone. However, their patients were much younger and so more likely to tolerate tricyclics. The routine administration of dosages of 200 mg without evident side-effects strengthens this view, thereby making comparisons difficult.

An increased requirement for ECT or combinations of treatment among deluded patients is supported by this study, although numbers were too small to evaluate the specific use of antidepressant/antipsychotic combinations. Furthermore, two of the controls, but none of the deluded patients, recovered without physical treatment. Spontaneous recovery has been cited as another distinction between these two types of depression (Glassman & Roose, 1981). Finally, ECT was ultimately required by two-thirds of those deluded, perhaps strengthening the view (Kantor & Glassman, 1977) that this may be the treatment of choice for such patients.

Again, illness severity is important since all treatment differences disappeared when this was controlled for. The finding that deluded patients had higher HRSD scores can be partly accounted for by the HRSD itself, which attributes higher scores for the sub-items of guilt and hypochondriasis where these are delusional. This is not, however, a complete explanation because, while these scores were, predictably, higher for the deluded group, so were the ratings for mood alone (Mann–Whitney test, $U = 165$, $Z = 2.51$, $P < 0.05$). However, the small numbers available in the matched-pair analysis should caution against ascribing all the treatment differences to severity alone, since genuine discrepancies may require much larger numbers to be statistically evident.

In summary, the evidence from this study suggests that some of the treatment differences which undoubtedly exist between delusional and non-delusional elderly people with depression may arise because delusional depression is a more severe form of depression. However, there is nevertheless reasonably compelling evidence from the nature of subsequent relapses that delusional depression may reflect a specific pathological vulnerability.

Conclusions

Delusional depression in the elderly is not uncommon in old age psychiatric practice, and ageing may exert a pathoplastic effect on the content of delusions, although the overall symptomatology is similar to that of non-delusional depression.

Although Schatzberg & Rothschild argued strongly for the retention of a separate category of delusional depression, or psychotic depression, their case was not accepted by the authors of DSM–IV. With regard to elderly patients with depression with psychotic features, the evidence is slimmer still, chiefly due to the lack of information at the biological level. There has been little work regarding neuro-endocrine evaluation, neuro-imaging or enzyme measures, and what there is has been inconclusive or liable to a type II error. There is a suggestion, consonant with data from younger individuals with psychotic depression, that cognitive impairment is measurably greater in delusional depression in later life, and our own recent research has demonstrated brain atrophy in subjects with psychotic depression. The best approach would be that of 'convergence' of evidence, based on clinical, neurobiological and outcome data.

The strongest evidence for differences comes from treatment studies. Treatment of delusional depression differs from that of the non-delusional form, and treatment data suggest that this is partly because it is a more severe illness. However, evidence from follow-up supports the view that there are more intrinsic differences, which supports a vulnerability model. One model of causation presupposes an interaction of stressors with a variety of critically situated endogenous brain changes, notably in the paralimbic regions and the reticular activating areas.

Although there is a high morbidity in the short term, there is evidence that delusional depression responds as well to treatment as non-delusional depression. Energetic treatment is needed with a combination of neuroleptic and either antidepressant therapy or ECT. Planned aftercare is essential as recurrences frequently require admission to hospital.

Patients with non-congruent delusional depression may constitute a particular subtype. Indeed, the search for differences between delusional and non-delusional depression might be hampered by treating all delusions in a homogeneous way.

Finally, the relevance of rather mundane variables, such as the patient's gender and civil status, especially being single, should not be overlooked, as these too may have an important influence on the expression of delusions within later-life depressive illness.

References

AMERICAN PSYCHIATRIC ASSOCIATION (1987) *Diagnostic and Statistical Manual of Mental Disorders* (3rd edn, revised) (DSM–III–R). Washington, DC: APA.
—— (1994) *Diagnostic and Statistical Manual of Mental Disorders* (4th edn) (DSM–IV). Washington, DC: APA.
BALDWIN, R. C. (1988) Delusional and non-delusional depression in late life: evidence for distinct subtypes. *British Journal of Psychiatry*, **152**, 39–44.
—— (1993) Late life depression and structural brain changes: a review of recent magnetic resonance imaging research. *International Journal of Geriatric Psychiatry*, **8**, 115–123.
—— (1995) Delusional depression in elderly patients: characteristics and relationship to age at onset. *International Journal of Geriatric Psychiatry*, **10**, 981–985.
—— & JOLLEY, D. J. (1986) The prognosis of depression in old age. *British Journal of Psychiatry*, **149**, 574–583.
—— & SIMPSON, S. (1997) Prognosis and outcome studies in late-life depression. *Clinical Neuroscience*, **4**, 16–22.
BLESSED, G., TOMLINSON, B. E. & ROTH, M. (1968) The association between quantitative measures of dementia and of senile change in the cerebral grey matter of elderly subjects. *British Journal of Psychiatry*, **114**, 797–811.
BRANDON, S., COWLEY, P., MCDONALD, C., *et al* (1984) Electroconvulsive therapy: results in depressive illness for the Leicestershire trial. *British Medical Journal*, **288**, 22–25.
BRODATY, H., HARRIS, L., PETERS, K., *et al* (1993) Prognosis of depression in the elderly: a comparison with younger patients. *British Journal of Psychiatry*, **163**, 589–596.
BURNS, A., JACOBY, R. & LEVY, R. (1990) Psychiatric phenomena in Alzheimer's disease. 1: Disorders of thought content *British Journal of Psychiatry*, **157**, 72–76.
BURVILL, P. W., HALL, W. D., STAMPFER, H. G., *et al* (1991) The prognosis of depression in old age. *British Journal of Psychiatry*, **158**, 64–71.
CHARNEY, D. S. & NELSON, J. C. (1981) Delusional and nondelusional unipolar depression: further evidence for distinct subtypes. *American Journal of Psychiatry*, **138**, 328–333.
CLINICAL RESEARCH CENTRE (1984) The Northwick Park ECT trial: predictors of response to real and simulated ECT. *British Journal of Psychiatry*, **114**, 227–237.
CORYELL, W. & TSUANG, M. T. (1982) Primary unipolar depression and the prognostic importance of delusions. *Archives of General Psychiatry*, **39**, 1181–1184.

——, GAFFNEY, G. & BURKHARDT, P. E. (1982) The dexamethasone suppression test and familial subtypes of depression: a naturalistic replication. *Biological Psychiatry*, **17**, 33–40.

——, ENDICOTT, J. & KELLER, M. (1987) The importance of psychotic features to major depression: course and outcome during a 2-year follow-up. *Acta Psychiatrica Scandinavica*, **75**, 78–85.

FEIGHNER, J. P., ROBINS, E. & GUZE, S. B. (1972) Diagnostic criteria for use in psychiatric research. *Archives of General Psychiatry*, **26**, 57–63.

FOLSTEIN, M. F., FOLSTEIN, S. E. & McHUGH, P. R. (1975) "Mini-Mental State": a practical method for grading the cognitive state of patients for the clinician. *Journal of Psychiatric Research*, **12**, 185–198.

FRANCES, A., BROWN, R., KOCSIS, J. H. & MANN, J. J. (1981) Psychotic depression: a separate entity? *American Journal of Psychiatry*, **138**, 831–833.

GLASSMAN, A. H. & ROOSE, S. P. (1981) Delusional depression: a distinct clinical entity? *Archives of General Psychiatry*, **38**, 424–427.

GLASSMAN, A. H., KANTOR, S. J. & SHOSTAK, M. (1975) Depression, delusions and drug response. *American Journal of Psychiatry*, **132**, 716–719.

HAMILTON, M. (1960) A rating scale for depression. *Journal of Neurology, Neurosurgery and Psychiatry*, **23**, 56–62.

HERLITZ, A. & FORSELL, Y. (1996) Episodic memory deficit in elderly adults with suspected delusional disorder. *Acta Psychiatrica Scandinavica*, **93**, 355–361.

HOCH, A. & McCURDY, J. T. (1922) The prognosis of involutional melancholia. *Archives of Neurology and Psychiatry*, **7**, 117.

HORDERN, A., HOLT, N. F., BURT, C. G. & GORDON, W. F. (1963) Amitriptyline in depressive states: phenomenology and prognostic considerations. *British Journal of Psychiatry*, **109**, 815–825.

HOWARTH, B. G. & GRACE, M. G. A. (1985) Depression, drugs, and delusions. *Archives of General Psychiatry*, **42**, 1145–1147.

JOHNSON, J., HORWATH, E. & WEISSMAN, M. M. (1991) The validity of major depression with psychotic features based on a community study. *Archives of General Psychiatry*, **48**, 1075–1081.

KANTOR, S. J. & GLASSMAN, A. H. (1977) Delusional depressions: natural history and response to treatment. *British Journal of Psychiatry*, **131**, 351–360.

KAY, D. W. K, COOPER, A. F. & GARSIDE, R. F. (1976) The differentiation of paranoid from affective psychoses by patients' premorbid characteristics. *British Journal of Psychiatry*, **129**, 207–215.

KIVELA, S. L. & PAHKALA, K. (1989) Delusional depression in the elderly: a community study. *Zeitschrift für Gerontologie*, **22**, 236–241.

KUNIK, M. E., CHAMPAGEN, L., HARPER, R. G. & CHACKO, R. C. (1994) Cognitive functioning in elderly depressed patients with and without psychoses. *International Journal of Geriatric Psychiatry*, **9**, 871–874.

LESSER, I. M., MILLER, B. L., BOONE, K. B., *et al* (1991) Brain injury and cognitive function in late-onset psychotic depression. *Journal of Neuropsychiatry and Clinical Neurosciences*, **3**, 33–40.

LEUTCHER, A. F. & SPAR, J. E. (1985) The late-onset psychoses: clinical and diagnostic features. *Journal of Nervous and Mental Disease*, **173**, 488–494.

MAJ, M., PIROZZI, R. & DI CAPRIO, E. L. (1990) Major depression with mood-congruent psychotic features: a distinct entity or a more severe subtype of depression. *Acta Psychiatrica Scandinavica*, **82**, 439–444.

MELTZER, H. Y., CHO, H. W., CARROLL, B. J., *et al* (1976) Serum dopamine-beta-hydroxylase activity in the affective psychoses and schizophrenia. *Archives of General Psychiatry*, **33**, 585–591.

MENDELWICZ, J. (1976) The age factor in depressive illness: some genetic considerations. *Journal of Gerontology*, **31**, 300–303.

MEYERS, B. S. & GREENBERG, R. (1986) Late-life delusional depression. *Journal of Affective Disorders*, 11, 133–137.

MILLER, B. L., LESSER, I. M., BOONE, K. B., *et al* (1991) Brain lesions and cognitive function in late-life psychosis. *British Journal of Psychiatry*, 158, 76–82.

MURPHY, E. (1983) The prognosis of depression in old age. *British Journal of Psychiatry*, 142, 111–119.

NELSON, J. C., CONWELL, Y., KIM, K. & MAZURE, C. (1989) Age at onset in late-life delusional depression. *American Journal of Psychiatry*, 146, 785–786.

O'BRIEN, J. T., AMES, D., SCHWEITZER, I., *et al* (1997) Clinical, magnetic resonance imaging and endocrinological differences between delusional and non-delusional depression in the elderly. *International Journal of Geriatric Psychiatry*, 12, 211–218.

PARKER, G., HADZI-PAVLOVIC, D., HICKIE, I., *et al* (1991) Distinguishing psychotic and nonpsychotic melancholia. *Journal of Affective Disorders*, 22, 135–148.

PEARLSON, G. D., RABINS, P. V., KIM, W. S., *et al* (1989) Structural brain CT changes and cognitive deficits in elderly depressives with and without reversible dementia (pseudodementia). *Psychological Medicine*, 19, 573–584.

PERRY, P. J., MORGAN, D. E., SMITH, R. E., *et al* (1982) Treatment of unipolar depression accompanied by delusions. *Journal of Affective Disorders*, 4, 195–200.

POST, F. (1967) Aspects of psychiatry in the elderly. *Proceedings of the Royal Society of Medicine*, 60, 249–254.

—— (1972) The management and nature of depressive illnesses in late life: a follow-through study. *British Journal of Psychiatry*, 121, 393–404.

RABINS, P. V., MERCHANT, A. & NESTADT, G. (1984) Criteria for diagnosing reversible dementia caused by dementia: validation by 2-year follow-up. *British Journal of Psychiatry*, 144, 488–492.

ROBINSON, D. G. & SPIKER, D. G. (1985) Delusional depression: a one year follow-up. *Journal of Affective Disorders*, 9, 79–83.

ROGERS, D., LEES, A. J., SMITH, E., *et al* (1987) Bradyphrenia in Parkinson's disease and psychomotor retardation in depressive illness. *Brain*, 110, 761–767.

ROSEN, J. & ZUBENKO, G. (1992) Emergence of psychosis and depression in the longitudinal evaluation of Alzheimer's disease. *Biological Psychiatry*, 29, 224–232.

ROTHSCHILD, A. J., BENES, F., HEBBEN, N., *et al* (1989) Relationship between brain CT findings and cortisol in psychotic and non-psychotic depressed patients. *Biological Psychiatry*, 26, 565–575.

SAPOLSKY, R., KREY, L. & McEWEN, B. (1986) The neuroendocrinology of stress and aging: the glucocorticoid cascade hypothesis. *Endocrine Reviews*, 7, 284–301.

SCHATZBERG, A. F. & ROTHSCHILD, A. J. (1992) Psychotic (delusional) major depression: should it be included as a distinct syndrome in DSM–IV? *American Journal of Psychiatry*, 149, 733–745.

SIMPSON, S., JACKSON, A., BALDWIN, R. C., *et al* (1997) Subcortical hyperintensities in late life depression: acute response to treatment and neuropsychological impairment. *International Psychogeriatrics*, 9, 257–275.

——, BALDWIN, R. C., JACKSON, A., *et al* (1999) The differentiation of DSM–III–R psychotic depression in later life from non-psychotic depression: comparison of cerebral atrophy measured by multispectral analysis of magnetic resonance brain images, neuropsychological findings and clinical features. *Biological Psychiatry*, 45, 193–204.

SMALL, G. W., KOMANDURI, R., GITLIN, M. & JARVIK, L. F. (1986) The influence of age on guilt expression in major depression. *International Journal of Geriatric Psychiatry*, 1, 121–126.

SPIKER, D. G., WEISS, J. C., DEALY, R. S., *et al* (1985) The pharmacologic treatment of delusional depression. *American Journal of Psychiatry*, 142, 430–436.

SWEENEY, D., NELSON, C., BOWERS, M., *et al* (1978) Delusional versus nondelusional depression: neurochemical differences. *Lancet*, ii, 100–101.

TARGUM, S. D., ROSEN, L. N., DeLISI, L. E., *et al* (1983) Cerebral ventricular size in major depressive disorder: association with delusional symptoms. *Biological Psychiatry*, **18**, 329–336.

VEITH, R. C. & RASKIND, M. A. (1988) The neurobiology of aging: does it predispose to depression? *Neurobiology of Aging*, **9**, 101–117.

WEINGARTNER, H., COHEN, R. M., BUNNEY, W. E., *et al* (1982) Memory-learning impairments in progressive dementia and depression. *American Journal of Psychiatry*, **139**, 135–136.

WING, J. K., COOPER, J. E. & SARTORIUS, N. (1974) *The Measurement and Classification of Psychiatric Symptoms*. London: Cambridge University Press.

WORLD HEALTH ORGANIZATION (1992) *The ICD-10 Classification of Mental and Behavioural Disorders*. Geneva: WHO.

ZUBENKO, G. S., MOOSSY, J., MARTINEZ, A. J., *et al* (1991) Neuropathologic and neurochemical correlates of psychosis in primary dementia. *Archives of Neurology*, **48**, 619–624.

6   Late-onset schizophrenia

LAURA L. SYMONDS and DILIP V. JESTE

Psychoses are among the most severe psychiatric disorders, and among them schizophrenia is arguably the most expensive one. Like other psychoses, schizophrenia can manifest in people of almost any age, including middle age and old age, and is characterised by delusions, hallucinations, bizarre behaviour and loss of touch with reality. The focus of most basic and clinical research has been on patients who have had an onset of psychosis early in life. This chapter specifically focuses on late-onset schizophrenia and compares it with the early-onset form of the disease.

The relatively sudden appearance of schizophrenia in an adult who had functioned rather normally throughout several decades of life is a puzzling phenomenon. The existence of late-onset schizophrenia raises a number of questions regarding its aetiology, pathophysiology and clinical appearance, and of schizophrenia in general. The following sections describe what is currently known about some of the clinical, neurocognitive and neuro-imaging aspects of late-onset schizophrenia.

Historical background

Schizophrenia was described by Kraepelin (1898), who called it dementia praecox. 'Praecox' denoted a young age of onset; 'dementia' was not intended in the sense that we use it today, but instead was used to imply a progressive deterioration of personality, especially of emotional and volitional functioning. Kraepelin also recognised a similar disorder, which he labelled 'paraphrenia', with a slightly different constellation of symptoms, and noted that the onset of this other disorder tended to occur between the ages of 30 and 50, and did not necessarily show a deteriorating course (Kraepelin, 1919a,b). Thus paraphrenia was described as a disorder not so much of emotion or volition but mainly of paranoid thinking. In addition, Kraepelin de-emphasised the inevitability of a deteriorating course as well as the necessity for a youthful onset. Indeed, Mayer (1921) followed up some of Kraepelin's patients with paraphrenia and concluded that both the symptoms and the course were very similar to those of dementia praecox. The term 'paraphrenia' was then dropped by Kraepelin, and fell into disuse.

E. Bleuler (1911) applied the term 'schizophrenia' to Kraepelin's patients dementia praecox and made it clear that he did not believe that either a young age at onset or a deteriorating course was central to the disease. M. Bleuler (1943) coined the term 'late-onset schizo-phrenia' to describe the subset of patients schizophrenia who develop the disorder after the age of 40; he was the first to make explicit that the symptoms of late-onset and early-onset schizophrenia were similar.

Paraphrenia as a diagnostic entity was revived by researchers in Great Britain in the 1950s and 1960s. Roth (1955) and others used the term 'paraphrenia' to describe a group of psychiatric patients whose first psychiatric symptoms appeared after the age of 60 and were paranoid in nature. Although the concept of 'paraphrenia' and then 'late paraphrenia' tended to evolve (see Roth, 1955; Kay & Roth, 1961; Harris & Jeste, 1988), late paraphrenia was primarily characterised by paranoid symptoms and some type of delusion, either with or without hallucinations, all in the absence of organic disorder, confusion or primary affective disorder.

Among the consequences of Roth and colleagues' research was that many patients with late-onset psychotic disorders were studied in Europe, while the study of similar patients in the USA went largely ignored. Many patients, however, were excluded because of the sometimes strict interpretation of the age-at-onset cut-off of 60; in addition, patients affected by illnesses other than schizophrenia (e.g. those with paranoid or delusional disorder) were commonly included because of the broader complex of symptoms in paraphrenia.

The diagnostic confusion has continued into the later part of this century (see Harris & Jeste, 1988; Riecher-Roessler *et al*, 1995, for reviews) and is reflected in the changing diagnostic criteria found in the ICD and DSM systems. In the latter, for example, between 1980 (American Psychiatric Association, 1980) and 1987 (American Psychi-atric Association, 1987) schizophrenia could not be diagnosed if the symptoms first appeared after age 45; such patients were given other diagnoses, such as psychosis not otherwise specified. Currently, DSM–IV (American Psychiatric Association, 1994), like DSM–I (American Psychiatric Association, 1952) and DSM–II (American Psychiatric Association, 1968), allows the diagnosis of schizophrenia at any age, unlike DSM–III (American Psychiatric Association, 1980), which did not allow the diagnosis after age 45, or DSM–III–R (American

Psychiatric Association, 1980), which specified a separate diagnosis of 'late-onset schizophrenia' after age 45. The revisions in criteria for diagnosis make it especially important when reviewing psychiatric research to take account of the diagnostic criteria which were used for the patients in a specific study.

Current diagnosis of schizophrenia

A diagnosis of schizophrenia can be made for a patient with late-onset schizophrenia if he or she meets all the DSM–IV criteria, including a duration of six months. ICD–10 criteria (World Health Organization, 1992) require a one-month duration of symptoms. In either case, this is to ensure that more acute disorders are excluded. Typically, patients with late-onset schizophrenia are middle aged or even elderly, and have functioned fairly well throughout adulthood, although premorbid paranoid or schizoid personality traits are common. The patients usually have auditory hallucinations and persecutory delusions. Low-dose treatment with neuroleptics generally results in improvement in these positive symptoms.

Epidemiology

The frequency of late-onset schizophrenia among consecutive admissions to psychiatric in-patient facilities has been reported to range from 3–4% (Fish, 1960; Yassa & Suranyi-Cadotte, 1993) to 8–10% (Roth, 1955; Leuchter & Spar, 1985). There are some difficulties, however, in interpreting these results. For example, the studies do not agree on the definition of late onset, which varies from 40 to 65 years. In addition, different investigators define onset of psychosis variously as the first psychiatric hospitalisation, the onset of positive symptoms, or the onset of prodromal symptoms. These events can be separated by several years (Maurer & Häfner, 1995). Finally, it is difficult objectively to determine events in an elderly person's history, or to evaluate premorbid functioning in the presence of premorbid schizoid personality traits.

Harris & Jeste (1988) reviewed data from the psychiatric literature to determine the proportion of schizophrenia patients who are diagnosed with late-onset schizophrenia. They found, based upon eight mostly European in-patient studies in which age at onset was determined by first hospitalisation, that approximately 77% of patients with schizophrenia had had onset at 40 years or younger, 13% between 41 and 50 years, 7% between 51 and 60 years, and 3% after age 60.

Most studies of late-onset schizophrenia report that a substantial majority of late-onset patients are women (Bleuler, 1943; Kay & Roth, 1961; Bland, 1977; Blessed & Wilson, 1982). Several explanations have been proposed for this, including greater longevity of women and neuro-endocrine changes (mainly depletion of oestrogen with menopause).

Clinical symptoms

Patients with a late onset of schizophrenia often present with delusions, which are predominantly persecutory and may be bizarre. Auditory hallucinations are also common. Less common, but not rare among such patients, are grandiose, erotic or somatic delusions, and Schneiderian first-rank symptoms (such as thoughts experienced as spoken aloud or voices heard commenting on the patient's thoughts). Finally, a number of patients with late-onset schizophrenia complain of depressive symptoms.

In contrast to patients with an earlier onset of schizophrenia, patients with late-onset schizophrenia are less likely to exhibit looseness of associations and inappropriateness of affect (Jeste *et al*, 1988; Pearlson & Rabins, 1988). Also more common in patients with early-onset schizophrenia than late-onset schizophrenia are negative symptoms, as assessed on the Scale for the Assessment of Negative Symptoms (SANS; Andreasen & Olsen, 1982) subscales of affective blunting and avolition/apathy (Jeste *et al*, 1995).

Unlike DSM–III–R, DSM–IV does not require a differential diagnosis to be made between early-onset and late-onset schizophrenia. To assign age at onset of the disease accurately, however, it is important to make sure that there were no earlier prodromal symptoms such as marked social isolation, blunted or inappropriate affect, or marked impairment in personal hygiene.

The relatively high incidence of paranoia in older patients (approximately 50% of geriatric in-patients, according to a study by Grief & Eastwood, 1993) makes it imperative to be able to differentiate late-onset schizophrenia from other disorders presenting with paranoia. For example, both delusional disorder and psychotic mood disorder commonly present with paranoia, and are also more likely to have an onset during middle age or old age than in early adulthood. Delusional disorder does not include, however, bizarre delusions or prominent auditory hallucinations, Schneiderian first-rank symptoms, or a deterioration in functioning outside the area of the delusions (Yassa & Suranyi-Cadotte, 1993). Mood disorders with psychotic features are most easily distinguished from late-onset schizophrenia by the predominance of affective symptoms and the periodicity of the illness. For a diagnosis of schizophrenia to be made, the total duration of all mood symptoms relative to that of the primary psychotic symptoms should be brief.

Neuropsychological functioning

The heterogeneity in behaviour that is such a hallmark of schizophrenia is less evident in the overall pattern of neuropsychological impairment in these patients. There have been numerous studies published on the neuropsychological abilities of patients with early-onset schizophrenia (e.g. Green & Walker, 1985; Levin *et al*, 1989; Saykin *et al*, 1991; Gur & Pearlson, 1993; Braff, 1993; Strauss, 1993). In general, patients with schizophrenia tend to perform worse than normal comparison subjects on tests of almost all ability areas, including verbal, perceptual motor, abstraction/flexibility, attention, verbal and visual learning, sensory perceptual and motor skills. Retention of information, however, tends to be relatively normal. The deficits apparent in schizophrenia are much less severe, however, than those in Alzheimer's disease, which additionally involves a severe impairment in retention of information (Heaton *et al*, 1994).

The differences between patients with late-onset schizophrenia and early-onset schizophrenia on neuropsychological tests are relatively unexplored. The evidence so far suggests that late-onset patients may be somewhat less impaired than early-onset patients, especially on measures of learning, abstraction/flexibility and organisation of semantic networks, but these conclusions are still tentative (Jeste *et al*, 1995; Paulsen *et al*, 1996). Like early-onset schizophrenia, late-onset schizophrenia does not appear to be a dementing disorder – patients followed for two years or more have shown no deterioration in neuropsychological functioning (Gladsjo *et al*, 1996).

Neuro-imaging

The advent of modern neuro-imaging techniques in the 1980s stimulated many investigators to search for structural abnormalities in the brains of psychotic patients. In contrast to the devastating behavioural and functional correlates of schizophrenia, the gross structure of the brain in these patients visualised by computerised tomography or magnetic resonance imaging is remarkably normal. There is no obvious anatomical abnormality that is seen in all patients with schizophrenia, and very few abnormalities which can be appreciated without the use of quantitative techniques. Nevertheless, there are some regions of the brain which have been more often found to be abnormal in patients with schizophrenia compared with normal controls. The most widely replicated result of structural neuro-imaging studies has been the finding that in patients with schizophrenia the cerebrospinal fluid spaces, including ventricles and sulci, are somewhat enlarged, though there is considerable variability between individuals (Crow, 1980; Jeste *et al*, 1982; Pfefferbaum *et al*, 1988; Andreasen *et al*, 1990a,b; Suddath *et al*, 1990; Swayze *et al*, 1990; Zipursky *et al*, 1992).

In addition, reduced volumes of several grey-matter regions of the brain have been reported. These include:

(a) the medial temporal lobe region, including the hippocampus and amygdala (Barta *et al*, 1990; Suddath *et al*, 1990; Jernigan *et al*, 1991a; Breier *et al*, 1992; Shenton *et al*, 1992a,b; Weinberger *et al*, 1992; Nasrallah *et al*, 1994);

(b) the lateral temporal lobe (Barta *et al*, 1990; Shenton *et al*, 1992a,b; Schlaepfer *et al*, 1994; Vladar *et al*, 1994);

(c) the prefrontal cortex, particularly the dorsolateral prefrontal region (Rosse *et al*, 1991; Breier *et al*, 1992; Raine *et al*, 1992; Andreasen *et al*, 1994b; Schlaepfer *et al*, 1994; Seidman *et al*, 1994; Wible *et al*, 1994; Maher *et al*, 1995). There have also been reports of volume reductions in the thalamic regions of patients with schizophrenia (Andreasen *et al*, 1990b, 1994a) as well as volume increases in nuclei of the basal ganglia, particularly the caudate and putamen nuclei (Jernigan *et al*, 1991b).

In contrast to the relative plethora of work on structural abnormalities in early-onset schizophrenia, very little is known about the brains of those who develop the disease for the first time later in life. In general, it appears that, compared with healthy individuals, the ventricle–brain ratio is elevated in patients with late-onset schizophrenia and early-onset schizophrenia (Rabins *et al*, 1987; Krull *et al*, 1991; Pearlson *et al*, 1993; Howard *et al*, 1994; Corey-Bloom *et al*, 1995). Patients with late-onset and early-onset schizophrenia do not appear to differ on this measure (Corey-Bloom *et al*, 1995). In addition, patients with late-onset schizophrenia have been reported to have more white-matter hyper-intensities than age-matched control subjects (Miller *et al*, 1986, 1989; Breitner *et al*, 1990). These pathological findings are, however, not specific to schizophrenia, but are also found in other late-onset diseases, including depression, and even in a proportion of normal subjects (Krishnan *et al*, 1988; Lesser *et al*, 1992, 1993).

Furthermore, other studies have not found differences between patients with late-onset schizophrenia and normal comparison subjects in incidence or severity of white-matter abnormalities (Krull *et al*, 1991; Symonds *et al*, 1997), though these studies differed significantly in method from those cited above. It is therefore still unresolved whether the brains of late-onset patients differ from those of normal comparison subjects in the number or size of white-matter hyperintensities. Even if such a finding is established, its clinico-pathological implication is not yet understood.

One of the more commonly reported results in neuro-imaging studies of patients with early-onset schizophrenia is a reduction in size of temporal lobe structures (Barta *et al*, 1990; Shenton *et al*, 1992a; Bogerts, 1993; Schlaepfer *et al*, 1994; Flaum *et al*, 1995). One study so far suggests that there may be a similar volume reduction for patients with late-onset schizophrenia (Barta *et al*, 1997). These investigators used quantitative measurement techniques to determine the volume of five separate regions within the temporal lobe. Four of the regions (entorhinal cortex, amygdala, left hippocampus and anterior superior temporal gyrus) were smaller in patients with late-onset schizophrenia than in healthy control subjects. Interestingly, one of the regions, the anterior superior temporal gyrus, was *not* smaller in patients with Alzheimer's dementia, suggesting that schizophrenia, including late-onset schizophrenia, may be associated with some specific brain abnormality not shared in other neurologically based diseases.

Finally, the thalamus has been reported to be smaller in patients with early-onset schizophrenia (Andreasen *et al*, 1990b, 1994a) than in normal comparison subjects. One study sought to determine whether the thalamus in late-onset schizophrenia is similarly affected (Corey-Bloom *et al*, 1995). The investigators used quantitative volume estimates of several brain regions in 16 patients with late-onset schizophrenia, 14 patients with early-onset schizophrenia and 28 normal comparison subjects. They determined that the thalamus in patients with late-onset schizophrenia was significantly larger than in early-onset patients, and that the volume measurements for normal comparison subjects were intermediate between early-onset and late-onset patients. Larger sample sizes are needed to reveal statistically significant differences between patients with late-onset schizophrenia and healthy control subjects. While the pathophysiological significance of abnormally large brain nuclei is not yet known, there are other reports in the literature of larger nuclei in patient populations (e.g. Jernigan *et al*, 1991b, reported larger lenticular nuclei in patients with early-onset schizophrenia than in normal subjects). Also, Dupont *et al* (1995) reported a significantly larger thalamus in bipolar patients than in unipolar patients; as in the Corey-Bloom *et al* (1995) study, the thalamic volume in normal comparison subjects was intermediate, though in this study the difference was statistically significant (possibly because of the larger sample sizes).

In summary, results from neuro-imaging studies suggest that patients with late-onset schizophrenia share several of the brain abnormalities found in patients with early-onset schizophrenia. Similarities include larger ventricles and smaller temporal lobe regions than in healthy control subjects. There are also differences (e.g. larger thalamus) between those patients who are affected later in life and those with an onset in young adulthood. Many of the brain regions reported to be abnormal in volume in younger patients with schizophrenia have not been investigated yet in either early-onset patients who are older or in patients with late-onset schizophrenia. However, neuro-imaging studies of normal ageing indicate that the volumes of most brain regions show increased variability among older compared with younger individuals (Jernigan *et al*, 1990). It is, therefore, more difficult to detect a significant difference, if one exists, between patients with late-onset schizophrenia and age-comparable normal subjects. It may be possible in future studies to sort out the relative contributions of ageing and psychosis in patients with late onset of psychosis. Studies which include both larger numbers of subjects and more refined measurement techniques would help to do this.

In this chapter, we have considered late-onset schizophrenia and early-onset schizophrenia to be one diagnosis, with the essential difference between them being the age at onset of the disease. It is, however, unclear at present how far to take this assumption. The role of brain lesions in the aetiology of schizophrenia is relevant to whether late-onset and early-onset schizophrenia are the same or separate clinical entities. Several investigators have suggested that the lesions seen on magnetic resonance images of patients with late-onset psychosis (including white-matter abnormalities) are the cause of the psychosis. Miller and his colleagues, for example, have documented several cases where this was probably the case (Miller *et al*, 1986, 1989). It appears, however, that late-onset schizophrenia can occur in the absence of such brain lesions (Symonds *et al*, 1997). The role that brain lesions play in the pathophysiology of late-onset psychotic disorders is not known, and it will be important to learn how brain lesions contribute to the development of late-onset schizophrenia.

Treatment

As with other types or forms of schizophrenia, neuroleptic or anti-psychotic drugs constitute the mainstay of treatment for late-onset schizophrenia.

Conventional or typical neuroleptics

Clinical experience and anecdotal reports suggest that neuroleptic therapy produces a positive outcome (remission or reduction in symptoms, and earlier discharge from hospital) in a majority of older patients with schizophrenia (Jeste *et al*, 1993). Nevertheless, few studies have documented the efficacy of conventional antipsychotics with well designed, placebo-controlled clinical trials in patients with late-onset schizophrenia.

Neuroleptic medications do have a number of side-effects that occur more frequently in older subjects, including sedation, orthostatic hypotension, anticholinergic reactions, extrapyramidal symptoms and tardive dyskinesia.

Sedation

Low-potency neuroleptics with sedative side-effects are excellent sleep inducers and may be helpful for the elderly patient with insomnia or severe daytime sedation. Sedation, however, persists for many hours after the drug has been given, and may interfere with the older patient's level of arousal during the day.

Orthostatic hypotension

This may lead to falls and could result in fractures or other injuries.

Anticholinergic reactions

Dryness of mouth, urinary retention, constipation, worsening of glaucoma and mental confusion may result from anticholinergic toxicity.

Neuroleptic-induced acute and subacute extrapyramidal symptoms

Of all the acute extrapyramidal side-effects, acute dystonic reactions are the only ones that are less common in older, compared with younger, patients. Parkinsonism and akathisia may last for weeks, months, or even longer, if neuroleptic treatment continues. Extrapyramidal symptoms are usually managed by a reduction of the conventional neuroleptic, or use of an anticholinergic (e.g. benztropine), a beta-blocker (e.g. propranolol) or a dopaminergic (e.g. amantadine) drug, or switching to an atypical antipsychotic.

Tardive dyskinesia

Tardive dyskinesia is characterised by abnormal involuntary movements, typically involving the orofacial region, limbs and trunk (Kane *et al*, 1992). Movements may be choreiform (i.e. rapid, jerky, non-repetitive), athetoid (i.e. slow, sinuous, continual), or rhythmic (i.e., stereotypies) and must be present for at least four weeks. According to DSM–IV, at least one month of exposure to neuroleptic medication is required for a diagnosis of tardive dyskinesia in the elderly (as opposed to a minimum of three months' exposure in younger individuals). Prevalence estimates of tardive dyskinesia in patients over the age of 60 being treated with 'typical' neuroleptic drugs are 50% or even higher (Yassa & Jeste, 1992). Not only is the incidence higher but so also is the risk of severe and persistent tardive dyskinesia greater in the elderly than in younger patients, especially if neuroleptics are continued.

While tardive dyskinesia is usually mild, severe dyskinesia can produce physical and psychosocial complications such as dental and denture problems and gait disturbances. Psychosocially, ambulatory patients with obvious tardive dyskinesia may experience shame, guilt, anxiety and depression.

There is no proven way to prevent tardive dyskinesia in patients receiving long-term treatment with typical antipsychotic medications. The best strategy involves restricting these drugs to well defined indications, using them in the lowest effective doses and assessing the patient at frequent intervals for early signs of abnormal movements. Discontinuation of antipsychotic therapy, although the most desirable treatment method, may be impractical for some patients with severe, chronic or relapsing psychosis. Typical antipsychotic medications can temporarily suppress symptoms of tardive dyskinesia, but since symptoms quickly return when treatment is withdrawn, use of these drugs specifically for treating tardive dyskinesia is not recommended except in severe cases.

The patient and family should be educated regarding the risks and benefits associated with treatment with antipsychotic medications. If withdrawal and discontinuation of the antipsychotic medication is not clinically feasible when abnormal movements are observed, switching to clozapine or other atypical antipsychotic medications may be considered. If treatment of the tardive dyskinesia is indicated or attempted, benign modalities should be employed initially (e.g. vitamin E) (Lohr *et al*, 1988).

Atypical antipsychotics

Atypical antipsychotic medications represent an advance in our pharmacotherapeutic armamentarium for schizophrenia. Very few studies, however, have documented the efficacy of antipsychotic drugs in clinical trials with patients with late-onset schizophrenia.

The primary indication for the use of clozapine is generally considered to be antipsychotic-resistant schizophrenia. Clozapine has been found significantly to improve disorganisation, positive symptoms and negative symptoms in this group, and the incidence of tardive dyskinesia appears to be very low (Buchanan, 1995). Unfortunately, the side-effects of clozapine make its use in older populations problematic (Salzman *et al*, 1995). The mandatory weekly blood samples can be a problem for the older patient, because of decreased mobility and increased bruising. Other side-effects include lethargy, sedation, postural hypotension, confusion and anticholinergic toxicity.

In small, open studies, risperidone has been reported to produce clinical improvement, in terms of a reduction in psychosis, aggression, agitation and other severe behavioural disturbances in elderly patients diagnosed with a variety of conditions, including schizophrenia (Jeste *et al*, 1996). The most commonly reported side-effects associated with risperidone include somnolence and postural hypotension. The threshold at which the elderly experience extrapyramidal symptoms is lower than that in younger adults. In the absence of long-term studies of risperidone the incidence of tardive dyskinesia with this drug is currently unknown. Preliminary data suggest that low-dose risperidone may improve the cognitive performance of some elderly psychotic patients.

Neuroleptic dosage

While there is a wide variability in the dosage requirements of the elderly, starting dosages of neuroleptics for older patients are often approximately one-quarter of those prescribed for younger adults. Dosage should be increased gradually or decreased according to clinical response or development of side-effects. The neuroleptic dose in older patients with schizophrenia tends to correlate inversely with current age and age at onset of illness. Thus, elderly patients with late-onset schizophrenia require lower doses than younger or early-onset older patients (Jeste *et al*, 1993). As patients with chronic schizophrenia who have been taking neuroleptics for many years continue to age, their dosage requirements often decrease. Doses must therefore be monitored and calibrated according to the clinical needs of the individual patient at different times.

Supportive psychosocial therapy should be an integral part of the overall management of patients with late-onset schizophrenia.

Acknowledgements

This work was supported by the National Institute of Mental Health (grants P30 MH49671, MH 43693, and MH 45131), the Department of Veterans Affairs, National Alliance for Research on Schizophrenia and

Depression (grant 96-5697), and Scottish Rite Benevolent Foundation's Schizophrenia Research Program, NMJ USA (grant 96-6520).

References

AMERICAN PSYCHIATRIC ASSOCIATION (1952) *Diagnostic and Statistical Manual of Mental Disorders.* Washington, DC: APA.

—— (1968) *Diagnostic and Statistical Manual of Mental Disorders* (2nd edn) (DSM–II). Washington, DC: APA.

—— (1980) *Diagnostic and Statistical Manual of Mental Disorders* (3rd edn) (DSM–III). Washington, DC: APA.

—— (1987) *Diagnostic and Statistical Manual of Mental Disorders* (3rd edn, revised) (DSM–III–R). Washington, DC: APA.

—— (1994) *Diagnostic and Statistical Manual of Mental Disorders* (4th edn) (DSM–IV). Washington, DC: APA.

ANDREASEN, N. & OLSEN, S. (1982) Negative vs positive schizophrenia: definition and validation. *Archives of General Psychiatry*, **39**, 789–794.

——, SWAYZE, V. W., FLAUM, M., *et al* (1990a) Ventricular enlargement in schizophrenia evaluated with computed tomographic scanning. *Archives of General Psychiatry*, **47**, 1008–1015.

——, EHRHARDT, J. C., SWAYZE, V. W., *et al* (1990b) Magnetic resonance imaging of the brain in schizophrenia. *Archives of General Psychiatry*, **47**, 35–44.

——, ARNDT, S., SWAYZE, V. W., *et al* (1994a) Thalamic abnormalities in schizophrenia visualized through magnetic resonance image averaging. *Science*, **266**, 294–298.

——, FLASHMAN, L., FLAUM, M., *et al* (1994b) Regional brain abnormalities in schizophrenia measured with magnetic resonance imaging. *Journal of the American Medical Association*, **272**, 1763–1769.

BARTA, P. E., PEARLSON, G. D., POWERS, R. E., *et al* (1990) Auditory hallucinations and smaller superior temporal gyral volume in schizophrenia. *American Journal of Psychiatry*, **147**, 1457–1462.

BARTA, P. E., POWERS, R. E., AYLWARD, W. H., *et al* (1997) Quantitative MRI volume changes in late-onset schizophrenia and Alzheimer's disease compared to normal controls. *Psychiatry Research*, **68**, 65–75.

BLAND, R. C. (1977) Demographic aspects of functional psychoses in Canada. *Acta Psychiatrica Scandinavica*, **55**, 369–380.

BLESSED, G. & WILSON, I. D. (1982) The contemporary natural history of mental disorder in old age. *British Journal of Psychiatry*, **141**, 59–67.

BLEULER, E. (1911) *Dementia Praecox, or the Group of Schizophrenias* (trans. J. Zinkin, 1950). New York: International Universities Press.

BLEULER, M. (1943) Late schizophrenic clinical pictures. *Fortschritte der Neurologie–Psychiatrie*, **15**, 259–290.

BOGERTS, B. (1993) Recent advances in the neuropathology of schizophrenia. *Schizophrenia Bulletin*, **19**, 431–445.

BRAFF, D. L. (1993) Information processing and attention dysfunctions in schizophrenia. *Schizophrenia Bulletin*, **19**, 233–259.

BREIER, A., BUCHANAN, R. W., ELKASHEF, A., *et al* (1992) Brain morphology and schizophrenia: a magnetic resonance imaging study of the limbic, prefrontal cortex, and caudate structures. *Archives of General Psychiatry*, **49**, 921–926.

BREITNER, J., HUSAIN, M., FIGIEL, G., *et al* (1990) Cerebral white matter disease in late-onset psychosis. *Biological Psychiatry*, **28**, 266–274.

BUCHANAN, R. W. (1995) Clozapine: efficacy and safety. *Schizophrenia Bulletin*, **21**, 579–591.

COREY-BLOOM, J., JERNIGAN, T., ARCHIBALD, S., *et al* (1995) Quantitative magnetic resonance imaging in late-life schizophrenia. *American Journal of Psychiatry*, **152**, 447–449.

CROW, T. J. (1980) Molecular pathology of schizophrenia: more than one dimension of pathology? *British Medical Journal*, **280**, 66–68.

DUPONT, R. M., JERNIGAN, T. L., HEINDEL, W., *et al* (1995) Magnetic resonance imaging and mood disorders. Localization of white matter and other subcortical abnormalities. *Archives of General Psychiatry*, **52**, 747–755.

FISH, F. (1960) Senile schizophrenia. *Journal of Mental Science*, **106**, 938–946.

FLAUM, M., SWAYZE, V. W., O'LEARY, D. S., *et al* (1995) Effects of diagnosis, laterality, and gender on brain morphology in schizophrenia. *American Journal of Psychiatry*, **152**, 704–714.

GLADSJO, J. A., HEATON, R. K., PAULSEN, J. S. & JESTE, D. V. (1996) Relationship of neuropsychological functioning and psychiatric symptoms in schizophrenia: a one-year follow-up (abstract). *International Neuropsychological Society*, **2**, 55.

GREEN, M. & WALKER, E. (1985) Neuropsychological performance and positive and negative symptoms in schizophrenia. *Journal of Abnormal Psychology*, **94**, 460–469.

GRIEF, C. & EASTWOOD, R. M. (1993) Paranoid disorders in the elderly. *International Journal of Geriatric Psychiatry*, **8**, 681–684.

GUR, R. E. & PEARLSON, G. D. (1993) Neuroimaging in schizophrenia research. *Schizophrenia Bulletin*, **19**, 337–353.

HARRIS, M. J. & JESTE, D. V. (1988) Late-onset schizophrenia: an overview. *Schizophrenia Bulletin*, **14**, 39–55.

HEATON, R., PAULSEN, J., MCADAMS, L. A., *et al* (1994) Neuropsychological deficits in schizophrenia: relationship to age, chronicity and dementia. *Archives of General Psychiatry*, **51**, 469–476.

HOWARD, R. J., ALMEIDA, O., LEVY, R., *et al* (1994) Quantitative magnetic resonance imaging volumetry distinguishes delusional disorder from late-onset schizophrenia. *British Journal of Psychiatry*, **165**, 474–480.

JERNIGAN, T. L., PRESS, G. A. & HESSELINK, J. R. (1990) Methods for measuring brain morphologic features on magnetic resonance images: validation and normal aging. *Archives of Neurology*, **47**, 27–32.

——, ARCHIBALD, S. L., BERHOW, M. T., *et al* (1991a) Cerebral structure on MRI. Part I: Localization of age-related changes. *Biological Psychiatry*, **29**, 55–67.

——, ZISOOK, S., HEATON, R. K., *et al* (1991b) Magnetic resonance imaging abnormalities in lenticular nuclei and cerebral cortex in schizophrenia. *Archives of General Psychiatry*, **48**, 881–890.

JESTE, D. V., KLEINMAN, J. E., POTKIN, S. G., *et al* (1982) Ex uno multi: subtyping the schizophrenia syndrome. *Biological Psychiatry*, **17**, 199–222.

——, HARRIS, M. J., PEARLSON, G. D., *et al* (1988) Late-onset schizophrenia: studying clinical validity. *Psychiatric Clinics of North America*, **11**, 1–14.

——, LACRO, J. P., GILBERT, P. L., *et al* (1993) Treatment of late-life schizophrenia with neuroleptics. *Schizophrenia Bulletin*, **19**, 817–830.

——, HARRIS, M. J., KRULL, A., *et al* (1995) Clinical and neuropsychological characteristics of patients with late-onset schizophrenia. *American Journal of Psychiatry*, **152**, 722–730.

——, EASTHAM, J. H., LACRO, J. P., *et al* (1996) Management of late-life psychosis. *Journal of Clinical Psychiatry*, **57**, 39–45.

KANE, J. M., JESTE, D. V., BARNES, T. R. E., *et al* (1992) *Tardive Dyskinesia: A Task Force Report of the American Psychiatric Association*. Washington, DC: APA.

KAY, D. W. K. & ROTH, M. (1961) Environmental and hereditary factors in the schizophrenias of old age ("late paraphrenia") and their bearing on the general problem of causation in schizophrenia. *Journal of Mental Science*, **107**, 649–686.

KRAEPELIN, E. (1898) Zur Diagnose und Prognose der Dementia praecox: Heidelberger Versammlung 26/27, November 1898. *Zeitschrift für die Neurologie und Psychiatrie*, **56**, 262.

—— (1919a) On paranoid diseases [in German]. *Zeitschrift für Gesamte Neurologie und Psychiatrie*, **11**, 617–638.

—— (1919b) *Dementia Praecox and Paraphrenia* (trans. R. M. Barclay, 1971). Huntington: Krieger.

KRISHNAN, K. R. R., GOLI, Z., ELLINWOOD, E. H., *et al* (1988) Leukoencephalopathy in patients diagnosed as major depressives. *Biological Psychiatry*, **23**, 519–522.

KRULL, A. J., PRESS, G., DUPONT, R., *et al* (1991) Brain imaging in late-onset schizophrenia and related psychoses. *International Journal of Geriatric Psychiatry*, **6**, 651–658.

LESSER, I. M., JESTE, D. V., BOONE, K. B., *et al* (1992) Late-onset psychotic disorder, not otherwise specified: clinical and neuroimaging findings. *Biological Psychiatry*, **31**, 419–423.

——, MILLER, B. L., SWARTZ, J. R., *et al* (1993) Brain imaging in late-life schizophrenia and related psychoses. *Schizophrenia Bulletin*, **19**, 773–782.

LEUCHTER, A. F. & SPAR, J. E. (1985) The late-onset psychoses. *Journal of Nervous and Mental Disease*, **173**, 488–494.

LEVIN, S., YURGELUN-TODD, D. & CRAFT, S. (1989) Contributions of clinical neuropsychology to the study of schizophrenia. *Journal of Abnormal Psychology*, **98**, 341–356.

LOHR, J. B., CADET, J. L., LOHR, M. A., *et al* (1988) Vitamin E in the treatment of tardive dyskinesia: the possible involvement of free radical mechanisms. *Schizophrenia Bulletin*, **14**, 291–296.

MAHER, B. A., MANSCHRECK, T. C., WOODS, B. T., *et al* (1995) Frontal brain volume and context effects in short-term recall in schizophrenia. *Biological Psychiatry*, **37**, 144–150.

MAURER, K. & HÄFNER, H. (1995) Methodological aspects of onset assessment in schizophrenia. *Schizophrenia Research*, **15**, 265–276.

MAYER, W. (1921) On paraphrenic psychoses [in German]. *Zeitschrift fur die Gesamte Neurologie und Psychiatrie*, **71**, 187–206.

MILLER, B. L., BENSON, F. D., CUMMINGS, J. L. & NESHKES, R. (1986) Late-life paraphrenia: an organic delusional system. *Journal of Clinical Psychiatry*, **47**, 204–207.

——, LESSER, I. M., BOONE, K., *et al* (1989) Brain white-matter lesions and psychosis. *British Journal of Psychiatry*, **155**, 73–78.

NASRALLAH, H. A., SKINNER, T. E., SCHMALBROCK, P. & ROBITAILLE, P. M. (1994) Proton magnetic resonance spectroscopy (1H MRS) of the hippocampal formation in schizophrenia: a pilot study. *British Journal of Psychiatry*, **165**, 481–485.

PAULSEN, J. S., ROMERO, R., CHAN, A., *et al* (1996) Impairment of the semantic network in schizophrenia. *Psychiatry Research*, **63**, 109–121.

PEARLSON, G. & RABINS, P. (1988) The late-onset psychoses: possible risk factors. In *The Psychiatric Clinics of North America: Psychosis and Depression in the Elderly* (ed. D. V. Jeste & S. Zisook), pp. 15–32. Philadelphia: Saunders.

——, TUNE, L. E., WONG, D. F., *et al* (1989) Quantitative D2 dopamine receptor PET and structural MRI changes in late onset schizophrenia. *Schizophrenia Bulletin*, **19**, 783–795.

PFEFFERBAUM, A., ZIPURSKY, R. B., LIM, K. O., *et al* (1988) Computed tomographic evidence for generalized sulcal and ventricular enlargement in schizophrenia. *Archives of General Psychiatry*, **45**, 633–640.

RABINS, P., PEARLSON, G., JAYARAM, G., *et al* (1987) Increased ventricle-to-brain ratio in late-onset schizophrenia. *American Journal of Psychiatry*, **144**, 1216–1218.

RAINE, A., LENCZ, T., REYNOLDS, G. P., *et al* (1992) An evaluation of structural and functional prefrontal deficits in schizophrenia: MRI and neuropsychological measures. *Psychiatry Research: Neuroimaging*, **45**, 123–137.

RIECHER-RÖSSLER, A., RÖSSLER, W., FÖRSTL, H., *et al* (1995) late-onset schizophrenia and late paranoia. *Schizophrenia Bulletin*, **21**, 345–354.

ROSSE, R. B., SCHWARTZ, B. L., MASTROPAOLO, J., *et al* (1991) Subtype diagnosis in schizophrenia and its relation to neuropsychological and computerized tomography measures. *Biological Psychiatry*, **30**, 63–72.

ROTH, M. (1955) The natural history of mental disorder in old age. *Journal of Mental Science*, **101**, 281–301.

SALZMAN, C., VACARRO, B., LIEFF, J. & WEINER, A. (1995) Clozapine in older patients with psychosis and behavioral disruption. *American Journal of Geriatric Psychiatry*, **3**, 26–33.

SAYKIN, A. J., GUR, R. C., GUR, R. E., *et al* (1991) Neuropsychological function in schizophrenia: selective impairment in memory and learning. *Archives of General Psychiatry*, **48**, 618–624.

SCHLAEPFER, T. E., HARRIS, G. J., TIEN, A. Y., *et al* (1994) Decreased regional cortical gray matter volume in schizophrenia. *American Journal of Psychiatry*, **151**, 842–848.

SEIDMAN, L. J., YURGELUN-TODD, D., KREMEN, W. S., *et al* (1994) Relationship of prefrontal and temporal lobe MRI measures to neuropsychological performance in chronic schizophrenia. *Biological Psychiatry*, **35**, 235–246.

SHENTON, M. E., KIKINIS, R., JOLESZ, F. A., *et al* (1992a) Left-lateralized temporal lobe abnormalities in schizophrenia and their relationship to thought disorder: a computerized, quantitative MRI study. *New England Journal of Medicine*, **327**, 604–612.

——, ——, ——, *et al* (1992b) Abnormalities of the left temporal lobe and thought disorder in schizophrenia: a quantitative magnetic resonance imaging study. *New England Journal of Medicine*, **327**, 604–612.

STRAUSS, M. E. (1993) Relations of symptoms to cognitive deficits in schizophrenia. *Schizophrenia Bulletin*, **19**, 215.

SUDDATH, R. L., CHRISTISON, G. W., TORREY, E. F., *et al* (1990) Anatomical abnormalities in the brains of monozygotic twins discordant for schizophrenia. *New England Journal of Medicine*, **322**, 789–794.

SWAYZE, V. W., ANDREASEN, N. C., ALLIGER, R. J., *et al* (1990) Structural brain abnormalities in bipolar affective disorder: ventricular enlargement and focal signal hyperintensities. *Archives of General Psychiatry*, **47**, 1054–1059.

SYMONDS, L. L., OLICHNEY, J. M., JERNIGAN, T. L., *et al* (1997) Lack of clinically significant structural abnormalities in MRIs of older patients with schizophrenia and related psychoses. *Journal of Neuropsychiatry and Clinical Neurosciences*, **9**, 251–258.

VLADAR, K., KULYNYCH, J. J., JONES, D. W., *et al* (1994) An MRI study of the superior temporal gyrus in monozygotic twins discordant for schizophrenia and in healthy twins (abstract). *Society for Neuroscience Abstracts*, **20**, 261.5.

WEINBERGER, D. R., BERMAN, K. F., SUDDATH, R. & TORREY, E. F. (1992) Evidence of dysfunction of a prefrontal limbic network in schizophrenia: a magnetic resonance imaging and regional blood flow study of discordant monozygotic twins. *American Journal of Psychiatry*, **149**, 890–897.

WIBLE, C. G., SHENTON, M. E., HOKAMA, H., *et al* (1994) Parcellation of human prefrontal cortex using high resolution MRI: a volumetric study of schizophrenic and control subjects (abstract). *Society for Neuroscience Abstracts*, **20**, 261.3.

WORLD HEALTH ORGANIZATION (1992) *The ICD–10 Classification of Mental and Behavioural Disorders*. Geneva: WHO.

YASSA, R. & JESTE, D. V. (1992) Gender differences in tardive dyskinesia: a critical review of the literature. *Schizophrenia Bulletin*, **18**, 701–715.

—— & SURANYI-CADOTTE, B. (1993) Clinical characteristics of late-onset schizophrenia: comparison with delusional disorder with and without hallucinations. *Schizophrenia Bulletin*, **19**, 701–707.

ZIPURSKY, R. B., LIM, K. O., SULLIVAN, E. V., *et al* (1992) Widespread cerebral gray matter volume deficits in schizophrenia. *Archives of General Psychiatry*, **49**, 195–205.

7 Late-onset schizoaffective disorders

ANDREAS MARNEROS

The neglected area

"The time is ripe for further confirmatory research in this neglected area," wrote Pitt in 1990 about schizoaffective disorders in the elderly. This area seems to be neglected. In the last 10 years very few papers have been registered with the key words 'late-onset schizoaffective disorders'. Some have mentioned late-onset schizoaffective disorders, but only peripherally (e.g. Howard *et al*, 1994; Angst & Preisig, 1995). Only two papers have dealt with late-onset schizoaffective disorders specifically (Pitt, 1990; Marneros *et al*, 1992).

Reasons for the neglect

Two factors may explain this neglect: the uncertainty regarding the definition of schizoaffective disorders in general; and the late-onset schizoaffective disorders themselves.

Uncertainty of definition

The definition of the schizoaffective disorders is still evolving, although clinical states corresponding to what we today call schizoaffective disorders were first described over 130 years ago. Perhaps the first description of schizoaffective disorders was given by Karl Kahlbaum in 1863 (see Chapter 1). Kraepelin himself – the father of the dichotomy of the 'endogenous' psychoses into schizophrenia (dementia praecox) and manic–depressive illness – accepted, in a very interesting paper published in 1920, the existence of what we call schizoaffective disorders as a weakness in his dichotomy. In the same period (in 1886) Magnan in France described the *bouffée délirante*, with essential similarities to schizoaffective disorders (see Pichot, 1986). Later in France the term 'dysthymic schizophrenia' was coined, which is very close to the concept of schizoaffective disorders (Pichot, 1986). Kurt Schneider's definition of the 'cases inbetween' (*Zwischen-Fälle*) is practically identical to modern definitions of schizoaffective disorders (Schneider, 1973; Marneros, 1983).

The term 'schizoaffective', introduced by Kasanin in 1933, soon became established. However, the criteria used by Kasanin for schizoaffective disorders are no longer valid. Only the word 'schizo-affective' and the criterion 'mixture of schizophrenic and affective symptoms' remain from Kasanin's concept. Nevertheless, a group of disorders named 'schizoaffective' began to become established in the various diagnostic systems. As Pichot (1986) pointed out, the official American history of schizoaffective disorder can be followed in the successive editions of the *Diagnostic and Statistical Manual of Mental Disorders*. DSM–I (American Psychiatric Association, 1952) described, among the 'schizophrenic reactions', the 'schizo-affective type'. The criteria used in DSM–I are different from Kasanin's original description. No mention is made of sudden onset, shortness of episode, or complete recovery.

DSM–II (American Psychiatric Association, 1968) included the category 'schizophrenia, schizoaffective type'. The definition, however, had become brief and non-committal: "Patients showing a mixture of schizophrenic symptoms and pronounced elation and depression". ICD–8, published in the same year, contained the same category (World Health Organization, 1968).

In 1978, the Task Force on Nomenclature and Classification of the American Psychiatric Association (APA) published the draft of DSM–III. It included a special category, schizoaffective disorders, completely distinct from schizophrenic disorders. The criteria proposed as essential were "a depressive or manic syndrome ... that preceded or develops concurrently with certain psychotic symptoms thought to be incompatible with a purely affective disorder". The DMS–III draft stated:

> "The term schizoaffective has been used in many different ways ... at the present time there is a controversy as to whether this disorder represents a variant of Affective Disorder of Schizophrenia, a third independent nosological entity, or part of a continuum between pure Affective Disorder and pure Schizophrenia."

The separate listing was justified by:

> "the accumulated evidence that individuals with a mixture of 'affective' and 'schizophrenic' symptoms, as compared with

individuals diagnosed as having schizophrenia, have a better prognosis, a tendency towards acute onset and resolution, more likely recovery to premorbid level of functioning, and an absence of an increase of prevalence of schizophrenia among family members."

Two years later, in the final printed edition of DSM–III (American Psychiatric Association, 1980), the category had practically disappeared. The manic episode and the major depressive episode now included cases "with mood-incongruent psychotic features" which, in the draft, would have belonged to the schizoaffective disorders. It is true that DSM–III formally retained a category called schizoaffective disorders but, being without diagnostic criteria, it was considered as a residual class "for those instances in which the clinician is unable to make a differential diagnosis between Affective Disorders and either Schizophreniform Disorder or Schizophrenia".

A new category, schizophreniform disorder, appeared. As Pichot (1986) pointed out, this category was very similar to Kasanin's original schizoaffective psychosis as far as its course was concerned: "The duration … is less than six months, … [there is] a tendency towards acute onset and resolution, … recovery to premorbid levels of functioning", but the symptomatic criteria are those of schizophrenia, with the exception of "a greater likelihood of emotional turmoil and confusion". No mention was made of affective symptoms (Pichot, 1986).

In DSM–III–R, published by the APA in 1987, schizoaffective disorders were born again – this time classified independently from both schizophrenia and affective disorders, in the category 'psychotic disorders not elsewhere classified', and with their own diagnostic criteria as well as with subtypes, namely bipolar type and depressive type. In DSM–IV, published by the APA in 1994, schizoaffective disorders belong to the category 'other psychotic disorders', with almost the same diagnostic criteria and the same subtypes as in DSM–III–R. This time the mixed bipolar syndromes are also recognised.

The tradition of ICD–8 was continued in ICD–9 (World Health Organization, 1978). In ICD–10 (World Health Organization, 1992), after bouncing like a ping-pong ball during successive draft publications, schizoaffective disorders landed in a category of their own, within schizophrenia and delusional disorders, with extensive description and with five subcategories:

(a) schizoaffective disorders at the present manic;
(b) schizoaffective disorders at the present depressive;
(c) mixed schizoaffective disorders;
(d) other schizoaffective disorders; and
(e) schizoaffective disorders not otherwise specified.

The evaluation of the concept and the definition of schizoaffective disorders continues. Many aspects remain to be clarified many questions still require answers. Most diagnostic systems recognise only the concurrent form of schizoaffective disorders, not the sequential one. But operational research has found no differences on any dimension between concurrent and sequential schizoaffective disorders (Marneros *et al*, 1988a,b,c, 1991).

We have lost valuable time ignoring the sequential type of schizoaffective disorders. Nevertheless, the ongoing evolution of concepts and definitions of schizoaffective disorder also means continuing uncertainty. The question 'What are the schizoaffective disorders?' remains unanswered.

That is the first reason why late-onset schizoaffective disorders constitute a neglected area.

Intrinsic reasons

The second reason for the assumed neglect are the late-onset schizoaffective disorders themselves. Pitt (1990) stated: "The topic of schizoaffective disorders in the elderly has been largely overlooked since Post's (1971) study, though such disorders are not rare".

We asked whether it is really the case that schizoaffective disorders in the elderly – in contrast to schizophrenia (Marneros & Deister, 1984) – have been overlooked? Felix Post, in his monographs *The Significance of Affective Symptoms in Old Age* (1962) and *Persistent Persecutory States of the Elderly* (1966), found that 38% of elderly patients with depression occasionally exhibited paranoid symptoms and that 58% of patients with late paraphrenia had, at some time, depressive admixtures. However, the states described by Post are sometimes far removed from schizoaffective disorders as they are currently defined. In 1971 Post published his paper "Schizo-affective symptomatology in late life". He investigated all patients aged over 60 years treated in Bethlem and Maudsley hospitals over five years. Post found that 29 patients, 4% of those involved, presented a problem of differential diagnosis between paraphrenic and affective illnesses. However, the criteria he used were broad.

Pitt himself reported that only 7 (1.4%) of 500 psychogeriatric patients "were significantly depressed as well as paranoic and could (retrospectively) be classified as schizoaffective" (Pitt, 1990). Holden (1987) identified 5 of 47 patients over 60 years old as schizoaffective.

In 1994 Howard *et al* applied ICD–10 criteria to a group of 101 patients diagnosed as having 'late paraphrenia'. Seven of them met the criteria for the depressive type of schizoaffective disorder and one for the mixed type.

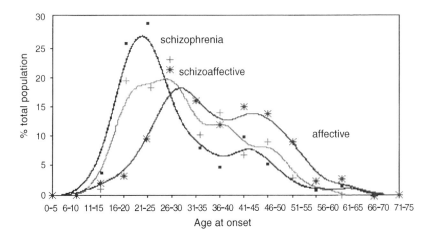

Fig. 7.1. Age at onset of schizophrenia, schizoaffective disorder and affective disorder (% of total population) (data from Marneros et al, 1989a,b, 1991).

Marneros and co-workers, in the Cologne Study, compared schizo-phrenic, schizoaffective and affective patients longitudinally (Marneros *et al*, 1989a,b, 1991; see also Marneros & Tsuang, 1986, 1990). Regarding age at onset, a peak was found for schizophrenia between 21 and 25 years of age, and for schizoaffective disorder between 26 and 30 years. For affective disorders a bimodal distribution was found, with the first peak between 31 and 35 years and the second peak between 41 and 45 years (Fig. 7.1). Patients with bipolar disorder became ill younger than those with unipolar disorder. This was true for both affective and schizoaffective disorders (Marneros *et al*, 1989c,d,e, 1991).

The mean age at onset of schizoaffective disorder was 30 years, the median 29.5 years, with a range of 15–58 years. No patient was found to have a first manifestation of a schizoaffective disorder after the sixth decade of life.

These results of the Cologne study have been confirmed by our findings in the Psychiatric Department of the Martin-Luther University Halle-Wittenberg. In three years there were 2236 admissions of 1505 patients, 602 of them first admissions. As Fig. 7.2 shows, 2.5% of first admissions were diagnosed as having a schizoaffective disorder, 7.5% schizophrenia and 26.4% affective disorders.

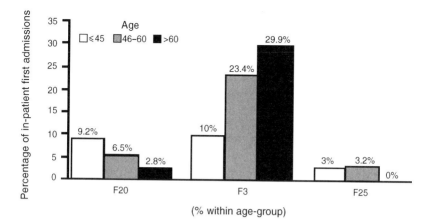

Fig. 7.2. In-patient first admissions at the Psychiatric Department of the Martin-Luther University Halle-Wittenberg (1993–95) (n=602), by ICD–10 diagnoses (F0, organic, including symptomatic, mental disorders; F1, mental and behavioural disorders due to psychoactive substance use; F20, schizophrenia; F3, affective disorder; F4, neurotic, stress-related and somatoform disorder; F25, schizoaffective disorder).

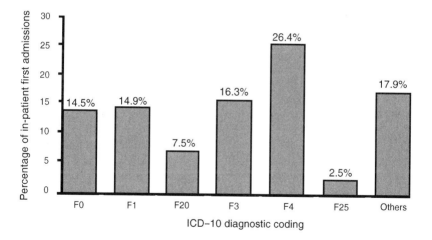

Fig. 7.3. In-patient first admissions at the Psychiatric Department of the Martin-Luther University Halle-Wittenberg (1993–95) (n=602): ICD–10 diagnoses as a percentage of each age group (F20, schizophrenia; F3, affective disorder; F25, schizoaffective disorder).

Splitting the three diagnostic groups according to age at onset (Fig. 7.3), we found that 2.8% of those with schizophrenia and 29.9% of those with affective disorders, but none of those with schizoaffective disorders, were older than 60 years.

It seems, then, that Pitt's statement that schizoaffective disorders in the elderly are "not rare" cannot be confirmed. This presents a paradox, because so-called 'atypical' mental disorders in the elderly are not uncommon and depressive symptoms in the elderly are common. Logically, therefore, schizoaffective symptoms – which are somewhat 'atypical' – could be expected to be more common, but it seems that this is a false expectation.

Conclusion

The reason for the neglect of schizoaffective disorders in the elderly seems then to be very simple: schizoaffective disorders with first onset in the elderly are extremely rare or even non-existent. Of course, the boundaries between young and old are ill-defined and the line between youth and age is different in every human being. Therefore we need to decide where to draw the borderline. Perhaps the most convenient compromise is the mean age of retirement. In most industrialised countries this is between the beginning and the middle of the seventh decade of life. It is evident that first onset of schizoaffective disorders beyond this time is extremely rare. Post's assumption that schizo-affective disorders in the elderly are not rare is based on broad definitions and elastic diagnostic criteria. Applying narrow diagnostic criteria, Post's assumption cannot be confirmed.

Marneros *et al* (1992) questioned whether it was justified to distin-guish between schizoaffective disorders with an onset after the 45th year of life and schizoaffective disorders with an earlier onset. Comparative studies showed no statistically significant differences between the two groups in premorbid and sociodemographic character-istics or in course, pattern of illness, or outcome.

Our conclusion is that there is no reason to distinguish between late-onset and early-onset schizoaffective disorders.

References

AMERICAN PSYCHIATRIC ASSOCIATION (1952) *Diagnostic and Statistical Manual of Mental Disorders.* Washington, DC: APA.
—— (1968) *Diagnostic and Statistical Manual of Mental Disorders* (2nd edn) (DSM–II). Washington, DC: APA.

—— (1980) *Diagnostic and Statistical Manual of Mental Disorders* (3rd edn) (DSM–III). Washington, DC: APA.

—— (1987) *Diagnostic and Statistical Manual of Mental Disorders* (3rd edn, revised) (DSM–III–R). Washington, DC: APA.

—— (1994) *Diagnostic and Statistical Manual of Mental Disorders* (4th edn) (DSM–IV). Washington, DC: APA.

ANGST, J. & PREISIG, M. (1995) Outcome of a clinical cohort of unipolar, bipolar and schizoaffective patients. Results of a prospective study from 1959 to 1985. *Schweizer Archiv für Neurologie und Psychiatrie*, **146**, 17–23.

HOLDEN, N. L. (1987) Late paraphrenia or the paraphrenias. A descriptive study with a 10-year follow-up. *British Journal of Psychiatry*, **150**, 635–639.

HOWARD, R., ALMEIDA, O. & LEVY, R. (1994) Phenomenology, demography and diagnosis in late paraphrenia. *Psychological Medicine*, **24**, 397–410.

KAHLBAUM, K. (1863) *Die Gruppirung der psychischen Krankheiten und die Eintheilung der Seelstörungen*. Danzig: Kafemann.

KASANIN, J. (1933) The acute schizoaffective psychoses. *American Journal of Psychiatry*, **13**, 97–126.

KRAEPELIN, E. (1920) Die Erscheinungsformen des Irreseins. *Zentralblatt für die gesamte Neurologie und Psychiatrie*, **62**, 1–29.

MARNEROS, A. (1983) Kurt Schneider's "Zwischen-Fälle", "mid-cases" or "cases-in-between". *Psychiatria Clinica*, **16**, 87–102.

—— & DEISTER, A. (1984) The psychopathology of 'late schizophrenia'. *Psychopathology*, **17**, 264–274.

—— & TSUANG, M. T. (eds) (1986) *Schizoaffective Psychoses*. Berlin: Springer.

—— & —— (eds) (1990) *Affective and Schizoaffective Disorders*. Berlin: Springer.

——, ——, ROHDE, A., *et al* (1988a) Long-term course of schizoaffective disorders. Part I: Definitions, methods, frequency of episodes and cycles. *European Archives of Psychiatry and Neurological Sciences*, **237**, 264–275.

——, ROHDE, A., DEISTER, A., *et al* (1988b) Long-term course of schizoaffective disorders. Part II: Length of cycles, episodes and intervals. *European Archives of Psychiatry and Neurological Sciences*, **237**, 276–282.

——, ——, ——, *et al* (1988c) Long-term course of schizoaffective disorders. Part III: Onset, type of episodes and syndrome shift, precipitating factors, suicidality, seasonality, inactivity of illness and outcome. *European Archives of Psychiatry and Neurological Sciences*, **237**, 283–290.

——, DEISTER, A., ROHDE, A., *et al* (1989a) Long-term outcome of schizoaffective and schizophrenic disorders: a comparative study. Part I: Definitions, methods, psychopathological and social outcome. *European Archives of Psychiatry and Neurological Sciences*, **238**, 118–125.

——, STEINMEYER, E. M., DEISTER, A., *et al* (1989b) Long-term outcome of schizoaffective and schizophrenic disorders: a comparative study. Part III: Social consequences. *European Archives of Psychiatry and Neurological Sciences*, **238**, 135–139.

——, DEISTER, A. & ROHDE, A. (1989c) Unipolar and bipolar schizoaffective disorders: a comparative study. I. Premorbid and sociodemographic features. *European Archives of Psychiatry and Neurological Sciences*, **239**, 158–163.

——, ROHDE, A. & DEISTER, A. (1989d) Unipolar and bipolar schizoaffective disorders: a comparative study. II. Long-term course. *European Archives of Psychiatry and Neurological Sciences*, **239**, 164–170.

——, DEISTER, A., ROHDE, A. & JÜNEMANN, H. (1989e) Unipolar and bipolar schizoaffective disorders: a comparative study. III. Long-term outcome. *European Archives of Psychiatry and Neurological Sciences*, **239**, 171–176.

——, —— & —— (1991) *Affektive, Schizoaffektive und Schizophrene Psychosen: Eine vergleichende Langzeitstudie*. Berlin: Springer.

——, —— & —— (1992) Schizophrenic, schizoaffective and affective disorders in the elderly: a comparison. In *Delusions and Hallucinations in Old Age* (eds C. Katona & R. Levy) pp. 136–152. London: Gaskell.

PICHOT, P. (1986) A comparison of different national concepts of schizoaffective psychosis. In *Schizoaffective Psychoses* (eds A. Marneros & M. T. Tsuang), pp. 8–17. Berlin: Springer.

PITT, B. (1990) Schizoaffective disorders in the elderly. In *Affective and Schizoaffective Disorders. Similarities and Differences* (eds A. Marneros & M. T. Tsuang), pp. 102–106. Berlin: Springer.

POST, F. (1962) *The Significance of Affective Symptoms in Old Age. A Follow-up Study of One Hundred Patients.* London: Oxford University Press.

—— (1966) *Persistent Persecutory States of the Elderly.* Oxford: Pergamon.

—— (1971) Schizo-affective symptomatology in late life. *British Journal of Psychiatry*, **118**, 437–445.

SCHNEIDER, K. (1973) *Klinische Psychopathologie* (10th edn). Stuttgart: Thieme.

WORLD HEALTH ORGANIZATION (1968) *International Classification of Diseases* (8th edn) (ICD–8). Geneva: WHO.

—— (1978) *International Classification of Diseases* (9th edn) (ICD–9). Geneva: WHO.

—— (1992) *International Classification of Diseases* (10th edn) (ICD–10). Geneva: WHO.

8 Dysthymia, somatisation disorder and generalised anxiety in the elderly

DAN G. BLAZER

A discussion of late-onset dysthymia, somatisation disorder and generalised anxiety would appear, at first glance, to aggregate a group of disorders which have, inherently, little in common. In fact, these disorders have a number of characteristics in common and these characteristics provide a useful opportunity to compare the aetiology of less severe but chronic psychiatric disorders of late onset with the same disorders of early onset. In addition to being chronic and less severe, dysthymia, somatisation disorder and generalised anxiety are not usually considered stress-related disorders but rather disorders of uncertain aetiology. Nevertheless, most clinicians would emphasise psychosocial, personality and developmental factors interacting over many years as driving the onset of these disorders in late life. In addition, these disorders are less easily diagnosed in older adults than more severe disorders such as major depression or panic disorder, and they are often therefore relegated to the status of a 'default' diagnosis if a more clearly defined disorder cannot be justified. Somatisation disorder is the exception to this rule. The criteria for somatisation disorder are clear (see below) and the multiple symptoms across multiple organ systems required for diagnosis rarely leave doubt in the clinician's mind regarding the presence or absence of the disorder.

Is there evidence that these disorders may, in fact, have a different aetiology if first onset occurs in late life compared with mid-life? Empirical data are sparse. One could hypothesise, however, that dysthymia and generalised anxiety disorder with onset in late life are more likely to be derived from biological abnormalities than psychosocial factors than is the case with persons in mid-life. Somatisation disorder, by definition (see below), usually has its onset early in life, yet the symptoms of the disorder may certainly appear in late life for the first time and a clear biological explanation of the symptoms frequently is not forthcoming. If these symptoms do have their first appearance in late life, then biological factors perhaps contribute more to the symptom onset than earlier in the life cycle.

After a brief review of the epidemiology and diagnosis of these three less severe psychiatric disorders in late life, a case will be made for a more biological contribution to their aetiology if first onset occurs in late life compared with onset earlier in life.

Dysthymic disorder

Sub-syndromal depression, a depressive syndrome that does not meet criteria for major depression yet is considered clinically significant in that it contributes to disability in older adults, is a common problem encountered by primary-care physicians in out-patient practice (Blazer, 1994). A variety of sub-syndromal depressions may be diagnosed, including: prodromal or partially recovered major depressive disorders; mood disorders due to a general medical condition but not reaching criteria for major depression; minor depression; brief recurrent mood disorders; depressive personality; and dysthymic disorder or neurotic depression. Dysthymic disorder is described in DSM–IV as "a chronically depressed mood that occurs for most of the day more days than not for at least two years" (American Psychiatric Association, 1994). In addition, two symptoms must be present among the following: poor appetite or overeating; insomnia or hypersomnia; low energy or fatigue; low self-esteem, poor concentration or difficulty making decisions; feelings of hopelessness; the permanent presence of low interest; and self-criticism. To make the diagnosis of dysthymic disorder, these symptoms should have become "a part of the individual's day-to-day experience". It should be recognised that no empirical data truly validate this psychopathological construct (unlike many statistical and psychobiological studies which provide some validation of major depression). Nevertheless, every clinician working with adults experiencing mood disturbances recognises patients who present with chronic, less severe depressive symptoms to which the DSM–IV criteria for dysthymic disorders can be applied.

Few argue that the frequency of clinically significant depressive symptoms in community populations is higher than the frequency of major depression. For example, most investigators have found that between 10% and 15% of subjects in the community experience clinically significant depressive symptoms (Blazer & Williams, 1980; Berkman *et al*, 1986; Blazer *et al*, 1991a). These estimates are much higher than the estimates for major depression which range from 1%

to 3% (Blazer & Williams, 1980). Of these individuals, a substantial percentage will meet criteria for dysthymic disorder.

Devenand *et al* (1994), in a clinical study of persons 60–92 years of age treated in an out-patient mental health clinic, found that 18% were diagnosed with dysthymic disorder. The mean age at onset was 55 (generally older than one expects to see in the onset of dysthymic disorder) and the average duration of illness was 12.5 years. Most of these persons did not report a previous episode of major depression. Most risk factors for major depression were not found among persons experiencing dysthymic disorder. The one exception was stressful events, which were frequently associated with the onset or continuance of dysthymic disorder. The higher frequency of major depression among women was not found for dysthymic disorder in this study (and some others). The chronicity required for diagnosis may decrease the reporting of some risk factors and may hamper a clear retrospective understanding of the cause–effect relationship between risk factors and onset of the disorder.

Are there reasons to believe that dysthymic disorder results from biological causes early in life? First, the apparent absence of an association between dysthymia and many of the psychosocial risk factors pertaining to major depression may indirectly suggest biological factors as causative. The gradual onset of depressive symptoms, resistant to treatment, with little psychosocial explanation, may also suggest a biological aetiology. Unfortunately, there are no data in the literature which demonstrate an association between dysthymic disorder in late life and neuropathological changes. In contrast to late-onset major depression, which has been associated with decreased cortisol secretion following dexamethasone, polysomnographic changes such as de-creased rapid eye movement latency and subcortical hyperintensities on magnetic resonance imaging, late-onset dysthymic disorder has not been associated with pathophysiological markers. These is no clear direct evidence of psychobiological factors leading to dysthymic disorder.

Perhaps something could be learned from the treatment of less severe depressions. In this case, unfortunately, methodological issues confound the exploration. For example, Paykel *et al* (1988) evaluated the use of amitriptyline in treating severe versus less severe depressive syndromes in primary care. The drug was effective in treating the more severe but not the less severe syndromes. The difficulty Paykel and his colleagues encountered in this study was a floor effect: persons treated with placebo and amitriptyline in the less severe depression category improved over a few weeks such that their symptom level was equivalent to those individuals who had recovered from more severe depression. Unfortunately, the changes in the scores from the onset of this study to its conclusion were not sufficient to demonstrate a statistically significant relationship between the medication and clinical improvement.

In another, much larger study, Quitkin *et al* (1988) found that persons with scores on the Hamilton Rating Scale for Depression (HRSD) of 10 or less responded to imipramine and phenelzine in a placebo-controlled trial. It is rare, however, that a well run clinical trial can be performed on a large number of subjects (over 400 out-patients in the Stewart study). Many psychiatrists and primary-care clinicians do treat persons with chronic, less severe depression with antidepressant medications, especially the selective serotonin reuptake inhibitors, and report 'success'. Few controlled studies, however, have documented such success, and none among the elderly. Nevertheless, the question remains open as to whether older persons might suffer from neuropathological abnormalities which can be corrected by pharmacological intervention.

In summary, there is little direct evidence for a relative predominance of biological over psychosocial risk factors contributing to the onset and persistence of late-onset dysthymic disorder. Nevertheless, the paucity of studies demonstrating a clear relationship between psychosocial risk factors or predisposing traits and the disorder leaves open the possibility. Further studies should help to clarify the relationship. Nevertheless, the difficulty with case identification and the floor effect in treatment studies will render such studies more difficult than studies exploring the aetiology of major depression.

Somatisation disorder

Somatisation disorder, according to DSM–IV, should rarely begin in late life. Specifically, persons "typically meet criteria by age 25". Yet many of the symptoms of somatisation disorder are frequent in late life and cannot be wholly explained by physiological changes. These include symptoms from each of the categories used to diagnose somatisation disorder: pain (joint pain); gastrointestinal (food intolerance, diarrhoea and constipation); sexual dysfunction (sexual indifference); and pseudo-neurological symptoms (localised weakness and urinary retention).

Somatisation disorder is a rare disorder, regardless of age (Swartz *et al*, 1991). The prevalence is approximately 0.1% across the life cycle in the United States and does not vary by age. There have been virtually no studies of somatisation disorder with onset in late life. In addition, to the knowledge of this author, there are no longitudinal studies of somatisation disorder of early onset in which subjects have been followed into late life. Nevertheless, conventional clinical wisdom suggests that somatisation disorder with early onset persists into later life.

There is little question, however, that the increasing frailty of late life coupled with hypochondriacal tendencies may lead some older adults to meet the criteria for somatisation disorder for the first time. In contrast to onset earlier in life, when actual physical problems are rarely a major contributor to this syndrome, frailty and physical difficulties play a major (though not a wholly explanatory) role in the onset of symptoms among older persons. Somatisation disorder therefore differs from dysthymia and generalised anxiety disorder in that neuropathological changes do not necessarily contribute to the aetiology more in late life than earlier in the life cycle. Biological factors, however, certainly contribute more, because actual but less severe physical problems are exaggerated by some older people, which may lead to late-onset somatisation disorder according to DSM–IV criteria.

The prognosis and management of the disorder in late life may differ from those of early-onset somatisation disorder. Further study will be needed to clarify the aetiology and treatment of late-onset somatisation disorder.

Generalised anxiety disorder

The frequency of generalised anxiety among older persons has been estimated to be high. Gurin *et al* (1983), in a survey of 2460 community-dwelling adults, found cognitive anxiety to be almost three times as frequent among persons 65 and older than among persons 21–40 years of age, and somatic anxiety nearly seven times more frequent. The combined frequency for both cognitive and somatic anxiety among the 65+ age group was 21.7%. The most comprehensive estimates of the prevalence of anxiety disorders and panic in late life, as defined by DSM–III, derive from the Epidemiologic Catchment Area (ECA) studies (Blazer *et al*, 1991b). In these studies, the prevalence of generalised anxiety disorder was 2.2% among older people when no exclusion criteria were considered in the diagnosis. When panic disorders and major depression were excluded, the frequency was 1.9%. If all other DSM–III disorders were excluded, the frequency was 1.1%. The ECA studies have been criticised for relatively low estimates of psychiatric disorders across the life cycle and especially in the elderly. For example, the frequency of major depression among the elderly in the community is approximately the same as that for generalised anxiety. Therefore, generalised anxiety is not an insignificant problem in older persons.

There is no consensus regarding the criteria for generalised anxiety disorder, although most clinicians believe that a syndrome of generalised anxiety disorder, uncomplicated by other disorders, does exist. This lack of consensus is reflected in the changing criteria for the disorder from DSM–III through DSM–III–R to DSM–IV. In DSM–IV, the central diagnostic criteria for generalised anxiety are divided into motor tension (such as restlessness and fatigue), autonomic hyperactivity (such as shortness of breath and palpitations) and vision/scanning (being keyed up or on edge as well as irritable).

The symptoms which are typically included in diagnostic criteria for generalised anxiety are common among older adults and certainly may derive from factors other than the syndrome of generalised anxiety. Frequently, however, the symptoms are concurrently of physiological and psychosocial aetiology. For example, in a study of symptoms most frequently reported to physicians during routine office visits by patients 75 years of age and older, many of the top 25 symptoms fell into the category of generalised anxiety (White *et al*, 1986). These included dizziness, chest pain, shortness of breath, general weakness, tiredness and exhaustion, nervousness, palpitations, nausea, and urinary frequency. 'Feeling shaky' may result from tremors associated with ageing, chest pain from costochondriasis or osteoarthritis, restlessness from medications, easy fatigability from frailty, shortness of breath from chronic pulmonary disease, dry mouth from medications, dizziness from postural hypotension, frequent urination from benign prostatic hypertrophy and difficulty concentrating from memory loss. In addition, older persons have more difficulty falling asleep than younger persons (Miles & Dement, 1980). Though the diagnosis of generalised anxiety cannot be established if an organic disorder is clearly identified as the cause of the symptoms (e.g. hyperthyroidism or medication intoxication can explain somatic anxiety), ruling out an organic disorder is difficult in older adults. Frequently psychosocial factors exaggerate symptoms that may have a biological aetiology, such as medication intoxication.

Biological changes inherent to ageing may lead to symptoms of anxiety. For many years, heightened perception of arousal and anxiety have been associated with increased symptoms of nervous system activation. The locus ceruleus has specifically been implicated (Redmond & Huang, 1979). Some studies have suggested a decline in noradrenaline levels with increasing ageing, leading to the assumption that late-onset generalised anxiety is less severe than earlier in life (Sunderland *et al*, 1991). Others have suggested, however, that noradrenaline levels decline only in the locus ceruleus, but remain stable elsewhere in the brain (Morgen & May, 1990).

Of more importance is the relationship of noradrenaline to stress. The mean noradrenaline level increases more with exercise in older adults than in younger adults. In addition, levels return to baseline after exercise more slowly among the elderly (Rowe & Troen, 1980). This physiological response to exercise may be associated with the altered ability of older adults to deal with stress as they age (Eisdorfer & Wilke, 1977).

In addition, there are some psychological studies suggesting that elderly persons may in fact be 'protected' against the development of the symptoms of generalised anxiety. Jarvik & Russell (1979) found that older persons may develop less adaptive strategies to deal with stress. One of these strategies is a passive stance, which the authors termed 'freeze'. This 'freeze' response in the midst of stress may enable the older adult to conserve energy while at the same time attempting to 'buy time', so that a more appropriate response can be mustered to the stressful situation. In the midst of freeze, the symptoms of generalised anxiety do not emerge.

Kastenbaum (1980) has suggested a means of dampening anxiety with ageing. As individuals age, novel events and situations are treated as though they are repetitions of the familiar, leading to habituation. In other words, novel stimuli are treated as if they are normal and the older person does not react as if the stimuli are novel. Older persons therefore find it easier to cope with the new stimuli, whether they be new situations, new people, or new events.

Conclusions

Though the data are sparse, the less severe and generally assumed psychosocially derived disorders of dysthymia, somatisation disorder and generalised anxiety with onset in later life may be more biologically determined than earlier in the life cycle. Further empirical studies are necessary to explore this hypothesis. Enough evidence exists to mount such studies. In addition, if this theory is correct, then psychopharmacological therapy may be appropriate for these disorders despite the difficulty in designing and implementing clinical trials.

There is a caveat to this conclusion. First, it must be recognised that older persons frequently experience stressful events which can lead to adjustment disorders with depression, anxiety and somatisation. Given that the stressors may continue over relatively long periods of time (such as the stress of living in an unsafe neighbourhood or fear of recurrence of a life-threatening physical illness), the symptoms may persist over extended periods as well. The consequent stress-related constellations of symptoms, even if they meet criteria for generalised anxiety, somatisation and dysthymia, can be clearly delineated through a careful psychiatric interview. These stress-related cases probably account for a minority of individuals who meet criteria for these disorders. Therefore the majority of persons who meet symptom criteria for these disorders probably fall into a category which is difficult to classify in terms of aetiology. For these individuals, psychobiological explanations should be sought, though psychobiological probes must be more refined than those currently available.

References

AMERICAN PSYCHIATRIC ASSOCIATION (1994) *Diagnostic and Statistical Manual of Mental Disorders* (4th edn) (DSM–IV). Washington, DC: APA.

BERKMAN, L. F., BERKMAN, C. S., KASL, S., *et al* (1986) Depressive symptoms in relation to physical health and functioning in the elderly. *American Journal of Epidemiology*, **124**, 372–388.

BLAZER, D. G. (1994) Dysthymia in community and clinical samples of older adults. *American Journal of Psychiatry*, **151**, 1567–1569.

—— & WILLIAMS, C. D. (1980) The epidemiology of dysphoria and depression in an elderly population. *American Journal of Psychiatry*, **137**, 439–444.

——, BURCHETT, D., SERVICE, C. & GEORGE, L. K. (1991a) The association of age and depression among the elderly: an epidemiologic exploration. *Journal of Gerontology*, **46**, 210–215.

——, HUGHES, D. A., GEORGE, L. K., *et al* (1991b) Generalized anxiety disorder. In *Psychiatric Disorders in America: The Epidemiologic Catchment Area Study* (eds L. N. Robins & D. A. Regier), pp. 180–203. New York: Free Press.

DEVENAND, D. P., NOBLER, M. S., SANGER, T., *et al* (1994) Is dysthymia a different disorder in the elderly? *American Journal of Psychiatry*, **151**, 1592–1599.

EISDORFER, C. & WILKE, F. (1977) Stress, disease and aging and behavior. In *Handbook of the Psychology of Aging* (eds J. E. Birren & K. W. Schaie), pp. 251–275. New York: Van Nostrand Rineholt.

GURIN, G., VEROFF, J. & FELD, S. (1983) *Americans View their Mental Health.* New York: Basic Books.

JARVIK, L. F., & RUSSELL, D. (1979) Anxiety, aging and the third emergency reaction. *Journal of Gerontology*, **34**, 197–200.

KASTENBAUM, R. J. (1980) Habituation as a model of human aging. *International Journal of Aging and Human Development,* **12**, 159–170.

MILES, L. E. & DEMENT, W. C. (1980) Sleep in aging. *Sleep*, **3**, 119–220.

MORGEN, D. G. & MAY, P. C. (1990) Age-related changes in neurochemistry. In *Handbook of the Biology of Aging* (3rd edn) (eds E. L. Schneider & J. W. Rowe), pp. 219–254. New York: Academic Press.

PAYKEL, E. S., HOLLIMAN, J. A., FREELING, P., *et al* (1988) Predictors of therapeutic benefits from amitriptyline in mild depression: a general practice placebo-control trial. *Journal of Affective Disorders*, **14**, 83–95.

QUITKIN, F. M., STEWART, J. W., MCGRATH, P. J., *et al* (1988) Phenelzine versus imipramine in probable atypical depression: defining syndrome boundaries of selective MAOI responders. *American Journal of Pychiatry*, **145**, 306–312.

REDMOND, D. E. & HUANG, H. Y. (1979) New evidence for locus-ceruleus–norepinephrine connection with anxiety. *Life Sciences*, **25**, 2149–2162.

ROWE, J. W. & TROEN, B. R. (1980) Sympathetic nervous system and aging in man. *Endocrine Review*, **1**, 165–175.

SUNDERLAND, T., LAWLOR, B. & MARTINEZ, R. (1991) Anxiety in the elderly: neurobiological and clinical interface. In *Anxiety in the Elderly* (eds C. Salzman & B. D. Liebowitz), pp. 105–129. New York: Springer.

SWARTZ, M., LANDERMAN, R., GEORGE, L. K., *et al* (1991) Somatization disorder. In *Psychiatric Disorders in America* (eds L. Robins & D. Regier), pp. 220–257. New York: Free Press.

WHITE, L. R., CARTWRIGHT, W. S. & CORNONI-HUNTLEY, J. (1986) Geriatric epidemiology. *Review of Gerontology and Geriatrics*, **6**, 215–221.

9 Sleep and sleep disturbances in the elderly

ULRICH VODERHOLZER
and MATHIAS BERGER

Changes of sleep with ageing

It is a well known fact that from infancy to adulthood there is a gradual reduction in time spent sleeping, from on average 16 hours in infancy to between seven and eight hours in early adulthood. It was also presumed that the need for sleep was reduced as the adult progressed into the senium (Roffwarg *et al*, 1966). This assumption can no longer be sustained. Epidemiological data obtained by questionnaire in large community samples have revealed that subjectively estimated sleep duration does not decrease with increasing age (Miles & Dement, 1980). Telemetric studies over 72 hours in healthy elderly subjects did not show an essentially reduced total sleep time per 24 hours (Spiegel, 1981). This discrepancy with the earlier assumption can be explained by the higher frequency of daytime napping in the elderly (Reynolds *et al*, 1991). In his investigation Spiegel (1981) found that the mean amount of daytime sleep was 50 min.

On the other hand, there is no doubt that the elderly do show a significant diminution of sleep efficiency, that is, a marked increase in waking periods. Changes in the sleep–wake rhythm with ageing may therefore be summarised as follows:

(a) decrease of sleep efficiency, but with no essential decrease of total sleep time per 24 hours;
(b) increase in incidence of daytime napping;
(c) increase in micro-arousals, with lowering of waking threshold;
(d) reduction of slow-wave sleep/delta-wave activity;
(e) increased variability of rapid eye movement (REM) sleep;

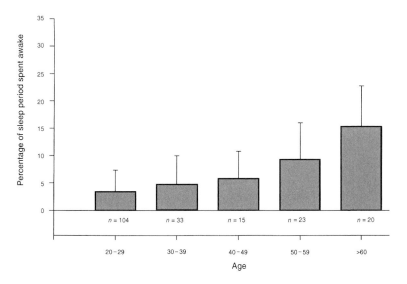

Fig. 9.1. Percentage of night-time sleep period spent awake, as a function of age, in 195 healthy subjects who did not complain of insomnia. Sleep maintenance progressively declines with age. Many old individuals do not, however, experience this natural phenomenon as sleep disturbance.

(f) reduced amplitude of circadian rhythms such as body temperature and cortisol secretion;
(g) decreased secretion of sleep-related hormones (growth hormone, melatonin).

Young adults usually show less than 10% of time spent awake during a night-time polysomnographic recording, whereas this percentage increases in the elderly to over 20% (Miles & Dement, 1980; Monk *et al*, 1991; Hoch *et al*, 1994). Figure 9.1 demonstrates the age-dependent increase in the percentage of time spent awake during the sleep period in healthy subjects without subjective complaints of disturbed sleep, as recorded in the sleep laboratory of the University of Freiburg. These findings indicate that ageing is associated with a decreased ability to maintain sleep continuity. The sleep deficit, or part of it, is attenuated by an increase in daytime sleep or a prolongation of time spent in bed, so that the total sleep time over a 24-hour period is not essentially reduced. This finding does not support the assumption that elderly people require less sleep than young people, nor that the ability of the central nervous system to generate sleep is impaired in old age.

The polysomnographic findings of increased daytime sleep in the elderly were also supported by a large epidemiological study of general practice patients. This study showed an increase in the frequency of midday sleep in those above the age of 65 years (Hohagen *et al*, 1994a). Apart from an increase of waking periods, several typical alterations of sleep have been consistently found in the aged (see Bliwise, 1993, 1994, for reviews), as summarised above. These age-dependent changes seem to occur somewhat earlier in men than in women (Hoch *et al*, 1988). In a meta-analysis of 27 studies addressing gender differences in the sleep of persons 58 years of age and older, Rediehs *et al* (1990) concluded that men tended to show more objective changes from the patterns of healthy, youthful sleep. In contrast, however, subjective complaints of disturbed sleep are more frequent in elderly women than in elderly men (Hohagen *et al*, 1994a). The observed polysomnographic variations of sleep in the elderly should be carefully examined to determine whether they are caused by organic factors such as respiratory, cardiovascular or movement disorders, as these causes of variations are not related to the age-specific changes in sleep patterns.

It was thought that increased frequency of nocturnal awakening and daytime napping in the elderly indicated a regression of their sleep patterns to that of infants, who show a polyphasic pattern of frequent changes between sleep and waking during a 24-hour period. However, such a polyphasic pattern does not seem to be restricted to infancy or – as a tendency – to the senium. Zulley & Bailer (1988) found a recurrence of ultradian sleep cycles of about four hours in healthy subjects under constant and monotonous bedrest conditions over 72 hours. This observation indicates that the monophasic rhythm of sleep and waking is conditioned and maintained by *zeitgebers* ('time cues'). In the aged, factors such as social contact, work, physical activity and light exposure during the day are frequently reduced (Table 9.1). This diminution of external *zeitgebers* may – especially in those physically ill who are restricted to monotonous bedrest conditions – unmask ultradian rhythms of sleep and waking, and disrupt the usual monophasic sleep–wake cycle of adulthood.

TABLE 9.1
Circadian rhythms with ageing

External factors (weakening of time cues)	Internal factors (weakening of circadian rhythm)
Reduced physical activity	Reduced amplitude of endocrine and
Reduced social contact	temperature rhythms
Reduced light exposure	Enhanced susceptibility to phase shifts and
	internal desynchronisation

Stability of the circadian system is an additional important factor for the stability of the sleep–wake rhythm. A strong oscillator regulates the circadian rhythm of body temperature, cortisol secretion and the propensity to REM sleep. Usually the sleep–wake rhythm is synchronised with this oscillator (Wever, 1979). In complete isolation, without external *zeitgebers*, a desynchronisation of sleep–wake and circadian body temperature rhythms can occur, a phenomenon which is called 'internal desynchronisation'. Elderly subjects have been described as regularly showing desynchronisation of circadian rhythms in isolation studies, whereas the majority of younger subjects maintain the synchronisation of their sleep–wake and temperature rhythm (Wever, 1979). An explanation for this enhanced vulnerability to desynchronisation in the elderly is a substantially reduced amplitude of circadian rhythms (Richardson *et al*, 1982; Copinschi & Van Cauter, 1995; Myers & Badia, 1995). The amplitude of circadian rhythms is negatively correlated to the day-to-day variability of the rhythms and the ability to shift phases. Since vigilance and performance are inversely correlated with the circadian rhythm of body temperature, a weakening of the circadian system has a strong impact on nocturnal sleep quality and on daytime vigilance. This was supported in studies by Wever (1979), who found a significant correlation between the amplitude of body temperature and sleep duration.

Prevalence of sleep disorders in the elderly

As shown by a variety of studies, insomnia is a frequent complaint among the elderly, and is more common in elderly women than in elderly men (Mellinger *et al*, 1985; Ford & Kamerow, 1989; Bliwise *et al*, 1992). As mentioned above, many investigations also report that elderly women describe their sleep as more disturbed than do men of the same age. Karacan *et al* (1976) found an increase of the complaint of disturbed sleep from 9% between the ages of 20 and 29 years to 21% between the ages of 60 and 69 years. Bixler *et al* (1979) found that 38% of all individuals between 51 and 80 years of age reported having problems with falling asleep, staying asleep, or waking too early. Livingston *et al* (1993) evaluated the prevalence of insomnia among elderly people in an inner-London community. Insomnia was present in 33%. These authors also reported that the best predictor of future depression in elderly people who were not depressed was current sleep disturbance. In a recent report on the frequency of sleep disturbances in elderly residents of nursing homes, 65% of the residents studied had one or more sleep-related complaint (Monane *et al*, 1996). Not all studies have found such high prevalence rates. Henderson *et al* (1995) found a prevalence of insomnia of only 15.8% after interviewing a sample of people aged 70 years or more. Even though the comparison of the various studies is limited by differences in evaluation and diagnostic criteria for insomnia, there can be no doubt that geriatric insomnia is common, especially in women.

An epidemiological study of the prevalence and treatment of sleep disorders

We have conducted a study of patients of general practitioners (GPs) in Germany (Hohagen *et al*, 1993, 1994a). Since more than 80% of all Germans visit a GP at least once a year, these patients reflect a representative sample of the whole population. In this investigation a total of 2842 patients above the age of 18 years, of whom 330 were older than 65 years, received a questionnaire covering sociodemographic data, sleep disturbances and their duration, drug and alcohol use, physical diseases and life events during the past six months. Patients were also asked what they believed to be the cause of their sleep disturbances. The GPs provided information on psychiatric and organic disorders, medication, frequency of consultations and whether or not they knew about the patient's sleep problem.

Sleep disturbances were differentiated into slight, moderate and severe insomnia. As set out in the DSM–III–R classification (American Psychiatric Association, 1987), severe insomnia was assumed if the patient reported that it had lasted for more than four weeks and had occurred on at least three of seven nights during the week, and if impairment of daytime performance was present. Moreover, to diagnose severe insomnia the total sleep time had to be less than six hours, with the time required to fall asleep longer than 30 minutes.

In this study, increasing age correlated clearly with an increase of insomnia, although this reached a plateau at the age of 60 years. The proportion of individuals with severe insomnia was higher in women than in men in all age groups. Eighty-eight per cent of the patients above 65 years reported that their insomnia had lasted for at least one year. In 64% of this group, insomnia had already persisted for more than five years. Table 9.2 shows the causes of insomnia according to patients. The elderly frequently reported that physical diseases, occupation with daily events, personal problems, disturbance by noise and life events during the past six months were the causes for their sleep problems. Compared with the reports of younger individuals, physical disease and noise were clearly more frequent causes of disturbed sleep in elderly individuals. Furthermore, the proportion of those who had experienced a life event during the past six months, a factor contributing to insomnia, was higher above the age of 65 compared with the individuals between 36 and 65 years. Life events, however, were also a frequent cause of insomnia in persons aged 18 to 35 years. The higher proportion of elderly subjects reporting noise as a cause of disturbed sleep might be explained by the flattening of the sleep electroencephalogram (EEG) and the lowering of the 'waking threshold'.

The interviews with the GPs also revealed that they did not know about the sleep problem of about half the patients who reported them. This unawareness of the patients' sleep disturbances was even more prominent in the individuals aged between 18 and 65 years, where the doctor knew about the problem in only a third of this age group. One explanation for this finding may be that the patients do not expect any other support than sleeping pills, and therefore may not report their sleep disturbances.

As shown in Fig. 9.2, the various age groups differed with regard to the prescription of sleeping pills. Whereas in the younger groups few patients took hypnotics despite having sleep disturbances, 57% of the elderly patients reported using hypnotics for their insomnia. The drugs most commonly used were benzodiazepines. The patients were also asked how long they had been regularly taking these hypnotic drugs. Sixty-three per cent reported a time span of more than one year, and 25% more than five years. However, the long-term administration of benzodiazepines for the treatment of insomnia should be avoided whenever possible, because of the risk of tolerance, dependence and rebound insomnia (Kales *et al*, 1983).

The over-prescription of hypnotic drugs clearly reveals the discrepancy between commonly used treatment modalities and state-of-the-art sleep medicine. A consensus conference in

TABLE 9.2
Patients' attributions of the causes of their severe insomnia

	18–35 years	36–50 years	51–65 years	> 65 years
Personal problems	72%	50%	32%	41%
Professional problems	64%	37%	17%	7%
Occupied with daily events	62%	46%	47%	57%
Important life events	38%	23%	22%	34%
Care of children or others	23%	17%	12%	15%
Noises	25%	29%	25%	39%
Own physical illness	24%	43%	53%	52%

Data from an epidemiological study of 2842 general practice patients (Hohagen *et al*, 1993, 1994a).

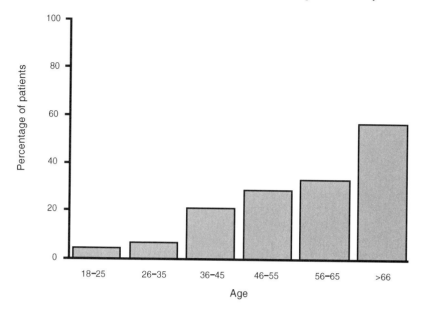

*Fig. 9.2. Percentage of patients with severe insomnia
in different age groups taking hypnotics.*

Germany in 1991 (Rüther *et al*, 1992) recommended a therapeutic time span of three weeks when treating insomnia with hypnotics. In a report from a World Health Organization (WHO) symposium on the treatment of insomnia (Costa *et al*, 1996) the authors state that on the basis of efficacy and safety two weeks or less of nightly use of sleep-promoting medications are appropriate.

Two results from our epidemiological study support the assumption that many of those individuals who chronically used sleeping pills had problems of tolerance and dependence. Thus most of them had had several unsuccessful trials of medication withdrawal and furthermore only 20% reported that their sleep quality had been significantly improved by the medication. A somewhat improved sleep was reported by 30%. However, 42% experienced no change, while the remainder suffered a worsening of their sleep problem in spite of using sleeping pills. This finding is supported by an epidemiological report by Ohayon & Caulet (1995), who found a similar pattern of chronic consumption of hypnotics in the metropolitan area of Montreal. The authors reported that 66% of these consumers continued to complain about their sleep despite taking hypnotic drugs. These observations support the assumption that some elderly people with sleep disturbances use sleeping pills to avoid withdrawal reactions such as rebound insomnia.

Causes and treatment of sleep disorders in the elderly

Insomnia in the elderly can have many different causes, frequently in combination (Prinz, 1995). A precise differential diagnosis is therefore required for appropriate treatment. Common causes of insomnia in the elderly are:

(a) psychiatric illness – depression, dementia, *and* agitated dementia;
(b) organic problems – cardiovascular symptoms, nocturia, chronic pain, bronchitis and asthma;
(c) sleep apnoea and sleep-disordered breathing;
(d) restless legs syndrome and periodic limb movements during sleep;
(e) maladaptive sleep habits.
(f) drug and alcohol use;
(g) persistent psychophysiological insomnia ('behavioural insomnia') with sleep-preventing associations, increased somatised tension.

In all age groups, insomnia often occurs secondary to psychiatric disorders such as depression, psychosis or dementia. Depressive insomnia can be treated with the tricyclic antidepressant trimipramine (Ware *et al*, 1989) or by other antidepressants with sedative potential such as amitriptyline, doxepine or trazodone. The usage of neuroleptics should be restricted to patients with psychosis and for agitated demented patients.

Physical disorders (e.g. nocturia, cardiac failure, respiratory diseases and chronic pain) are further common causes of disrupted sleep, especially in the elderly. Thus, severe physical disease, a secondary depression and extensive bed rest may further contribute to sleep disturbance. An appropriate analgesic medication can help to manage insomnia in chronic pain patients. Rescheduling the intake of diuretics may help to reduce nocturia.

An additional important cause of reduced sleep quality is a disturbance of nocturnal respiratory function, such as sleep apnoea syndrome. Ancoli-Israel *et al* (1991) and Ancoli-Israel & Coy (1994) reported that 10% of randomly selected elderly subjects had 10 or more apnoeas per hour of sleep and 24% had five or more per hour. Sleep-related breathing disorders are associated with hypertension, cardiac arrhythmias, heart failure, impaired memory and frequent napping during the daytime, and may enhance the risk of brain infarction (Neau *et al*, 1995). Ingram *et al* (1994) reported that vigilance may be impaired only in those older adults suffering from more severe sleep apnoea.

An important differential diagnosis in patients complaining of insomnia is restless legs syndrome (RLS) (Montplaisir *et al*, 1994). The prevalence of this disorder increases with ageing, and is present in about 5% of the elderly. These patients experience uncomfortable sensations, typically located in the legs. These sensations encompass pain, burning, tingling, 'insects crawling over the skin' and an urge to move one's legs; they usually occur in the late evening and early night. The afflicted usually have severe sleep disturbances, and poly-somnographic recording frequently shows a massive disruption of the sleep profile, as well as many periodic leg movements (PLMs), inducing arousals during sleep or preventing sleep onset (Coleman *et al*, 1980). It is important to consider RLS in differential diagnosis, as this disorder often remains undiagnosed, with its sensory symptoms attributed to other disorders such as polyneuropathy and various orthopaedic problems. Restless legs syndrome can be effectively treated by dopa-minergic agents such as L-dopa (Brodeur *et al*, 1988). The prevalence of PLMs during sleep as an isolated phenomenon without the symptoms of RLS is as high as about 30% in elderly individuals (Bliwise *et al*, 1995), but there is still some controversy over the relevance of this to insomnia.

Many old people acquire poor sleep habits such as spending too much time in bed and frequent daytime napping. These practices were often introduced by the patients in response to their sleeping problem. Very often expectations of sleep are far too high. This was shown in our epidemiological study (Hohagen *et al*, 1994a), in which 46% of the elderly individuals wished for a sleeping time of nine hours or more.

Educating patients in good sleep habits and changing maladaptive sleeping habits is therefore an essential component of insomnia management, especially in the elderly (Table 9.3). The behavioural measures should include restriction and regulation of time spent in bed, avoidance of daytime napping, enhancement of daytime activities and exposure to daylight. Campbell & Dawson (1991) and Campbell *et al* (1993) reported beneficial effects of light therapy for geriatric insomnia with significant effects on sleep EEG and daytime per-formance (Murphy & Campbell, 1996). Behavioural treatments for insomnia might also include muscle relaxation therapy, stimulus control therapy, cognitive techniques such as cognitive relaxation, discontinuation of ruminations, and reorganisation of sleep-in-compatible thoughts (Morin, 1993; Bliwise *et al*, 1995, Ancoli-Israel *et al*, 1997).

The use of hypnotics for elderly patients should be much more fastidious than that described by the epidemiological data. Sedative medication can induce daytime carryover effects, and thus promote inactivity and daytime napping. Benzodiazepines rapidly induce

TABLE 9.3
Management of sleep disorders in the elderly after exclusion of psychiatric and organic disorders

Type of management	Specific steps
Information	Education about the characteristic changes in sleep with ageing Modifying patients' expectations
Sleep habits	Restriction of time spent in bed Regular sleep–wake schedule Avoidance of excessive daytime napping Enhancement of daytime activities Enhancement of exposure to sunlight during the daytime Reduction of sedative medication and alcohol
Behavioural treatments	Progressive muscle relaxation Cognitive relaxation Stimulus control techniques Cognitive restructuring
Pharmacological approaches	Herbal drugs Benzodiazepines only for short-term, situational or intermittent conditions Sedating antidepressants Melatonin

tolerance and rebound insomnia after discontinuation of the drug (Kales *et al*, 1983). Impaired memory, a characteristic side-effect of benzodiazepines, and an increased risk of hip fractures (Ray *et al*, 1989) due the muscle-relaxing effect of the substances must also be given special consideration.

Alternative drugs for insomnia include herbal substances and sedative antidepressants, which may be useful not only for depressive insomnia but also for primary insomnia (Hohagen *et al*, 1994b). The effect of melatonin on sleep disturbances is currently being evaluated in a large number of studies. The secretion of melatonin, which is inversely correlated with ageing (Reiter, 1995), plays an important role in the entrainment of the circadian system to external time cues. With the concurrent weakening of the circadian rhythm in old age, melatonin might be especially useful for the treatment of insomnia in the elderly. Haimov *et al* (1995) and Garfinkel *et al* (1995) reported a significant amelioration of sleep problems in elderly insomniacs following melatonin replacement therapy. However, information on the effectiveness and side-effects after long-term use of melatonin are still lacking, so that recommendations cannot presently be given.

In summary, the complaint of insomnia is very common in older individuals, and is frequently caused by multiple factors such as the physiological changes of sleep in ageing, disturbances of the circadian rhythm, psychiatric and organic disease, sleep apnoea syndrome, RLS and maladaptive sleep habits. A differential therapy can be improved if all these factors are considered.

References

AMERICAN PSYCHIATRIC ASSOCIATION (1987) *Diagnostic and Statistical Manual of Mental Disorders* (3rd edn, revised) (DSM–III–R). Washington, DC: APA.

ANCOLI-ISRAEL, S. & COY, T. (1994) Are breathing disturbances in the elderly equivalent to sleep apnea syndrome? *Sleep*, **17**, 77–83.

——, KRIPKE, D. F., KLAUBER, M. R., *et al* (1991) Sleep disordered breathing in community-dwelling elderly. *Sleep*, **14**, 486–495.

——, POCETA, J. S., STEPNOWSKY, C., *et al* (1997) Identification and treatment of sleep problems in the elderly. *Sleep Medicine Reviews*, **1**, 3–17.

BIXLER, E. O., KALES, A., SOLDATOS, C. R., *et al* (1979) Prevalence of sleep disorders in the Los Angeles metropolitan area. *American Journal of Psychiatry*, **136**, 1257–1262.

BLIWISE, D. L. (1993) Sleep in normal aging and dementia. *Sleep*, **16**, 40–81.

—— (1994) Normal aging. In *Principles and Practice of Sleep Medicine* (2nd edn) (eds M. H. Kryger, T. Roth & W. C. Dement), pp. 26–39. Philadelphia: Saunders.

——, PRINZ, P. N. & VITIELLO, M. V. (1992) *Sleep and Physical Health in the Elderly. Status of Current Literature. Recommendations for the Future.* (Invited position paper: Report of the National Commission on Sleep Disorders Research.) Washington, DC: Government Printing Office.

——, FRIEDMAN, L., NEKICH, J. C. & YESAVAGE, J. A. (1995) Prediction of outcome in behaviorally based insomnia treatments. *Journal of Behaviour Therapy and Experimental Psychiatry*, **26**, 17–23.

BRODEUR, C., MONTPLAISIR, J., GODBOUT, R. & MARINIER, R. (1988) Treatment of restless legs syndrome and periodic movements during sleep with L-dopa: a double-blind controlled study. *Neurology*, **38**, 1843–1845.

CAMPBELL, S. S. & DAWSON, D. (1991) Bright light treatment of sleep disturbance in older subjects. *Sleep Research*, **20**, 448.

——, —— & ANDERSON, M. (1993) Alleviation of sleep maintenance insomnia with timed exposure to bright light. *Journal of the American Geriatric Society*, **41**, 829–836.

COLEMAN, R. M., POLLAK, C. P. & WEITZMAN, E. D. (1980) Periodic movements in sleep (nocturnal myoclonus): relation to sleep disorders. *Annals of Neurology*, **8**, 416–421.

COPINSCHI, G. & VAN CAUTER, E. (1995) Effects of ageing on modulation of hormonal secretions by sleep: a circadian rhythmicity. *Hormone Research*, **43**, 20–24.

COSTA, E., SILVA, J. A., CHASE, M., *et al* (1996) Special report from a symposium held by the World Health Organization and the World Federation of Sleep Research Societies: an overview of insomnias and related disorders – recognition, epidemiology, and rational management. *Sleep*, **19**, 412–416.

FORD, D. E. & KAMEROW, D. B. (1989) Epidemiologic study of sleep disturbances and psychiatric disorders. *Journal of the American Medical Association*, **262**, 1479–1484.

GARFINKEL, D., LAUDON, M., NOF, D. & ZISAPEL, N. (1995) Improvement of sleep quality in elderly people by controlled-release melatonin. *Lancet*, **346**, 541–543.

HAIMOV, I., LAVIE, P., LAUDON, M., *et al* (1995) Melatonin replacement therapy of elderly insomniacs. *Sleep*, **18**, 598–603.

HENDERSON, S., JORM, A. F., SCOTT, L. R., *et al* (1995) Insomnia in the elderly: its prevalence and correlates in the general population. *Medical Journal of Australia*, **162**, 22–24.

HOCH, C. C., REYNOLDS, C. F. III, KUPFER, D. J. & BERMAN, S. R. (1988) Stability of EEG sleep and sleep quality in healthy seniors. *Sleep*, **11**, 521–527.

——, DEW, M. A., REYNOLDS, C. F. III, *et al* (1994) A longitudinal study of laboratory- and diary-based sleep measures in healthy 'old old' and 'young old' volunteers. *Sleep*, **17**, 489–496.

HOHAGEN, F., RINK, K., KÄPPLER, C., *et al* (1993) Prevalence and treatment of insomnia in general practice. A longitudinal study. *European Archives of Psychiatry and Clinical Neuroscience*, **242**, 329–336.

——, KÄPPLER, C., SCHRAMM, E., *et al* (1994a) Prevalence of insomnia in elderly general practice attenders and the current treatment modalities. *Acta Psychiatrica Scandinavica*, **90**, 102–108.

——, FRITSCH-MONTERO, R., WEISS, E., *et al* (1994b) Treatment of primary insomnia with trimipramine: an alternative to benzodiazepine hypnotics? *European Archives of Psychiatry and Clinical Neurosciences*, **244**, 65–72.

INGRAM, F., HENKE, K. G., LEVIN, H. S., *et al* (1994) Apnea and vigilance performance in a community-dwelling older sample. *Sleep*, **17**, 248–252.

KALES, A., SOLDATOS, C. R., BIXLER, E. O. & KALES, J. D. (1983) Rebound insomnia and rebound anxiety. A review. *Pharmacology*, **26**, 121–137.

KARACAN, I., THORNBY, J. I., ANCH, M., *et al* (1976) Prevalence of sleep disturbance in a primarily urban Florida county. *Social Science and Medicine*, **10**, 239–244.

LIVINGSTON, G., BLIZARD, B. & MANN, A. (1993) Does sleep disturbance predict depression in elderly people? A study in inner London. *British Journal of General Practice*, **43**, 445–448.

MELLINGER, G. D., BALTEN, M. G. & UHLENHUTH, E. H. (1985) Insomnia and its treatment. *Archives of General Psychiatry*, **42**, 225–232.

MILES, L. & DEMENT, W. C. (1980) Sleep and aging. *Sleep*, **3**, 119–220.

MONANE, M., GLYNN, R. J. & AVORN, J. (1996) The impact of sedative-hypnotic use on sleep symptoms in elderly nursing home residents. *Clinical Pharmacology and Therapeutics*, **59**, 83–92.

MONK, T. H., REYNOLDS C. F. III, BUYSSE, D. J., *et al* (1991) Circadian characteristics of healthy 80-year-olds and their relationship to objectively recorded sleep. *Journal of Gerontology: Medical Sciences*, **46**, 171–175.

MONTPLAISIR, J., GODBOUT, R., PELLETIER, G. & WARNES, H. (1994) Restless legs syndrome and periodic limb movements during sleep. In *Principles and Practice of Sleep Medicine* (2nd edn) (eds M. H. Kryger, T. Roth & W. C. Dement), pp. 589–597. Philadelphia: Saunders.

MORIN, C. M. (1993) *Insomnia: Psychological Assessment and Management*. New York: Guilford Press.

MURPHY, P. J. & CAMPBELL, S. S. (1996) Enhanced performance in elderly subjects following bright light treatment of sleep maintenance insomnia. *Journal of Sleep Research*, **5**, 165–172.

MYERS, B. L. & BADIA, P. (1995) Changes in circadian rhythms and sleep quality with aging: mechanisms and interventions. *Neuroscience and Biobehavioral Reviews*, **19**, 553–571.

NEAU, J. PH., MEURICE, J. C., PAQUEREAU, J., *et al* (1995) Habitual snoring as a risk factor for brain infarction. *Acta Neurologica Scandinavica*, **92**, 63–68.

OHAYON, M. M. & CAULET, M. (1995) Insomnia and psychotropic drug consumption. *Progress in Neuropsychopharmacology and Biological Psychiatry*, **19**, 421–431.

PRINZ, P. (1995) Sleep and sleep disorders in older adults. *Journal of Clinical Neurophysiology*, **12**, 139–146.

RAY, W. A., GRIFFIN, M. R. & DOWNEY, W. (1989) Benzodiazepines of long and short elimination half-life and the risk of hip fracture. *Journal of the American Medical Association*, **262**, 3303–3307.

REDIEHS, M. A., REIS, J. S. & CREASON, N. S. (1990) Sleep in old age: focus on gender differences. *Sleep,* **13**, 410–424.

REITER, R. J. (1995) The pineal gland and melatonin in relation to aging: a summary of the theories and of the data. *Experimental Gerontology,* **30**, 199–212.

REYNOLDS, C. F. III, JENNINGS, J. R., HOCH, C. C., *et al* (1991) Daytime sleepiness in the healthy "old old": a comparison with young adults. *Journal of the American Geriatrics Society,* **39**, 957–962.

RICHARDSON G. S., CARSKADON M. A. & ORAV, E. J. (1982) Circadian variation of sleep tendency in elderly and young adult subjects. *Sleep,* **5**, 82–94.

ROFFWARG, H. P., MUZIO, J. N. & DEMENT, W. C. (1966) Ontogenetic development of the human sleep–dream cycle. *Science,* **152**, 604–619.

RÜTHER, E., BERGER, M., FREIBURG, H., *et al* (1992) Epidemiologie, Pathophysiologie, Diagnostik und Therapie von Schlafstörungen. Ergebnisse einer Consensus-Konferenz der Arbeitsgemeinschaft Klinischer Schlafzentren (AKS) und der Arbeitsgemeinschaft für Neuropsychopharmakologie (AGNP). *Münchner Medizinische Wochenschrift,* **134**, 460–466.

SPIEGEL, R. (1981) Sleep and sleeplessness in advanced age. In *Advances in Sleep Research* (ed. E. D. Weitzman). New York: Spectrum.

WARE, J. C., BROWN, F. W., MOORAD, P. J., *et al* (1989) Effects on sleep: a double blind study comparing imipramine to the sedating tricyclic antidepressant trimipramine in depressed insomniac patients. *Sleep,* **12**, 537–549.

WEVER, R. A. (1979) *Circadian System of Man: Results of Experiments under Temporal Isolation.* New York: Springer.

ZULLEY, J. & BAILER, J. (1988) Polyphasic sleep/wake patterns and their significance to vigilance. In *Vigilance: Methods, Models and Regulation* (ed. J. P. Leonard), pp. 167–180. Frankfurt: Peter Lang.

10 Neuropsychiatric features of dementia

ALISTAIR BURNS

The clinical syndrome of dementia comprises three main elements:

(a) a neuropsychological syndrome, characterised by memory loss and disorders of higher cortical function such as apraxia, aphasia and agnosia;
(b) a neuropsychiatric cluster of symptoms, often divided into disorders of mood, disorders of perception, disorders of thought content and disorders of behaviour;
(c) problems with activities of daily living.

It is the neuropsychiatric expressions of dementia which form the basis for this contribution.

Early descriptions of dementia confirm the presence of neuropsychiatric features as an integral part of the dementia syndrome. The first symptom of Alzheimer's first case (Alzheimer, 1907) was of delusional jealousy and there is a clear description of severe behavioural disturbance, with screaming and dragging bedding around the ward in the later stages of the illness. In vascular dementia, the Hachinski score (Hachinski *et al*, 1975) embodies the main features which differentiate that dementia from a primary or Alzheimer's dementia and the neuropsychiatric features include the relative preservation of personality, depression, somatic complaints and emotional lability. The recently described fronto-temporal dementia (Lund & Manchester Groups, 1994) has behavioural disorder and affective symptoms as the first two defining characteristics of the syndrome and Lewy-body dementia (McKeith *et al*, 1992) has visual and auditory hallucinations as part of the diagnostic criteria.

Prevalence

The neuropsychiatric features of Alzheimer's disease can be divided into four main types:

(a) disorders of mood (usually depressed mood but rarely mania);
(b) disorders of perception (hallucinations and misidentifications);
(c) disorders of thought content (delusions and paranoid ideas);
(d) disorders of behaviour (aggression, wandering, sexual disinhibition).

These features occur commonly in dementia (*Lancet*, 1989). The proportion of patients who become depressed has been described as up to two-thirds, while about one-third have persecutory ideas, and hallucinations occur in about 15% and aggression in about 20%. Generally speaking, psychiatric symptoms occur early in the disease and behavioural disturbances later (Burns *et al*, 1990a–d). There is ample evidence that these features are related to biological changes in the brain (e.g. Förstl *et al*, 1992, 1993, 1994). Correlations have been found between their presence and plaque and tangle counts in Alzheimer's disease and appearances on neuro-imaging. Depression in Alzheimer's disease is said to occur at two distinct stages of the disease – in the early stages as an almost natural reaction to loss of memory, and later as a result of pathological changes in the brain (e.g. Förstl *et al*, 1992).

Measurement

A number of scales have been described to measure these features in dementia (see Appendix). BEHAVE–AD (Reisberg *et al*, 1987) was one of the first and describes the main characteristics of behavioural disturbance as well as having a global rating of impairment. The particular usefulness of this instrument is that it can measure changes over time and therefore can be used in drug trials. The Alzheimer's disease Assessment Schedule 'non-cog' scale (ADAS; Rosen *et al*, 1984) measures characteristics including depression, tearfulness, delusions, hallucinations, pacing, increased motor activity and appetite changes. Ratings are on a scale of 1–5 and the instrument takes about 45 minutes to complete, with an interview and symptom pairings over the preceding week. The Columbia University Scale for Psychopathology in Alzheimer's disease (CUSPAD; Devanand *et al*, 1992) measures a similar array of symptoms and is meant to be used direct with a caregiver; it examines symptoms in the last month and takes up to 25 minutes to administer. The Neuropsychiatric Inventory (NPI; Cummings *et al*, 1994) assesses the usual range of symptoms. It has the advantage of having both severity and frequency rating scales, measures symptoms in the last month as well as at any time since the onset of dementia and, because of nested questions, takes 7–10 minutes to administer. The Present Behavioural Examination (Hope & Fairbairn, 1992) measures in great detail aspects of behaviour associated with advanced dementia. It is too long an instrument for routine use.

Based on work in a previous set of studies (Burns *et al*, 1990a–d), Manchester and Oxford University combined to produce the psycho-pathology scale called the MOUSEPAD (Manchester and Oxford University Scales for the Evaluation and Psychopathological Assessment of Dementia; Allen *et al*, 1996). The scale rates both severity and frequency and dates the symptoms of dementia since the onset of the syndrome or, alternatively, solely within the last month. It takes up to 30 minutes to administer. It does not contain any items dealing with depression; this needs to be assessed separately, in the form of the Cornell Scale for Depression in Dementia (Alexopoulos *et al*, 1988). The MOUSEPAD enables one to assess the temporal relationship of symptoms to the evolution of the dementia, allowing the hypothesis to be tested that psychiatric symptoms tend to cluster in discrete periods of time during the initial and moderate stages of dementia, with behavioural disturbance occurring towards the end. Two specific syndromes of psychiatric morbidity in dementia will be discussed in more detail – depression and misidentifications.

Depression

The proportion of patients with dementia who develop depression varies widely. In a recent analysis of 20 studies (Allen & Burns, 1995) with sample sizes varying from 28 to 1258, the prevalence of symptoms of depression ranged from zero to 87% and of the syndrome of depression between zero and 86%. Using National Institute for Neurological and Communicative Disorders and Stroke and the Alzheimer's disease and Related Disorders Association diagnostic criteria for Alzheimer's disease (NINCDS/ADRDA; McKhann *et al*, 1984), the prevalence of depressive symptoms went down to an average of 30% (range 7–63%) and the proportion with a depressive syndrome to 19% (range 12–24%). In multi-infarct dementia, the prevalence of symptoms varied between 0% and 60% and of the syndrome between 6% and 27%. Patients with multi-infarct dementia tend to have higher ratings of depression than patients with Alzheimer's disease, particularly on neuro-vegetative items.

TABLE 10.1

Clinical and neuropathological correlates of depression in Alzheimer's disease

	Dementia with depression (n=14)		Dementia without depression (n=38)	
Mean (s.d.) age at onset (years)	77.1	(7.5)	75.0	(7.4)
Mean (s.d.) duration (years)	8.2	(5.6)	7.5	(4.1)
Mean (s.d.) MMSE score	7.4	(6.8)	4.2	(5.1)
Mean (s.d.) CAMCOG total score	24.6	(21.7)	12.6	(16.1)
Mean (s.d.) CAMCOG language score	11.1	(9.1)	5.8	(7.0)
Mean (s.d.) neuronal count:				
Locus ceruleus	36.9	(14.0)	51.4	(28.0)
Substantia nigra	495.5	(294.6)	478.1	(312.0)
Basal nucleus of Meynert	95.1	(56.7)	71.2	(49.3)

The relationship between depression and cognitive impairment has been described by many authors – generally it is accepted that there is an inverse relationship between the two. In nine studies described by Allen & Burns (1995) there were 190 non-depressed patients with dementia alone who were compared with 192 patients with dementia and depression. The mean score on the Mini-Mental State Examination (MMSE; Folstein *et al*, 1975) was 1.51 points higher in the depressed group ($P < 0.000001$, Mann–Whitney U test).

The biological basis of depression in Alzheimer's disease has been examined by a number of authors. The author's personal experience is summarised in the series of studies (Burns, 1996; Burns & Förstl, 1996; Förstl *et al*, 1992) where patients coming to postmortem with proven Alzheimer's disease were examined in relation to the presence of depression during life. Results are summarised in Table 10.1, which shows that 14 patients with Alzheimer's disease in depression were no different in terms of age of onset or duration of illness to 38 patients with Alzheimer's disease but no depression. Those with depression were significantly less cognitively impaired as measured on the CAMDEX (Roth *et al*, 1986) and the MMSE. Mean neuronal counts in the locus ceruleus, substantia nigra and basal nucleus of Meynert showed that there was relative preservation in the basal nucleus of Meynert neurons with specific fall-out in noradrenergic neurons in the locus ceruleus but no difference in the substantia nigra. These findings support a neurochemical hypothesis of depression in Alzheimer's disease.

Misidentifications

Essentially, misidentifications are a form of misperception with the resultant false belief held, and often acted upon, with delusional intensity. Other types of delusional misidentification described in the literature include the Capgras syndrome, the Fregoli syndrome and various forms of intermetamorphosis. Misidentifications occur in up to 30% of patients with dementia at some point in their illness (Allen & Burns, 1995). Burns *et al* (1990a–d) described four main types of misidentification – the idea that people are in the house (17%), misidentification of self in the mirror (4%), misidentification of other people (12%) and misidentification of events on the television (6%). Patients with misidentification were younger and were more often men than women; they also had a decreased mortality after three-year follow-up. Förstl *et al* (1991) described the computerised tomography (CT) brain scans of patients with misidentifications. Of 128 patients, 40 showed evidence of misidentification and misidentification occurred more frequently in men (53%, compared with 24% in women) and visual hallucinations were significantly more common in patients with misidentifications (62% versus 38%). There was evidence of right/left frontal lobe asymmetry, with relative preservation of the left frontal lobe on CT scans. Neuronal counts in the hippocampus were significantly less in patients with misidentifications, suggesting that particularly severe dementia resulting in a failure to update memory may be one of the underlying mechanisms involved. However, there was no difference in mean MMSE score in the two groups, which shows that global cognitive impairment was not affected.

Stress in carers

Links between stress in carers and psychiatric symptoms in patients have been sought by a number of workers in order to identify factors which provoke stress and therefore may be amenable to intervention. There is some evidence that particular symptoms and signs in patients with dementia are associated with increased stress in their carers. Neuropsychiatric features such as memory loss, aphasia, apraxia and agnosia seem to be related to burden and depression. Neuropsychiatric features such as psychiatric symptoms and behavioural disturbances are associated with many problems, including perception of difficulties, restriction of activity, changes in the patient–carer relationship, as well as burden and depression. Problems with activities of daily living experienced by patients seem to be associated with physical health and restriction of activities in carers.

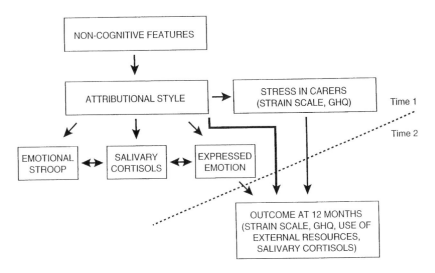

Fig. 10.1. How the effects of non-cognitive features could be manifest through a
number of intermediaries such as expressed emotion and attributional style,
to promote stress in carers.

A collaborative study between the Departments of Psychology and
Psychiatry at the University of Manchester (Professor Nicholas Tarrier
and Miss Cathy Donaldson) has investigated the relationship between
particular signs and symptoms in a patient with dementia and the effect
that has on carers. Causal attributions have been investigated in
schizophrenia and it may be that, in the same way that expressed
emotion (EE) can mediate relapse in that disorder, attributional style
and EE may predict use of services and strain in carers of patients with
dementia. A negative attributional stance would be suggested by the
belief that a behaviour was felt to be internal to the patient and
controllable by him or her. These negative attributions have been
related to stress in carers (Pagel *et al*, 1985). Figure 10.1 shows a
diagrammatic representation of how the effects of non-cognitive
features could be manifest through a number of intermediaries such
as EE and attributional style, to promote stress in carers. Biological
markers of the relationship would include changes in salivary cortisol,
and attentional bias (a psychophysiological measure) would be
assessed by the Stroop test (Watts *et al*, 1986). The study aims to
examine patients and carers and is following them over 12 months to
assess use of external services and to measure the relationship between
perceived strain and signs and symptoms in the patients. One hundred

patients (32 male, 68 female) have been examined, with an age range of 56–93 years. The duration of illness was approximately 4 years and the mean MMSE score of the sample is 14/30, indicating that the majority have a moderate degree of dementia of the Alzheimer type. One hundred carers (43 male and 57 female) with an age range of 32–86 years were seen. Fifty per cent were spouses and 36% were children or relatives. The duration of caring was approximately 27 months – male carers were all caring for female patients, while female carers were equally divided into those caring for male or female patients.

Initial results (Donaldson *et al*, 1998; Fearon *et al*, 1998) have shown: that high EE is positively associated with the level and severity of behavioural disturbance in the patients and the strain and psychological distress in carers; that high EE is not associated with a degree of cognitive impairment or global ratings of dementia severity and the patients' or carers' knowledge of dementia; that strain is associated with the degree of behavioural disturbance in patients and flattening of the normal diurnal variation in salivary cortisol levels. The study is forming the basis of an intervention trial in an attempt to identify carers at risk of strain and to develop strategies aimed at reducing it.

Dementia and schizophrenia

Cognitive decline was regarded as a feature of schizophrenia in early descriptions of the illness but heterogeneity in outcome is now well documented. A number of studies have documented high rates of cognitive impairment among geriatric in-patients with schizophrenia and the MMSE scores of some patients are compatible with dementia. The neuropsychological, pathological and neurochemical bases of cognitive impairment and dementia in elderly schizophrenic patients are unknown, although it seems clear that there is intellectual decline early in the course of schizophrenia. The issue is whether there is later intellectual decline and whether this accounts for the high rates of severe cognitive impairment among chronic in-patients. The evidence from cross-sectional studies of in-patient populations is contradictory. Davidson *et al* (1995) reported decreasing MMSE scores with age, while two other studies (Heaton *et al*, 1994; Hyde *et al*, 1994) failed to find evidence for a decline in cognitive function related to duration of illness or to age. All the cross-sectional studies have been carried out on in-patients and thus many sampling biases could account for the discrepant results. Longitudinal studies of in-patients are also contradictory, with no decline in MMSE scores in two years in one study (Harvey *et al*, 1992) but appreciable declines in a five-year and a ten-year follow-up study (Waddington *et al*, 1990; Nilsson *et al*, 1995).

Prohovnik *et al* (1993) reported age-dependent increases in the prevalence of Alzheimer's disease pathology among chronic schizo-phrenic patients. Recent studies, however, suggest that Alzheimer's disease is not the explanation for cognitive impairment among elderly patients with chronic schizophrenia (Powchik *et al*, 1993; Arnold *et al*, 1995; Grolier *et al*, 1995; Harrison, 1995). Earlier studies reported periventricular gliosis in schizophrenia but more recent studies raise doubts as to whether this is an invariable feature or whether it is associated with other pathologies coexisting with schizophrenia (Arnold *et al*, 1995). Gliosis is generally interpreted as indicating a persisting pathological/toxic process but its absence might not preclude a slow neurodegeneration. It is crucial to establish the relationship between gliosis and late cognitive changes.

While it is generally accepted that the core neuropathological features of schizophrenia predate the onset of symptoms and are non-progressive, this may not be true of the cognitive changes, which may be preventable with appropriate treatment. An epidemiologically based sample is necessary to establish whether there is a progressive decline in any aspect of cognitive function in ageing patients with schizophrenia and such a study is shortly to get under way in Manchester in collaboration with the Department of Psychiatry (Professors S. Lewis and J. F. W. Deakin and Dr A. Procter) and the Department of Neuropathology (Dr D. Mann). The hypotheses of the study are:

(a) the prevalence of clinically significant dementia will be greater in chronic schizophrenia than the normal population;

(b) dementia will be associated with early age at onset, negative symptoms, use of neuroleptic and anticholinergic drugs, structural brain changes, presence of neurological signs (including tardive dyskinesia) and possession of the apolipo-protein E4 allele;

(c) in non-demented elderly patients with schizophrenia there will be an age-related decline in verbal learning and memory greater than that seen in controls, whereas there will be no excess of age-related impairment in executive, frontal-lobe functions, which are impaired early in the illness;

(d) patients with schizophrenia and cognitive impairment, com-pared with those without deficits, will have greater atrophy of medial temporal lobe structures but will not differ in volumes of frontal cortical regions or ventricular size;

(e) in postmortem brains, loss of glutamate uptake sites, neuropeptide Y and somatostatin from medial temporal cortex and hippocampus will be greater in patients with dementia than in patients without dementia, whereas in the frontal cortex increased markers for glutamatergic synapses will be similar in the two groups.

Conclusion

The association between psychotic symptoms and cognitive impairment is a complex one – patients with a primary diagnosis of dementia suffer from a number of psychiatric symptoms and behavioural disturbances and patients with primarily functional disorders become cognitively impaired. There is increasing appreciation that a sharp distinction between functional and organic psychiatric diseases is less justified and this in part is due to more sophisticated techniques of investigation such as neuro-imaging and neuropathological examination.

Appendix

Columbia University Scale for Psychopathology in Alzheimer's disease (CUSPAD; Devanand *et al*, 1992)

This is a caregiver interview covering the past month. It takes 10–25 minutes to administer and covers the following points:

(a) delusions (including misidentifications);
(b) hallucinations;
(c) illusions;
(d) behaviour disturbance (wandering, agitation, confusion);
(e) depression (affecting sleep, appetite).

Neuropsychiatric Inventory (NPI; Cummings *et al*, 1994)

This comprises a severity scale (scored 1–3) and a frequency scale (scored 1–4), and relates to the past month (or other period). It takes 7–10 minutes to administer and covers the following points:

(a) delusions (including misidentifications);
(b) hallucinations;
(c) agitation/aggression;
(d) dysphoria;
(e) anxiety;
(f) euphoria;
(g) apathy;
(h) disinhibition;
(i) irritability;
(j) aberrant motor activity.

Manchester and Oxford University Scale for the Psychopathological Assessment of Dementia (MOUSEPAD; Allen *et al*, 1996)

This is based on the research results reported by Burns *et al* (1990a–d). It is a structured questionnaire completed with the caregiver and covers the following:

(a) psychiatric symptoms – delusions, hallucinations, reduplications, misidentifications;
(b) behavioural disturbance – aggression, wandering, sleep, eating, sexual behaviour.

Depression questions are also included. The scale rates the severity and frequency of symptoms since onset of dementia and over the last month. It takes 15–30 minutes to administer.

References

ALEXOPOULOS, G., ABRAMS, R., YOUNG, R. & SHAMOIAN, C. (1988) Cornell Scale for Depression in Dementia. *Biological Psychiatry*, **23**, 271–284.

ALLEN, H. & BURNS, A. (1995) Non-cognitive features in dementia. *Reviews in Clinical Gerontology*, **5**, 57–75.

——, GORDON, S., HOPE, T., *et al* (1996) Manchester and Oxford Universities scale for psychopathological assessment of dementia (MOUSEPAD). *British Journal of Psychiatry*, **169**, 293–307.

ALZHEIMER, A. (1907) Uber Eine Eigenartige Erkrankung Der Hirinde. *Allegemeine Zeitschrift fur Psykiatrie und Psychisch – Gerichtlich Medicin*, 64, 146–148.

ARNOLD, S. E., BRANZ, B. R., TROJANOWSKI, J. Q. & GUR, R. E. (1995) GFAP immuno-histochemical assessment of astrocytosis in ventromedial temporal lobe limbic cortices in elderly patients with schizophrenia. *Schizophrenia Research*, **15**, 25–26.

BURNS, A. (1996) The Institute of Psychiatry Alzheimer's disease cohort: Part 1 – Clinical observations. *International Journal of Geriatric Psychiatry*, **11**, 309–320.

——, A. & FÖRSTL, H. (1996) The Institute of Psychiatry Alzheimer's disease cohort: Part 2 – Clinical observations. *International Journal of Geriatric Psychiatry*, **11**, 321–327.

——, JACOBY, R. & LEVY, R. (1990a) Psychiatric phenomena in Alzheimer's disease 1. Disorders of thought content. *British Journal of Psychiatry*, **157**, 72–76.

——, —— & —— (1990b) Psychiatric phenomena in Alzheimer's disease 2. Disorders of perception. *British Journal of Psychiatry*, **157**, 76–81.

——, —— & —— (1990c) Psychiatric phenomena in Alzheimer's disease 3. Disorders of mood. *British Journal of Psychiatry*, **157**, 81–86.

——, —— & —— (1990d) Psychiatric phenomena in Alzheimer's disease 4. Disorders of behaviour. *British Journal of Psychiatry*, **157**, 86–94.

CUMMINGS, J., MEGA, M., GRAY, K., *et al* (1994) The Neuropsychiatric Inventory. *Neurology*, **44**, 2308–2314.

DAVIDSON, M., POWCHIK, P., GABRIEL, S. M., *et al* (1995) Correlations between temporal lobe synaptic protein immunoactivity and schizophrenic psychosis. *Schizophrenia Research*, **15**, 26.

DEVANAND, D., MILLER, L., RICHARDS, M., *et al* (1992) The Columbia University Scale for Psychopathology in Alzheimer's disease. *Archives of Neurology*, **49**, 371–376.

DONALDSON, C. TARRIER, N. & BURNS, A. (1998) Determinants of carer stress in Alzheimer's disease. *International Journal of Geriatric Psychiatry*, **13**, 48–56.

FEARON, M., TARRIER, N. & BURNS, A. (1998) Intimacy as a predictor of expressed emotion in carers of people with Alzheimer's disease. *Psychological Medicine*, **28**, 1085–1090.

FOLSTEIN, M., FOLSTEIN, S. & McHUGH, P. (1975) Mini-Mental State. *Journal of Psychiatric Research*, **12**, 189–198.

FÖRSTL, H., BURNS, A., JACOBY, R. & LEVY, R. (1991) Neuroanatomical correlates of misidentification and misperception in dementia of the Alzheimer type. *Journal of Clinical Psychiatry*, **52**, 268–271.

——, ——, LUTHERT, P., *et al* (1992) Clinical and neuropathological correlates of depression in Alzheimer's disease. *Psychological Medicine*, **22**, 877–884.

——, ——, LEVY, R., *et al* (1993) Neuropathological correlates of behavioural disturbance in confirmed Alzheimer's disease. *British Journal of Psychiatry*, **163**, 364–368.

——, ——, —— & CAIRNS, N. (1994) Neuropathological correlates of psychotic phenomena in confirmed Alzheimer's disease. *British Journal of Psychiatry*, **165**, 53–59.

GROLIER, J., DAVIDSON, M., HAROUTUNIAN, B., *et al* (1995) Neurpathological study of 101 elderly institutionalised schizophrenics. *Schizophrenia Research*, **15**, 28.

HACHINSKI, V., ILLIFF, L., ZILKHA, E., *et al* (1975) Cerebral blood flow in dementia. *Archives of Neurology*, **32**, 632–637.

HARRISON, P. (1995) On the neuropathology of schizophrenia and its dementia. *Neurodegeneration*, **4**, 1–12.

HARVEY, P., DAVIDSON, M., POWCHIK, P., *et al* (1992) Assessment of dementia in elderly schizophrenics with structured rating scales. *Schizophrenia Research*, **7**, 85–90.

HEATON, R., PAULSEN, J. S., McADAMS, L. A., *et al* (1994) Neuropsychological deficits in schizophrenics: relationship to age, chronicity and dementia. *Archives of General Psychiatry*, **51**, 469–476.

HOPE, T. & FAIRBAIRN, C. (1992) Present Behavioural Examination. *Psychological Medicine*, **22**, 223–230.

HYDE, T. M., NAWROZ, S., GOLDBERG, T. E., *et al* (1994) Is there cognitive decline in schizophrenia? A cross-sectional study. *British Journal of Psychiatry*, **164**, 494–500.

LANCET (1989) Psychotic symptoms in Alzheimer's disease (Editorial). *Lancet*, *ii*, 1193–1194.

LUND AND MANCHESTER GROUPS (1994) Clinical and neuropathological criteria for fronto-temporal dementia. *Journal of Neurology, Neurosurgery and Psychiatry*, **57**, 416–418.

McKEITH, I., PERRY, R., FAIRBAIRN, A., *et al* (1992) Operational criteria for senile dementia of the Lewy body type. *Psychological Medicine*, **22**, 911–922.

McKHANN, G. BLACKMAN, D. FOLSTEIN, M., *et al* (1984) Clinical diagnosis of Alzheimer's disease: report of the NINCDS/ADRDA work group. *Neurology*, **34**, 939–944.

NILSSON, M. N., BUNNEY, W. E., POTKIN, S. E. & SANDMAN, C. (1995) Cognitive decline in schizophrenic patients and normal control followed long term. *Schizophrenia Research*, **15**, 130–131.

PAGEL, M., BECKER, J. & COPPEL, D. (1985) Loss of control, self-blame and depression – an investigation of spouse caregivers of Alzheimer's disease patients. *Journal of Abnormal Psychology*, **94**, 169–182.

POWCHIK, P., DAVIDSON, M., NEMEROFF, C., *et al* (1993) Alzheimer's-disease-related protein in geriatric schizophrenic patients with cognitive impairment. *American Journal of Psychiatry*, **150**, 1726–1727.

PROHOVNIK, I., DWORK, A., KAUFMAN, M., *et al* (1993) Alzheimer type neuropathology in elderly schizophrenia patients. *Schizophrenia Bulletin*, **19**, 805–816.

REISBERG, B., BORANSTEIN, J., FRANSSEN, E., *et al* (1987) BEHAVE-AD. In *Alzheimer's Disease – Problems, Prospects and Perspective* (ed. H. J. Altman), pp. 1–16. New York: Plenum Press.

ROSEN, W., MOHS, R. & DAVIES, K. (1984) A new rating scale for Alzheimer's disease. *American Journal of Psychiatry*, **141**, 1356–1364.

ROTH, M., TYM, E., MOUNTJOY, C., *et al* (1986) CAMDEX. *British Journal of Psychiatry*, **149**, 698–709.

WADDINGTON, J. L., O'CALLAGHAM, E., LARKIN, C., *et al* (1990) Magnetic resonance imaging and spectroscopy in schizophrenia. *British Journal of Psychiatry*, **157**, 56–65.

11 Brain imaging in late-onset mental disorders: testing hypotheses

G. D. PEARLSON

If we select schizophrenia as a prime example of a late-life mental disorder, we are immediately faced with a paradox. 'Classic' schizophrenia is now most probably best characterised as a neurodevelopmental disorder, with early-adult onset (e.g. Weinberger, 1987). Because of the complex inheritance of the disorder (e.g. that the disease's proband-wise concordance for monozygotic twins is only around 50%), taken in concert with epidemiological evidence, schizophrenia is often hypothesised to be a 'two-hit disease'. In this model, the first, genetic hit (diathesis) is proposed to interact with a second, environmental hit (stress). The second is presumed to occur most usually in early neurodevelopment (e.g. maternal influenza, or an obstetric mishap). Is schizophrenia with onset late in life then the same disorder delayed until old age, or does it represent a different disorder with a separate aetiopathology? Restating these alternatives as competing hypotheses, one can posit first and most simply that early- and late-onset forms of schizophrenia represent the same disorder. In late-onset schizophrenia, the second hit presumably occurs in late life. An example of such a late-life second hit would be normal age-associated brain changes (e.g. age-related atrophy affecting a critical structure or pathway, or age-related changes in dopamine receptors). A second hypothesis would posit that late-onset schizophrenia is an organic phenocopy of the early-onset form with a one-hit, primarily age-associated aetiopathology, (e.g. microvascular disease, or the first manifestations of a primary dementing illness).

Combining the above hypotheses, it is feasible that late-onset schizophrenia as seen in clinical practice represents a diversity of aetiopathologies, perhaps a mixture of delayed 'classic' early-onset and 'organic' secondary cases. As we have noted previously (Pearlson & Petty, 1994), different studies of late-life schizophrenia have used widely different inclusion/exclusion criteria to select cases, with differing clinical onset ages and varying stringency in eliminating the possibility of organic disorders being only two of many prominent examples. Thus different investigators have standard samples which have varied widely in case composition.

Brain imaging has a clear potential to provide evidence to allow one to decide between the above competing hypotheses, by clarifying the types of brain changes in late-onset schizophrenia and perhaps shedding light on their aetiology. Using brain imaging in this manner allows the following questions to be posed. First, do patients with late-onset schizophrenia share brain changes with those described previously for classic, early-onset disease? Second, can one divide the disorder into, for example, 'organic phenocopies' and other subtypes of the disease? Third, is it feasible to identify the second hit in a two-hit scenario?

To address the first point, structural and functional brain imaging abnormalities have both been described for early-onset schizophrenia. These include the following: increased ventricle–brain ratios on computerised tomography (CT) and magnetic resonance imaging (MRI) (Johnstone *et al*, 1976; Weinberger *et al*, 1979; Pearlson *et al*, 1987); third-ventricle enlargement (Boronow *et al*, 1985); cortical atrophy on CT and MRI (Pfefferbaum *et al*, 1988; Gur *et al*, 1991); blood-flow abnormalities on single-photon emission CT (SPECT) (Gur *et al*, 1985; Matthew *et al*, 1988); increased dopamine D2 receptor subtype B_{max} on positron emission tomography (PET) scans (Wong *et al*, 1986a–c; Tune *et al*, 1994); and regional cerebral blood-flow abnormalities during provocative tasks, for example, those of working memory or set-shifting (Berman *et al*, 1992).

The neuro-imaging literature reveals that many of the same abnormalities have been reported in late-onset schizophrenia. These include increased ventricle–brain ratio on CT and MRI (Naguib & Levy, 1987; Rabins *et al*, 1987; Howard *et al*, 1992, 1994). Third-ventricle enlargement in late-onset schizophrenia has been described by Pearlson *et al* (1993), Breitner *et al* (1990) and Flint *et al* (1991). Cortical atrophy on CT and MRI has been described by Howard *et al* (1992, 1994), but not by Burns *et al* (1989). Cortical atrophy as judged by increased percentage of cerebral spinal fluid spaces has also been described by Pearlson *et al* (1993). Abnormalities of blood flow seen by SPECT in late-onset schizophrenia have been reported by Miller *et al* (1992). Increased dopamine subtype D2 receptor B_{max} levels have been demonstrated using PET by Pearlson *et al* (1993).

The question of the specificity, particularly disease-specificity, of the above brain-imaging changes is crucial. First, as we have noted previously (Pearlson & Petty, 1994), many of the reported findings in late-onset schizophrenia are non-specific, in the sense of being unlocalised in the brain. Second, somewhat similar brain findings have also been reported for patients suffering from late-onset depression. In that condition, for example, an increased ventricle–brain ratio on CT or MRI has been reported (Pearlson *et al*, 1987; Rabins *et al*, 1991). Third, ventricle enlargement has also been described in depressed elderly subjects (Coffey *et al*, 1989, 1990), as have MRI white-matter abnormalities (Krishnan *et al*, 1988; Coffey *et al*, 1989, 1990; Zubenko *et al*, 1990). Similarly, cortical atrophy on CT and MRI has been shown by Pearlson *et al* (1997).

A volumetric temporal-lobe MRI study by Barta *et al* (1997) compared 12 elderly patients with Alzheimer's disease with an age- and gender-matched comparison group of 11 patients with late-onset schizophrenia and 18 matched normal controls. Patients with Alzheimer's disease showed the expected widespread both general and regional cerebral atrophy. Patients with late-onset schizophrenia showed similar degrees of shrinkage of entorhinal cortex, hippocampus and amygdala to the patients with Alzheimer's disease but had significantly more volume loss in both superior temporal gyri. This last finding is similar to reports in patients with 'classic', early-onset schizophrenia (Barta *et al*, 1990). This study is particularly interesting since it suggests that at least some specific changes in temporal lobe reported for 'classic', early-onset schizophrenia but not early-onset affective disorder (Pearlson *et al*, 1997) may also be seen in late-onset schizophrenia. A further, related comparison was carried out by Rabins *et al* (unpublished data). Patients with late-onset depression and late-onset schizophrenia were each compared with elderly age- and gender-matched normal controls using the CERAD visual-analogue MRI rating scales. This revealed significant differences between normals and patients. Patients with late-onset schizophrenia differed from normal controls in having significant enlargement of the third ventricle and both temporal horns. By contrast, depressed patients did not show these abnormalities but differed uniquely from normals in showing enlargement of bilateral cerebral sulci, lateral ventricles and Sylvian fissures. Thus Rabins' data make the point that although there are similarities in terms of some non-specific brain changes in the two disorders, they are nevertheless distinct when directly compared.

Late-onset depression has some parallels to late-onset schizophrenia. Both diseases have less genetic contribution than early-onset cases of the same disorder, and there is a higher than normal prevalence of non-specific cerebral vascular disease. For depression this has been shown on MRI and SPECT (Coffey *et al*, 1989, 1990; Lesser *et al*, 1991; Rabins *et al*, 1991; Beats, 1992).

Pearlson *et al* (1993) compared patients with late-onset schizophrenia directly with elderly patients with early-onset schizophrenia. Eleven late-onset patients were compared with 11 early-onset individuals, group matched by age and gender. Onset age in the late-onset group was 68 ± 5 years compared with 41 ± 11 years in the early-onset group. The two populations were compared using the CERAD MRI rating scales for measures of third ventricle and left and right Sylvian fissures, temporal sulci, temporal horn, lateral ventricles, and cerebral sulci. No significant differences were found between the two groups, again emphasising similarity between pathological brain changes in the two populations.

What can we conclude from the above review of brain-imaging studies? First, more narrowly defined patients with late-onset schizophrenia seem to resemble those with early-onset schizophrenia with regard to neuroimaging differences with age-matched normal controls. Although 'psychosis', like 'depression', may be a limited final common path response to brain damage from a wide variety of causes, brain changes associated with late-onset schizophrenia differ in several important details from those seen in late-onset depression. Many of the studies of late-onset schizophrenia cited above included fairly narrowly defined patients, and these cases are less likely to include patients with a high likelihood of 'organic' or coarse brain disease. In contrast, studies choosing to accept more broadly defined patients will increase diagnostic heterogeneity, likely including a higher proportion of 'organic phenocopies', with consequently more evidence of cerebral vascular and other coarse brain pathology. Ultimately, several improvements in study design of imaging investigations will help to transcend some of the above limitations. Much larger study populations and longitudinal designs will address questions regarding aetiological subgrouping and the need for later diagnostic reclassification. Inclusion of suitable patient comparison groups (e.g. elderly affective disorder and elderly early-onset schizophrenia) will help to clarify issues related to disease specificity. Finally, neuropathological examination will help to elucidate the nature of the underlying pathology and aid the distinction between developmental and neurodegenerative processes.

References

BARTA, P. E., PEARLSON, G. D., POWERS, R. E., *et al* (1990) Reduced superior temporal gyrus volume in schizophrenia: relationship to hallucinations. *American Journal of Psychiatry*, **147**, 1457–1462.

——, ——, ——, *et al* (1997) Quantitative MRI volume changes in late-life onset schizophrenia compared to normal controls and Alzheimer's disease: a preliminary report. *Psychiatry Research Neuroimaging*, **68**, 65–75.

BEATS, B. (1992) Imaging and affective disorder in the elderly. *Clinical Geriatric Medicine*, **8**, 267–277.

BERMAN, K. F., TORREY, E. F., DANIEL, D. G. & WEINBERGER, D. R. (1992) Regional cerebral blood flow in monozygotic twins discordant and concordant for schizophrenia. *Archives of General Psychiatry*, **49**, 927–934.

BORONOW, J., PICKAR, D., NINAN, P. T., *et al* (1985) Atrophy limited to third ventricle only in chronic schizophrenic patients: report of a controlled series. *Archives of General Psychiatry*, **40**, 266–271.

BREITNER, J. C. S., HUSAIN, M. M., FIGIEL, G., *et al* (1990) Cerebral white matter disease in late-onset psychosis. *Biological Psychiatry*, **28**, 266–274.

BURNS, A., CARRICK, J., AMES, D., *et al* (1989) The cerebral cortical appearance in late paraphrenia. *International Journal of Geriatric Psychiatry*, **4**, 31–34.

COFFEY, C. E., FIGIEL, G. S., DJANG, W. T., *et al* (1989) White matter hyperintensity on magnetic resonance imaging: clinical and neuroanatomic correlates in the depressed elderly. *Journal of Neuropsychiatry and Clinical Neurosciences*, **1**, 135–144.

——, ——, ——, *et al* (1990) Subcortical hyperintensity on magnetic resonance imaging: a comparison of normal and depressed elderly subjects. *American Journal of Psychiatry*, **47**, 187–189.

FLINT, A. J., RIFAT, S. L. & EASTWOOD, M. R. (1991) Late-onset paranoia: distinct from paraphrenia? *Journal of Geriatric Psychiatry*, **6**, 103–109.

GUR, R. E., GUR, R. C., SKOLNICK, B. E., *et al* (1985) Brain functions in psychiatric disorders. III. Regional cerebral blood flow in unmedicated schizophrenics. *Archives of General Psychiatry*, **42**, 329–334.

——, MOZLEY, P. D., RESNICK, S. M., *et al* (1991) Magnetic resonance imaging in schizophrenia, I: volumetric analysis of brain and cerebrospinal fluid. *Archives of General Psychiatry*, **48**, 407–412.

HOWARD, R. J., FÖRSTL, H., ALMEIDA, O., *et al* (1992) First-rank symptoms of Schneider in late paraphrenia: cortical structural correlates. *British Journal of Psychiatry*, **160**, 108–109.

——, ALMEIDA, O., LEVY, R. & GRAVES, P. (1994) Quantitative magnetic resonance imaging volumetry distinguishes delusional disorder from late-onset schizophrenia. *British Journal of Psychiatry*, **165**, 474–480.

JOHNSTONE, E., CROW, T., FRITH, C., *et al* (1976) Cerebral ventricular size and cognitive impairment in chronic schizophrenia. *Lancet*, **ii**, 924–926.

KRISHNAN, K. R. R., GOLI, V., ELLINWOOD, E. H., *et al* (1988) Leukoencephalopathy in patients diagnosed as major depressive. *Biological Psychiatry*, **23**, 519–522.

LESSER, I. M., MILLER, B. L., BOONE, K. B., *et al* (1991) Brain injury and cognitive function in late-onset psychotic depression. *Journal of Neuropsychiatry and Clinical Neurosciences*, **3**, 33–40.

MATTHEW, R. J., WILSON, W. H., TANT, S. R., *et al* (1988) Abnormal resting regional cerebral blood flow patterns and their correlates in schizophrenia. *Archives of General Psychiatry*, **45**, 542–549.

MILLER, B. L., LESSER, I. M., MENA, I., *et al* (1992) Regional cerebral blood flow in late-life–onset psychosis. *Neuropsychiatry, Neuropsychology, and Behavioural Neurology*, **5**, 132–137.

NAGUIB, M. & LEVY, R. (1987) Late paraphrenia: neuropsychological impairment and structural brain abnormalities on computed tomography. *International Journal of Geriatric Psychiatry*, **2**, 83–90.

PEARLSON, G. D. & PETTY, R. G. (1994) Late-onset schizophrenia. In *Textbook of Geriatric Neuropsychiatry* (eds J. L. Cummings & C. E. Coffey), pp. 262–277. Washington, DC: American Psychiatric Press.

——, GARBACZ, D. J., TOMPKINS, R. H., *et al* (1987) Lateral cerebral ventricular size in late onset schizophrenia. In *Schizophrenia and Aging* (eds N. E. Miller & G. D. Cohen), pp. 246–248. New York: Guilford.

——, TUNE, L. E., WONG, D. F., *et al* (1993) Quantitative D2 dopamine receptor PET and structural MRI changes in late-onset schizophrenia. *Schizophrenia Bulletin*, **19**, 783–795.

——, BARTA, P. E., MENON, R. R., *et al* (1997) Medial and superior temporal gyral volumes and cerebral asymmetry in schizophrenia versus bipolar disorder. *Biological Psychiatry*, **41**, 1–14.

PFEFFERBAUM, A., ZIPURSKY, R. B., LIM, K. O., *et al* (1988) Computed tomographic evidence for generalized sulcal and ventricular enlargement in schizophrenia. *Archives of General Psychiatry*, **45**, 633–640.

RABINS, P. V., PEARLSON, G. D., JAYARAM, G., *et al* (1987) Elevated VBR in late-onset schizophrenia. *American Journal of Psychiatry*, **144**, 1216–1218.

——, ——, AYLWARD, E., *et al* (1991) Cortical magnetic resonance imaging changes in elderly inpatients with major depression. *American Journal of Psychiatry*, **148**, 617–620.

TUNE, L. E., WONG, D. F., PEARLSON, G. D., *et al* (1994) Dopamine D2 receptor density in schizophrenia patients: a PET study with 11C-N-methylspiperone. *Psychiatry Research*, **49**, 219–237.

WEINBERGER, D. R. (1987) Implications of normal brain development for the pathogenesis of schizophrenia. *Archives of General Psychiatry*, **44**, 660–669.

——, TORREY, E. F., NEOPHYTIDES, A. N., *et al* (1979) Lateral cerebral ventricular enlargement in chronic schizophrenia. *Archives of General Psychiatry*, **36**, 735–739.

WONG, D. F., GJEDDE, J. & WAGNER, H. N. Jr (1986a) Quantification of neuroreceptors in the living human brain, I: irreversible binding of ligands. *Journal of Cerebral Blood Flow Metabolism*, **6**, 146–177.

——, ——, ——, *et al* (1986b) Quantification of neuroreceptors in the living human brain, II: assessment of receptor density and affinity using inhibition studies. *Journal of Cerebral Blood Flow Metabolism*, **6**, 147–153.

——, WAGNER, H. N. JR, TUNE, L. E., *et al* (1986c) Positron emission tomography reveals elevated D2 dopamine receptors in drug-naive schizophrenics. *Science*, **234**, 1558–1563.

ZUBENKO, G. S., SULLIVAN, P., NELSON, J. P., *et al* (1990) Brain imaging abnormalities in mental disorders of late life. *Archives of Neurology*, **47**, 1107–1111.

12 Treatment of late-onset mental disorder with antidepressants and neuroleptics

H.-J. MÖLLER

Drug treatment of late-life depression or schizophrenia is of great importance, as the functional psychoses are among the most common psychiatric diseases in the elderly. It therefore seems astonishing that there are great deficits in the drug research that has been done with this age group. There are almost no studies specifically on the treatment of late-onset depression or schizophrenia. A few studies have evaluated the efficacy and safety of different antidepressants in elderly patients with depression, but there are extremely few on the efficacy and safety of neuroleptics in elderly patients with schizophrenia.

There is a broad consensus that the drug treatment of depression or schizophrenia in the elderly is in general both effective and safe. However, a high percentage of functional psychiatric diseases go unrecognised and untreated in the elderly. In consequence, longer hospital stays and increased morbidity and mortality from medical illness and from suicide may occur.

Pharmacokinetics in elderly patients

The drug treatment of elderly patients has to take into consideration certain pharmacokinetic alterations with age (Norman, 1993) (Table 12.1).

The chief features examined here are: absorption, distribution, metabolism, and excretion (Braithwaite, 1982; Crome & Dawling, 1989). All these processes may be affected in the elderly but the degree to which they are affected greatly varies in individual cases.

Absorption may be reduced owing to reductions in gastric acid production, in gastrointestinal motility, in gastrointestinal blood flow, and in absorptive surface. These processes are counteracted by a reduced first-pass clearance in the liver.

Distribution depends on body mass, which, as a rule, is reduced in the elderly, so that a higher tissue concentration should be expected for a given dose. The proportion of adipose tissue is also important. This proportion is increased in the elderly, which leads to a higher plasma concentration of water-soluble drugs and to the reverse effect for lipophilic compounds. Antidepressants are usually the latter. Most studies have shown a decline in plasma albumin with age, which can result in an increased free concentration of acidic drugs.

Metabolism mainly takes place in the liver. Drugs with a high hepatic excretion ratio depend on liver blood flow. This is reduced in the elderly, so that clearance may also be reduced. Drugs with a low hepatic excretion ratio are less affected by liver blood flow, but are more dependent on drug-metabolising capacity. This capacity is reduced in the elderly for processes like oxidation, reduction and hydrolysis, but not for reactions like conjugation (sulphate, glucuronide).

Excretion mainly concerns glomerular filtration, which falls by about half in old age. Compounds which are detoxified by renal elimination are therefore excreted much more slowly in the elderly.

The following study illustrates such alterations. Nies *et al* (1977) studied the relationship between age and plasma levels of amitriptyline and imipramine and their respective metabolites, nortriptyline and desipramine. Participants in the six-week, double-blind study of amitriptyline were depressed out-patients ($n=35$), whose ages ranged between 21 and 68 years. They were given 75 mg/day amitriptyline for the first five days, and that dose was subsequently increased to 150 mg/day. The imipramine study consisted predominantly of depressed in-patients ($n = 23$), whose ages ranged between 27 and 78 years. Most of these received 150 mg/day for a minimum of 21 days. Steady-state plasma levels of amitriptyline and imipramine showed a significant positive correlation with age; i.e. the levels were higher in older individuals. Levels of desipramine were also higher in the elderly; those of nortriptyline were not. Wide inter-subject variability was observed (Dunner, 1994).

There have been only a few reports on the relationship between plasma levels of neuroleptics and ageing in patients with schizophrenia, and these have reported inconsistent findings. Some authors found an age-related increase in the plasma levels of neuroleptics, while others did not (Tran-Johnson *et al*, 1992) (Table 12.2).

Pharmacodynamic changes in elderly patients

In vivo alterations to pharmacodynamics are difficult to demonstrate, as a synopsis of relevant studies in the literature attests. At the centre

TABLE 12.1

Some single-dose pharmacokinetic studies of antidepressants in the elderly (Norman, 1993; for references see source)

n	Age	Gender	Dose (mg)	Results	Reference
Amitriptyline					
6	72–83	F	125 p.o.	Absorption slower, plasma clearance reduced, $t_{1/2}$ increased, V_d reduced in elderly; c.f. literature	Henry *et al* (1981)
7	21–23	M	80–100 p.o.	Systemic clearance, bioavailability and free fraction not different between groups	Schulz *et al* (1983)
5	62–81	M	40–50 p.o.	$t_{1/2}$ increased in elderly (21.7 ± 2.9 h c.f. 16.2 ± 6.1 h); V_d increased in elderly (17.1 ± 2.4 l/kg c.f. 14.1 ± 2.0 l/kg)	Cutler *et al* (1981)
Desipramine					
7	69–92	F	25–50 p.o.	Terminal half-life ranged from 10.5 to 40.9 h, mean 25.5 h, similar to literature data in young	Abernethy *et al* (1985)
35	21–88	19M/16F	50 p.o.	Elimination half-life and t_{max} increase in elderly males; no other differences	
Dothiepin					
9	19–38	6M/3F	75 p.o.	Similar absorption, distribution and elimination in the elderly and young subjects	Bareggi *et al* (1990)
7	60–84	4M/3F		Slower clearance in the elderly (10.8 ± 5.0 ml/min/kg c.f. 21.6 ± 9 ml/min/kg)	
9	27–78	2M/7F	75 p.o.	No effect of age on kinetic parameters when data from this study combined with a previous study. Gender difference noted for dothiepin and northiaden half-life and V_d dothiepin	Maguire *et al* (1983)
Imipramine					
12	23–54	6M/6F	25 i.m.	C_{max} higher, $t_{1/2}$ longer in elderly than young subjects; clearance lower in elderly males only	Benetello *et al* (1990)
14	66–77	7M/F			
46	21–88	26M/20F	50 p.o. 12.5 i.v.	$t_{1/2}$ longer, clearance decreased, C_{max} higher in elderly compared to young. Absolute bioavailability not different between young and old	Aberenthy *et al* (1985)
5	75–83	F	125 p.o.	$t_{1/2}$ longer, plasma clearance decreased – c.f. literature data for young subjects	Henry *et al* (1980)

	Age	M/F	Dose	Findings	Reference
Maprotiline					
5	75–83	F	175 p.o.	No apparent differences with literature for young subjects	Henry et al (1980)
Mianserin					
8	60–83	4M/4F	60 p.o.	Absorption prolonged, elimination half-life longer in the elderly than in younger controls	Maguire et al (1983)
14	64–90	6M/8F	30 p.o.	Absorption prolonged, elimination half-life longer and apparent oral clearance decreased in the elderly – compared with younger controls	Shami et al (1983)
Nortriptyline					
16	69–100	F	75 p.o.	Decreased plasma clearance and increased elimination half-life relative to young controls ($t_{1/2}$ 23.5–79.0 h; CI = 8.3–38.4 l/h).	Dawling et al (1980)
10	66–79	8F/2M	100 p.o.	Kinetic parameters for elderly similar to literature data for young subjects. Wider inter-individual variability in elderly than in young	Turbott et al (1980)
Citalopram					
11	73–90	4M/7F	Steady-state	Increased $t_{1/2}$ and decreased systemic clearance in elderly compared with previous data for younger patients	Fredericson-Overo et al (1985)
Paroxetine					
21	60–85	7M/14F	20 mg p.o. 30 mg p.o.	Trends for increased $t_{1/2}$ in elderly against young; $t_{1/2}$ longer following mutiple doses than single dose	Lundmark et al (1989)
20	64–78	6M/14F	20 mg p.o.	C_{max} elderly c. $3\times C_{max}$ young; $t_{1/2}$ similar in both groups	Bayer et al (1989)
23	21–34	16M/7F		At steady-state C_{max}, AUC, $t_{1/2}$ and C_{min} higher in elderly; wide inter-individual variability; considerable overlap between groups	
Trazodone					
18	60–78	7M/11F	25 mg i.v.	V_d and $t_{1/2}$ increased and clearance decreased in elderly men compared with young men; V_d and $t_{1/2}$ increased in elderly women compared with young women	Greenblatt et al (1987)
25	18–40	12M/13F	50 mg p.o.		
10	65–74		100 mg p.o.	$t_{1/2}$ and AUC increased and clearance decreased in elderly, c.f. young subjects	Bayer et al (1983)

of pharmacodynamic changes in the elderly is a concept of gradual reduction of homeostatic reserve or ability to cope with environmental changes (Swift, 1990). For example, advancing age has been shown to increase the number of corrective movements involved in standing upright and has been related to a reduction in the number of dopamine D_2 receptors in the striatum (Sheldon, 1963). An increased sensitivity of older patients to postural hypotension induced by drugs with alpha-adrenoreceptor-blocking effects (e.g. tricyclic antidepressants) can be related to changes in the responsiveness of baroreceptors in the carotid sinus and elsewhere (Swift, 1990).

Although the mechanism is unknown, it is well established that the elderly are more sensitive to the effects of acute doses of benzo-diazepines than are young subjects. The effects of single oral doses of temazepam, nitrazepam, diazepam and others on psychomotor per-formance and other subjective measures have been shown to be accentuated despite similar total and free plasma levels of drug in young and old subjects (Castleden *et al*, 1977; Swift *et al*, 1985a,b). On the other hand, long-term administration of benzodiazepines ap-parently causes little psychomotor impairment, despite relatively high daytime plasma concentrations (Swift *et al*, 1984).

As a consequence of the alterations in old age mentioned above, most compounds have longer half-lives in elderly patients and can demonstrate stronger effects. As a general prescribing rule, elderly patients should receive doses of one-half to two-thirds of the doses that are usual in young patients.

Drug treatment of elderly patients with depression

There is a consensus that antidepressant therapy is effective and should be recommended for the treatment of depression in the elderly. Because of the pharmacokinetic changes in the elderly, the tolerability of antidepressants, especially of the classic tricyclics, is reduced compared with younger populations. However, this problem can be managed by a careful dosing regime and a careful selection of the drug (Stewart, 1993; Dunner, 1994; Schneider & Olin, 1995; Hampel *et al*, in press).

Efficacy of antidepressant treatment in elderly depressed patients

There have been approximately 30 randomised placebo-controlled, parallel-group clinical trials involving elderly patients that support the efficacy of acute treatment (Fig. 12.1). Medications used have included nortriptyline, imipramine, doxepin, bupropion,

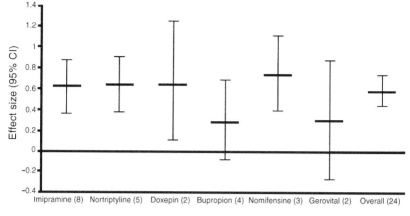

Fig. 12.1. *Effect sizes by drug treatment in geriatric depression – placebo-controlled comparisons. For each medication, the mean effect size is displayed as a horizontal bar; 95% confidence intervals are displayed as vertical bars. Effect sizes significantly greater than 0 are those with confidence intervals that do not encompass 0. The number of trials is indicated in parentheses. Total sample sizes for each medication are imipramine, 239; nortriptyine, 223; doxepin, 49; bupropion, 71; nomifensine, 114; procaine hydrochloride (Gerovital), 47 (Schneider & Olin, 1995; reproduced with permission from Springer Publishing Company).*

desipramine, nomifensine, phenelzine, fluoxetine, fluvoxamine and mirtazapin. In comparison with the results shown in Fig. 12.1, there is an approximate 30% placebo response rate (Plotkin *et al*, 1987; Halikas, 1995; Salzman *et al*, 1995).

The efficacy of antidepressants in the treatment of elderly depressed patients is also supported by a large amount of evidence from studies comparing different second-generation antidepressants with classic antidepressants, including mianserin, trazodone, fluoxetine, paroxetine, moclobemide, brofaromine and mirtazapin (Feighner & Cohn, 1985; Altamura *et al*, 1988; Feighner *et al*, 1988; De Vanna *et al*, 1990; Dunner *et al*, 1992; Volz *et al*, 1995; Hoyberg *et al*, 1996).

To collect some more precise information about studies performed since 1980, my group performed a careful review of the literature (Volz & Möller, 1994). Although we took into account only publications of an appropriate standard, we had to conclude that the methodological

TABLE 12.2, part I (see also below)

Selected pharmacokinetic studies of older psychotic patients treated with neuroleptics (Tran-Johnson et al, 1992; for references see source)

Study	n	Mean age (range)	Gender	Diagnosis	Neuroleptic	Mean dose (range) (mg/day)	Mean serum neuroleptic level (range) (ng/ml)
Axelsson & Martensson (1976)	169	56 (14–90)	M 66, F 103	Organic brain syndrome; alcoholic; neurotic; psychotic	Thioridazine	234 (30–600)	Trace to 2.17 ng/ml
Forsman & Ohman (1977) (3 groups)	18	65.2 (50–83)	Not reported	Chronic psychosis	Haloperidol	12.5 (1–90)	9.7 (0.6–121)
	25	77.9 (68–86)	Not reported	Dementia		2.4 (1–6)	3.4 (0.5–18.6)
	24	49 (21–76)	Not reported	Unspecified		5.0 (1–21)	4.9 (0.7–13.4)
Yesavage et al (1981) (2 groups)	28	30 (22–53)	Not reported	Schizophrenia	Thiothixene	20	Range 3–45
	25	41 (22–62)				10	Range 2–19
Jeste et al (1982) (2 groups)	29	18–49	Mostly men	Schizophrenia	Haloperidol Fluphenazine Chlorpromazine	Variable	Measured differently either by a radioreceptor assay or with an HPLC
	16	69.5 (s.e.m. 5 years)	All women	Schizophrenia (n=14) or organic brain syndrome (n=2)	Thioridazine (n=12) or mesoridazine (n=4)	278.2 (50–1000)	
Yesavage et al (1982)	30	30 (20–53)	All men	Schizophrenia and schizo-affective disorder	Thiothixene	80 (28 patients)	31 ng/ml in 2 patients > 45 years of age. 15.6 ng/ml in 25 patients <39 years of age
Movin et al (1990) (3 groups)	38	19–36	M 20, F 18	Schizophrenia	Remoxipride	200 mg twice daily of IR or CR x4 days	2.8 (s.d. 0.8)
		46–69		Schizophrenia			6.0 (s.d. 2.8)
		71–89		Psychotic illness		200 mg IR ×14 days	9.7 (s.d. 3.9)

IR, immediate release; CR, controlled release.

TABLE 12.2, part II

Selected pharmacokinetic studies of older psychotic patients treated with neuroleptics (Tran-Johnson et al, 1992; for references see source)

Study	Study design	Comments
Axelsson & Martensson (1976)	Open trial, medication given 3 times/day for 8 days prior to blood draw	Significant correlation between plasma levels and age. Most striking increase within age interval of 46–55 years of age
Forsman and Ohman (1977) (3 groups)	Medication given thrice daily, sampling at 7 a.m. after constant dose for 1 week	Authors found a tendency towards increasing serum concentration with age, but this was not statistically significant
Yesavage *et al* (1981) (2 groups)	Acute single dose test	Significant correlation between plasma levels and age. $r=0.43$; $P<0.02$; $r=0.41$; $P<0.05$
Jeste *et al* (1982) (2 groups)	Open trial ($n=29$), and open study ($n=16$) with 1-year follow-up	Older patients had a much higher ratio of serum neuroleptic level or activity to daily dose, compared to younger patients. Patients with tardive dyskinesia had higher ratio of level to dose, only in the older age group patients
Yesavage *et al* (1982)	Acute level 2.5 h after 20 mg dose; steady-state level after 10 days of therapy (80 mg/day)	Significant correlation between serum level and age ($r=0.43$; $P < 0.05$). Acute level correlated with positive changes in Brief Psychiatric Rating Scale score after 1 week of treatment ($r=0.51$; $P < 0.005$)
Movin *et al* (1990) (3 groups)	Comparative, randomised, double-blind, cross-over trials (2 groups), and open trial	Findings of increased plasma concentrations, area under the curve, half-life unbound concentration but constant unbound fraction suggested decreased hepatic intrinsic clearance of remoxipride in the elderly

standard in this field is not comparable with the general standard (Table 12.3, Fig. 12.2). As can be seen from Fig. 12.2, most compounds reduced the baseline total score on the Hamilton Rating Scale for Depression (HRSD) between 50% and 70%. Some of the studies are reported below.

Gerner *et al* (1980) showed a clear advantage of imipramine and trazodone over placebo. Considering the total number of side-effects, trazodone was comparable to placebo, while imipramine produced the most severe side-effects, which were mostly anticholinergic in nature. The total study duration of four weeks can be regarded as too short. Georgotas & McCue (1989), for example, reported that half of those elderly patients who did not respond to seven weeks of treatment with either phenelzine or nortriptyline responded during an additional two weeks. Furthermore, 26 dropouts (out of 60) seems high. In the imipramine group, as many as 60% of patients dropped out, which means that only eight out of 20 completed the trial in this group.

Scardigli & Jans (1982) compared mianserin with trazodone. The four-week period of the trial was too short. They postulated a quicker onset of action for mianserin, but due to the problematic use of multiple statistical testing without adjustment, this result does not seem to be acceptable. With mianserin, the total number of side-effects was considerably lower than with trazodone, which is mostly due to more anticholinergic side-effects in the trazodone group.

Gwirtsman *et al* (1983) compared maprotiline with doxepin in a six-week trial. They found maprotiline to be superior to doxepin, but this difference was apparent only after week 4 of the trial. Before this time, the two groups showed parallel improvement. The investigators undertook serum-level measurement but were not able to find a correlation between plasma level and recovery. There were no major differences regarding safety and tolerability. Since the authors state only the minimum dose given and the mean maximum daily dose, a mean daily dose is not clearly ascertainable.

Cohn *et al* (1984) were able to show the clear advantage of imipramine over placebo even with the small patient number in both groups ($n = 21$). In the imipramine group, a fairly high dose was used, which led to a side-effect ratio of 86% (19% in the placebo group). The most commonly reported side-effects were nervousness/restlessness, dry mouth and nausea/vomiting. This paper again shows the clear efficacy of this classic antidepressant drug, but also the poor tolerability of this compound in an elderly patient sample.

Merideth *et al* (1984) were able to show the superiority of imipramine over placebo in a small sample. The main side-effects in the imipramine group were dry mouth (36%), constipation (24%), drowsiness (18%), nervousness/restlessness (18%) and blurred vision (14%). The trial aimed primarily at the comparison of nomifensine and imipramine.

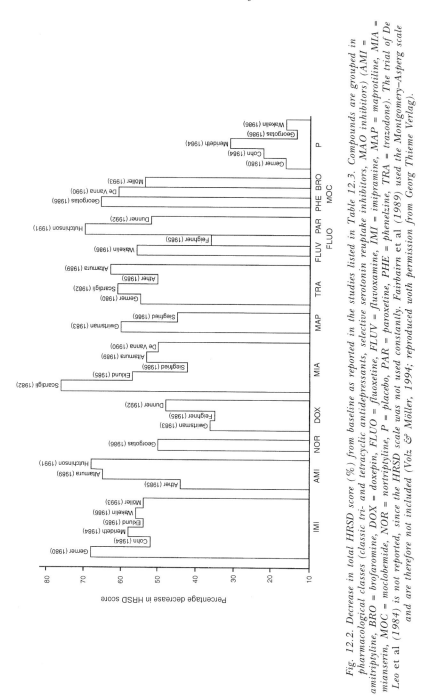

Fig. 12.2. *Decrease in total HRSD score (%) from baseline as reported in the studies listed in Table 12.3. Compounds are grouped in pharmacological classes (classic tri- and tetracyclic antidepressants, selective serotonin reuptake inhibitors, MAO inhibitors) (AMI = amitriptyline, BRO = brofaromine, DOX = doxepin, FLUO = fluoxetine, FLUV = fluvoxamine, IMI = imipramine, MAP = maprotiline, MIA = mianserin, MOC = moclobemide, NOR = nortriptyline, P = placebo, PAR = paroxetine, PHE = phenelzine, TRA = trazodone). The trial of De Leo et al (1984) is not reported, since the HRSD scale was not used constantly. Fairbairn et al (1989) used the Montgomery–Asperg scale and are therefore not included (Volz & Möller, 1994; reproduced with permission from Georg Thieme Verlag).*

TABLE 12.3

Controlled clinical trials on antidepressants in the elderly since 1980 (Volz & Möller, 1994)

Reference (index no. for Fig. 12.3)	n	Drugs used (mg/day)	Duration (weeks) and patient status i=in-patient o=out-patient	Efficacy	Safety
Gerner et al (1980) (1)	60	imipramine (145) trazodone (305) placebo	4 (o)	imipramine = trazodone > placebo	placebo = trazodone > imipramine
Scardigli & Jans (1982)[1] (2)	48	mianserin (up to 60) trazodone (up to 405)	4 (?)	mianserin ≥ trazodone	mianserin > trazodone
Gwirtsman et al (1983) (3)	49	maprotilin (>75) doxepin (>75)	6 (i & o)	maprotiline > doxepin	maprotiline = doxepin
Cohn et al (1984)[1] (4)	42	imipramine (136) placebo	4 (o)	imipramine > placebo	placebo > imipramine
De Leo et al (1984)	46	viloxazine (ca. 280) placebo	4	=	placebo > viloxazine
Merideth et al (1984)[1] (5)	41	imipramine (150) placebo	5 (o)	imipramine > placebo	placebo > imipramine
Eklund et al (1985) (6)	50	mianserin (45) imipramine (105)	4 (?)	=	mianserin > imipramine
Ather et al (1985) (7)	101	trazodone (>100) amitriptyline (>50)	6 (i & o)	=	=
Feighner & Cohn (1985) (8)	157	fluoxetine (20–80) doxepin (50–250)	6 1 year open follow-up (o)	=	fluoxetine > doxepin
Georgotas et al (1986) (9)	90	phenelzine (>45) nortriptyline (>75) placebo	7 (o)	phenelzine = nortriptyline > placebo	placebo > phenelzine = nortriptyline

Study	N	Drugs (dose)	Duration (weeks)		
Wakelin (1986)[2] (10)	76	fluvoxamine (161) imipramine (160) placebo	4 (i & o)	fluvoxamine = imipramine> placebo	placebo > fluvoxamine > imipramine
Siegfried & O'Connolly (1986)[1] (11)	50	mianserin (40) maprotiline (100)	4 (i)	=	mianserin > maprotiline
Altamura *et al* (1989)[3] (12)	106	trazodone (150) amitriptyline (75) mianserin (60)	5 (i)	=	trazolane > amitriptyline = mianserin
Fairbairn *et al* (1989)	48	lofepramine (140) dothiepin (100)	6 (i & o)	=	=
De Vanna *et al* (1990)[4] (13)	80	moclobemide (300–500) mianserin (75–125)	4	=	=
Hutchinson *et al* (1991) (14)	90	paroxetine (30) amitriptyline (100)	6 (o)	=	paroxetine > amitriptyline
Dunner *et al* (1992)[5] (15)	271	paroxetine (23) doxepin (105)	6 (o)	= (>)	paroxetine > doxepin
Möller & Volz (1993) (16)	189	brofaromine (85) imipramine (87)	8 1 year open follow-up (i & o)	=	brofaromine > imipramine

1. The nomifensine results of these trials are not reported because nomifensine was withdrawn from the market.
2. Data pooled retrospectively from three clinical trials.
3. The first published paper of Altamura *et al* (1988) is not reported here since there may be at least partly the same patients in both trials.
4. In this paper two trials are reported; only the first-mentioned trial meets our above-stated criteria.
5. Data pooled retrospectively from two clinical trials.

Eklund *et al* (1985) performed a comparison between mianserin and imipramine for four weeks, which seems too short. They found comparable efficacy. Because of a lower side-effect rate in the mianserin group, they concluded that mianserin is better tolerated. Since only completers were analysed, the fact that there were four dropouts with severe side-effects in the mianserin group (three with confusion and disorientation, one suicide) but none due to side-effects in the imipramine group is not represented in this analysis.

Ather *et al* (1985) report superiority of trazodone over amitriptyline in both efficacy and safety in a six-week trial. In the light of the fact that 76.5% of amitriptyline patients were on 50 mg a day during the whole trial period and that the "superior efficacy" was apparent at only one point of time (week 6) in one (current severity of patient's illness) out of five measurements of efficacy, this does not seem to be a well founded conclusion. In their paper, it is not stated which parameters were prospectively defined as primary efficacy parameters. In this trial, 10 mg/day diazepam was chosen as reference, and no marked differences were detected between the tranquilliser and the two antidepressants. This raises the question of sample selection.

Feighner & Cohn (1985) report interesting results with a comparative trial of fluoxetine and doxepin. Both drugs were effective, with advantages in the safety parameters for fluoxetine. Doxepin caused, in particular, dry mouth, drowsiness/sedation, constipation, and dizziness/lightheadedness, while nervousness/anxiety and drowsiness/sedation were predominant with fluoxetine. What is striking in this trial is the high percentage of dropouts in both groups: only 53% of the fluoxetine group and 39% of the doxepin group completed the trial.

Georgotas *et al* (1986) undertook a very interesting trial comparing nortriptyline, phenelzine and placebo. First of all, the duration of seven weeks is sufficient, which is also proved by the fact that it took five weeks to observe a significant antidepressant response. Secondly, the dose was optimised, either on the basis of plasma levels of nortriptyline or of the amount of monoamine oxidase (MAO) inhibition as measured by platelets (in the phenelzine group). Therefore the fairly high response rate of approximately 60% in both groups is not astonishing. The trial must have been supervised very well, as evidenced by the low dropout rate, which was highest in the placebo group. There was an overall good tolerability of the trial drugs, with certain advantages for phenelzine concerning anticholinergic side-effects, and certain advantages for nortriptyline concerning nasal congestion, urinary symptoms and dermatological problems. The most astonishing result therefore is that classical MAO inhibitors also seem to be safe and effective in this special patient population.

Wakelin (1986) reports the results of a pooled analysis from three independent trials comparing fluvoxamine, imipramine and placebo. The simultaneous use of retrospective data pooling and statistical hypothesis testing for the whole sample is a critical issue. The stated earlier onset of efficacy of the fluvoxamine group was not a prospectively defined aim of the trial, and it was found by multiple retrospective testing of subfactors of the HRSD. The claim that fluvoxamine is better tolerated than imipramine was proved only for orthostatic blood pressure regulation, but the number of adverse experiences did not differ significantly between the two active-treatment groups. The treatment duration of four weeks can be regarded as too short.

Siegfried & O'Connolly (1986) found comparable efficacy of mianserin and maprotiline. The trial duration of four weeks seems too short for such a conclusion. In the maprotiline group, considerably more side-effects occurred, but this could be due to the low dose of mianserin. The trial seems to have been performed on a more representative group of elderly depressed patients than in other studies because nearly all patients had concomitant somatic diseases. Although such inclusion criteria make the primary diagnosis slightly more uncertain, this approach increases the representativeness and the generalisability of the results. In this trial, a cognitive test battery was used to measure the cognitive effects of the drugs. In the critical flicker fusion frequency test and in the choice reaction task it was claimed that mianserin is superior to maprotiline.

Altamura *et al* (1989) found similar antidepressant effects for amitriptyline, mianserin and trazodone. The doses in the control groups (amitriptyline and mianserin) were rather low, so the result may be biased in favour of trazodone. Trazodone shows an advantage concerning the number of side-effects, especially anticholinergic and cardiovascular side-effects, which may be especially useful in patients with cerebral or cardiac diseases.

Fairbairn *et al* (1989) reported equal efficacy of lofepramine and dothiepin but better tolerability of lofepramine. These advantages were reported only for dry mouth, daytime drowsiness and blurred vision, and the results of the overall analysis of the total number of adverse events are not given.

De Vanna *et al* (1990) found no differences in the efficacy and tolerability of moclobemide and mianserin. The latter is true only for the overall evaluation of tolerability, because the frequency of adverse events was a disadvantage in the moclobemide group. The treatment period (four weeks) seems too short.

Hutchinson *et al* (1991) reported the results of a six-week trial with 90 patients to test paroxetine and amitriptyline (in a 2:1 randomisation). The statistical analysis is very good (intent-to-treat principle, power calculation), and the adverse events and patient withdrawals are also reported comprehensively. They state a comparable efficacy of the two treatments, but with a quicker onset in the paroxetine group. The latter statement is based on the fact that more patients in the paroxetine group showed a 50% reduction in HRSD score over weeks 1 and 2 (11% *v.* 3% and 27% *v.* 17%, respectively). This difference was not tested statistically and, taking the same figures for week 6 into consideration (76% *v.* 80%), one might even speculate that amitriptyline is more effective. The major side-effects in the paroxetine group were nausea, vomiting and dizziness, and in the amitriptyline group dry mouth, nausea, dizziness, somnolence and asthenia.

Dunner *et al* (1992) pooled the data of two independent trials of paroxetine versus doxepin, without reporting the results of the individual trials. They were able to show a similar efficacy to doxepin and even superiority in certain items (e.g. HRSD score, depressed mood or the CGIC severity of illness scale), although the dose of the comparator, as they state themselves, was fairly low. There were safety advantages of paroxetine, especially concerning anticholinergic side-effects, but in the paroxetine group more patients stopped the trial due to drug-related side-effects (19% *v.* 15%).

Möller & Volz (1993) reported on a total sample of 189 elderly patients who were randomised in a 2:1 ratio to either brofaromine or to imipramine. Brofaromine and imipramine were found to be similarly effective, but the lack of a placebo group makes it difficult to draw any final conclusion about overall efficacy. In terms of tolerability, brofaromine was superior to imipramine (not, however, in the intent-to-treat analysis), but there was no major difference concerning the relative number of adverse events (31.8% *v.* 35.9%). The major side-effects in the brofaromine group were restlessness, vertigo, nausea and headache, while in the imipramine group dryness of mouth, impaired vision, vertigo and headache were observed. Their paper discusses the problem of low dosing in the imipramine group (87 mg/day). A direct comparison with a result in a normal-aged group is possible, since the same design was used in another large trial (Möller & Volz, 1992).

Currently, few data are available to indicate for how long patients should take an antidepressant. Practice guidelines, however, suggest continuing the dose for six to eight weeks after the therapeutic dose has been satisfactorily established to determine an initial response. For the patient who has responded to the drug, it is recommended to continue for at least six months, to make certain that remission can be stabilised. Patients with histories of recurrent depression probably should be maintained on the antidepressant indefinitely to prevent recurrence. For bipolar patients, lithium should be the first choice for long-term treatment. With respect to elderly patients there are insufficient empirical data in this field, especially concerning long-term prophylactic treatment (McCue, 1992).

In cases of therapy resistance, strategies similar to those used for younger populations are suggested, among others augmentation therapy with lithium or, in cases of delusional depressions, combination with a neuroleptic. However, the empirical base is weaker than for younger populations. In cases of severe non-response, electroconvulsive therapy is indicated (Schneider & Olin, 1995) (Table 12.4).

Safety of antidepressant treatments for elderly patients

The safety of antidepressants is a very important issue, especially in the elderly. When choosing a tricyclic antidepressant to treat major depression in elderly patients, safety aspects influence the decision more than efficacy aspects.

Different pharmacological groups can be differentiated with respect to safety, as is the case with the antidepressant treatment of younger populations. The main groups are covered briefly below.

Tricyclic antidepressants. They have a well known complex side-effects profile, resulting from their interaction with several central nervous receptor sites. Blockade of muscarine receptors can cause dry mouth, tachycardia, sweating, urinary retention and confusion. Lack of tolerability can make it difficult to achieve the appropriate dose for an elderly patient. Postural hypotension and confusion, associated with tricyclics, can lead to falls, with devastating consequences in the elderly, such as hip fracture. Cognitive dysfunctions can be observed in the elderly treated with anticholinergic tricyclics. Because suicide is a potential risk in elderly depressed patients, the danger of overdosing must be recognised. A dose of more than 1500 mg of imipramine equivalents can be lethal. The secondary amine tricyclics nortriptyline (Hegerl & Möller, 1996) and desimipramine are considered safer than the tertiary amine tricyclics imipramine, amitriptyline and doxepine, and are preferred among the tricyclics for the treatment of the elderly depressed.

Selective serotonine reuptake inhibitors. Selective serotonin reuptake inhibitors (SSRIs) like fluoxetine, paroxetine, citalopram, fluvoxamine and sertraline may be especially beneficial for the elderly because of their selective mode of action (Phanjoo *et al*, 1991; Schöne & Ludwig, 1993). Their selectivity for serotonin receptors results in relatively few, mostly gastrointestinal side-effects, such as nausea. The SSRIs are usually free of cardiovascular effects; furthermore, they produce negligible, if any, anticholinergic, antihistaminic or alpha-adrenergic reactions. They do not interfere with cognitive function. There are

TABLE 12.4

Summary of acute treatments for major depression in elderly patients (adapted and modified from Schneider (1993) and Schneider & Olin (1995); for references refer to sources)

Treatment	Efficacy	Comments	References
Antidepressant medications	Numerous randomised, placebo-controlled trials of several tricyclics, bupropion, trazodone, and others. Trial results are for acute treatment responses	Adequate doses, plasma levels, and treatment duration are essential in order to maximise response. Response may take 6–12 weeks, somewhat longer than in younger patients. Side-effects may limit use	Plotkin *et al* (1987) Gerson *et al* (1988) Salzman (1994) Klawansky (1994) Schneider (1994) Georgotas *et al* (1986) Katz *et al* (1990) Nelson *et al* (1986) Friedhoff (1994)
Psychostimulants	Evidence of efficacy over the short term; onset of action is rapid; randomised trial results are limited; responders are usually converted to a standard antidepressant	Particularly in medically ill, hospitalised patients; when there is an increased risk from other antidepressants; and when rapid response may be needed	Satel & Nelson (1989) Pickett *et al* (1990)
Combined antidepressant and neuroleptic (anti-psychotic) medications	More effective than either medication alone for depression with delusions or severe agitation. However, electroconvulsive therapy is more effective than the combination		Nelson *et al* (1986) Abrams (1992)

Augmentation of antidepressants with lithium, thyroid medication, carbamazepine	Patients non-responsive to several weeks of treatment with standard antidepressant medications may respond rapidly after these medications are added. Evidence is based on case series and reports	May be useful for patients who are not responding or are only partially responding to standard antidepressant medications. Constitutes acceptable clinical practice	Finch & Katona (1989) Van Marwijk *et al* (1990) Zimmer *et al* (1991)
Electroconvulsive therapy	Clearly effective for severe depression, depression with melancholia or with delusions, and when antidepressants are not fully effective. Sometimes combined with antidepressants	In medication-resistant patients, acute response rate is approximately 50%. Relapse rate is high, requiring attention to maintenance antidepressant treatment. Favourable effect of increasing age	Abrams (1992) Sackheim (1994)
Combined antidepressant medication and psychotherapy	Effective in out-patients using manual-based therapies; the relative contributions of each component are not well understood	Combined therapy has not been adequately studied in the elderly	Reynolds *et al* (1992) Reynolds *et al* (1994) Gallagher-Thompson & Steffan (1994)

Percentage of reported side-effects/adverse events

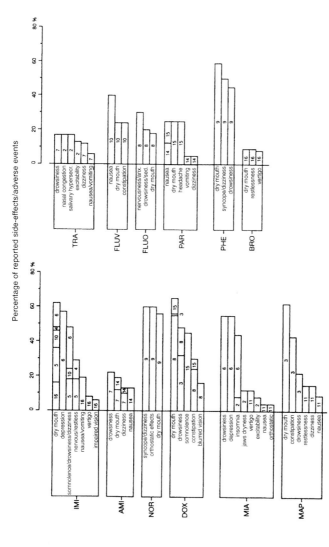

Fig. 12.3. *Percentages of reported side-effects or adverse events. Note that the percentages are not cumulative. The numbers in the columns are the index numbers shown in Table 12.3. The trials of Gerner et al (1980), De Leo et al (1984), Altamura et al (1989) and Fairbairn et al (1989) used different instruments for the documentation of side-effects and are not represented here, since these scores are not comparable with the (spontaneously) reported adverse experiences and side-effects. Since De Vanna et al (1990) did not report exact numbers, these results are also not represented (Volz & Möller, 1994; reproduced with permission from Georg Thieme Verlag).*

some data showing that in a group of patients with depressive illness, treatment with paroxetine produces more improvement of cognitive function than does fluoxetine (Dunner *et al*, 1992). In contrast, significant impairment of cognitive function was observed with tricyclics (Hindmarch, 1992). Safety in overdose might be of particular importance in the treatment of elderly patients.

Monoamine oxidase inhibitors. These drugs interact with thiamine-rich food, thus limiting their use in elderly patients (problem of hypertensive crisis). However, the selective MAO-A inhibitor moclobemide does not induce such problems and is generally well tolerated by elderly patients.

Coming back to our own review of the studies published since 1980, Fig. 12.3 gives an overall impression of safety and tolerability. This can only be an outline, since the ways in which the side-effects were ascertained differed significantly from trial to trial. The tricyclics show a clear predominance of anticholinergic side-effects, above all dry mouth and sedating effects, whereas the SSRIs show a predominance of nausea and vomiting, although dry mouth is also one of the most important side-effects in this group. This was also the most common symptom in the trials with MAO inhibitors, followed by syncopes and dizziness in the phenelzine trial and by restlessness in the brofaromine trial. Compared with classic antidepressants, there appear to be safety and tolerability advantages for SSRIs or MAO inhibitors, and this should have an effect on clinical practice since non-compliance – a practical problem in elderly patients – is often caused by side-effects. The new generation of antidepressants seems to possess a certain advantage in this field, so that their use in this patient group might especially increase compliance(Volz & Möller, 1994). However, some authors assume that the efficacy of an SSRI will be inferior to that of tricyclics in the treatment of severe depression (Roose *et al*, 1994).

Neuroleptic treatment of schizophrenia in the elderly

Neuroleptics are commonly used to treat schizophrenia and also exogenic psychosis in elderly patients (Harrington *et al*, 1992; Woerner *et al*, 1995). However, there are extremely few methodologically sound controlled trials of neuroleptic drugs in this population, especially of functional psychosis (Salzman, 1987).

Clinical experience and case reports indicate that the efficacy proven in younger schizophrenic patients may be extrapolated to elderly psychotic patients (Rabins *et al*, 1984; Makanjuola, 1985; Jeste *et al*, 1993). Whereas a few studies have documented the efficacy of antipsychotic drugs with well designed, placebo-controlled clinical

TABLE 12.5
Subject characteristics at study entry (n=166) (Woerner et al, 1995)

Mean (s.d.) age		
at study entry	76.8	(9.2)
at onset of neurological/psychiatric symptoms	72.6	(13.5)
at first in-patient treatment	73.0	(13.8)
Mean (s.d.) years of education	10.6	(3.6)
Gender: *n* (%)		
male	67	(25)
female	199	(75)
Primary presenting complaint: *n* (%)		
medical	11	(4)
neurological	62	(23)
psychiatric	151	(57)
multiple	41	(16)
Organic mental syndrome diagnosis: *n* (%)[1]		
none	93	(35)
dementia (Alzheimer's or multi-infarct)	84	(32)
other or mixed syndromes	88	(33)
Other axis I psychiatric diagnosis: *n* (%)[1]		
none	148	(56)
schizophrenia or schizoaffective disorder	13	(5)
affective disorder	81	(30)
other	24	(9)

1. Thirty patients had both an organic mental syndrome diagnosis and another axis I psychiatric diagnosis; six had neither.

trials in older patients with schizophrenia, little is known about the treatment of schizophrenia in patients over the age of 75 years. Data concerning the use of the newer drugs in late-life psychosis are extremely limited. There are initial studies suggesting that clozapine and also risperidone are efficacious (Jeste *et al*, 1996).

The American epidemiological survey by Saltz *et al* (1991) (see also Woerner *et al*, 1995), which included patients from different institutions like psychiatric and geriatric medical services, demonstrated that treatment of schizophrenia or schizoaffective disorders is only a small part of neuroleptic treatment in this population (Table 12.5). The study also gives certain impressions about neuroleptics of first choice for these patients (Table 12.6). A clear drug of choice at all sites included in the study was haloperidol, prescribed for 68% of the patients.

TABLE 12.6
Neuroleptics of choice (neuroleptic first prescribed) (n=266) (Woerner et al, 1995)

Drug	No. of patients	%
Haloperidol	182	68
Perphenazine	34	13
Thioridazine	24	9
Thiothixene	17	6
Chlorpromazine	4	2
Molindone	2	1
Mesoridazine	1	
Loxapine	1	1
Prochlorperazine	1	

Efficacy of neuroleptic treatment in elderly patients

A Department of Veterans' Affairs cooperative project, involving 13 hospitals and 308 men with schizophrenia aged 54–74 years (medium 66 years), investigated the role of phenothiazines in the treatment of schizophrenia (Honigfeld *et al*, 1965). In this 24-week, double-blind, placebo-controlled study, acetophenazine and trifluoperazine were significantly more effective than placebo in treating symptoms of schizophrenia.

In a sample of 50 psychogeriatric patients, with chronic schizophrenia representing the largest group, Tsuang *et al* (1971) compared the antipsychotic efficacy of haloperidol and thioridazine in a 12-week, double-blind study of actively psychotic patients over the age of 60 years. The authors reported significant decreases in a number of areas of schizophrenic psychopathology for both groups.

Branchey *et al* (1978) compared the efficacy of orally administered fluphenazine with thioridazine in patients with chronic schizophrenia (mean age 67 years) in a double-blind crossover study. Both of these phenothiazines produced modest but significant improvements in schizophrenic psychopathology compared with the ratings at the end of the placebo wash-out period.

Some other investigators (Janzarik, 1957; Kay & Roth, 1961; Post, 1966; Herbert & Jacobson, 1967; Rabins *et al*, 1984; Craig & Bregman, 1988; Jeste *et al*, 1988) have also reported the response of older patients with schizophrenia to neuroleptics. These studies, however, are limited in their scientific value because of their open, uncontrolled design. Nevertheless, in most of these studies, the neuroleptic therapy produced a positive outcome in terms of remission or reduction of symptoms.

The available data suggest that all the commonly prescribed antipsychotic medications are equally efficacious: there is no evidence that any one class of neuroleptics is more effective in reducing symptoms of schizophrenia when given in equivalent dosages (Jeste *et al*, 1993). Therefore the selection of antipsychotics for elderly patients should be based primarily on the side-effect profile of the particular drug.

Ageing of patients with schizophrenia is associated with remission or a marked improvement in at least one-third of subjects (McGlashan, 1988). This fact, coupled with a high risk of tardive dyskinesia in older patients, suggests that neuroleptic withdrawal should be an important therapeutic consideration in this patient population. Unfortunately, the literature on the subject of neuroleptic withdrawal in older patients with schizophrenia (over 45 years) is sparse. Furthermore, the published studies have several methodological problems, including the lack of specific diagnostic criteria in some studies, variable methods and materials, relatively small sample sizes and incomplete presentation of data. There are only six double-blind controlled studies that include patients with schizophrenia of mean age over 45 years (Table 12.7).

The mean rate of relapse for the neuroleptic-withdrawn groups in the six studies was about 40%, while that for the neuroleptic-maintained groups was about 11%. Nevertheless, given that almost 60% of the patients withdrawn from neuroleptics did not relapse over a mean period of six months, it seems feasible to discontinue neuroleptic medication from a selected population of older patients with schizophrenia, if it is done carefully with adequate monitoring on follow-up (Jeste *et al*, 1993).

Safety of neuroleptic treatment in the elderly

The side-effect profiles of individual neuroleptics differ considerably and such differences may be important when prescribing a particular medication to a patient for whom the occurrence of a particular side-effect might prove dangerous. For example, in patients with Parkinsonian symptoms, high-potency antipsychotics may worsen tremor and rigidity. On the other hand, high-potency neuroleptics are reported to cause less cardiovascular toxicity than low-potency neuroleptics (Ereshefsky & Richards, 1992). Hence highly potent drugs like haloperidol may be a better choice than low-potency neuroleptics among patients with cardiovascular disorders. Low-potency neuroleptics also have marked anticholinergic activity and should be avoided in patients with prostatic hypertrophy or in those who are already on other anticholinergics.

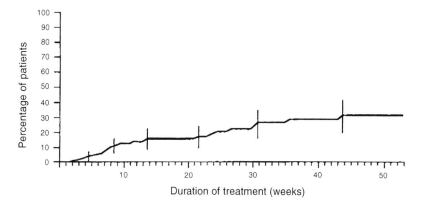

Fig. 12.4. Percentage of patients developing tardive dyskinesia by weeks of neuroleptic treatment. Vertical bars indicate 95% confidence intervals (Saltz et al, 1991; reproduced with permission from the American Medical Association).

There is mounting evidence that geriatric patients are especially sensitive to neuroleptic side-effects, specifically the anticholinergic side-effects of the phenothiazine type of neuroleptic and the extra-pyramidal side-effects, especially of the butyrophenone type of neuroleptic. The risk of tardive dyskinesia, in particular, should be considered. In the study by Saltz *et al* (1991), 31% of patients developed tardive dyskinesia after about 43 weeks of cumulative neuroleptic exposure (Fig. 12.4). It should be noted that these results were obtained with comparatively low doses of neuroleptic, because in most cases the indication for the neuroleptic treatment was not functional psychosis but behavioural disturbance. Within elderly populations, the duration of exposure to neuroleptics is the strongest predictor of risk for tardive dyskinesia, and this risk increases rapidly within the first year of total lifetime neuroleptic use (Sweet *et al*, 1995).

To avoid extrapyramidal side-effects and especially tardive dys-kinesia, clozapine has been suggested as an alternative treatment (Oberholzer *et al*, 1992). However, the severe anticholinergic side-effects of clozapine and also the disturbance of cardiovascular regulation and problems like delirium, falls, bradycardia and so on limit the administration of this drug in elderly patients (Pitner *et al*, 1995).

The basic principle in treating elderly patients with antipsychotics is to start low and go slow. Titration rates of antipsychotic drugs depend

TABLE 12.7 (part I, see also below)

Literature review on neuroleptic withdrawal in patients with schizophrenia over the age of 45 (Jeste et al, 1993; for references see source)

Authors	n	Mean age	Mean hospital stay (years)	Neuroleptic	Concurrent medications	Study design
Olson & Peterson (1962)	60	51	1.5	CPZ, thioridazine	NS	Double-blind with placebo
Whittaker & Hoy (1963)	26	50	15.5	Perphenazine	Antiparkinsonian or phenadrine	Double-blind with placebo
Rassidakis et al (1970)	43 (33 with SZ)	49.3	NS	Thioridazine, haloperidol, CPZ	Antiparkinsonian	Open
Hershon et al (1972)	32	57	NS	Trifluoperazine	Antiparkinsonian	Double-blind with placebo
Andrews et al (1976)	17	About 57	6	CPZ	NS	Double-blind with placebo
Ruskin & Nyman (1991)	10	60	NS	Haloperidol	NS	Double-blind with placebo

Note: CPZ, chlorpromazine; NS, not specified; SZ, schizophrenia; BPRS, Brief Psychiatric Rating Scale.

TABLE 12.7 (part II)
Literature review on neuroleptic withdrawal in patients with schizophrenia over the age of 45 (Jeste et al, 1993; for references see source)

Authors	Follow-up (months)	% Relapse (time: months)	Predictors of relapse	Other findings
Olson & Peterson (1962)	6	29% (6 with placebo)	Higher ratings of 'moderate depression' on the 'Distress' scale	Phenothiazines may have an activating effect on chronic patients
Whittaker & Hoy (1963)	2.5	39% (2.5)	None identified	Four patients were seen to regress "to a state markedly worse" than before
Rassidakis *et al* (1970)	9	58.1% (9)	Younger age at onset, younger current age, and non-paranoid subtype	No withdrawal effects were noted
Hershon *et al* (1972)	4	28.1% (4)	Younger current age, longer duration of neuroleptic treatment, higher previous neuroleptic dose	Motor restlesness, but not parkinsonism or dyskinesia, increased after neuroleptic withdrawal
Andrews *et al* (1976)	10.5	35% (10.5)	Higher previous neuroleptic dose	Relapsers had increased social withdrawal after neuroleptic discontinuation
Ruskin & Nyman (1991)	6	50% (6)	Younger age, higher previous neuroleptic dose, higher baseline BPRS, recent psychiatric hospitalisation	Patients who relapsed reconstituted rapidly after neuroleptics were restarted

BPRS, Brief Psychiatric Rating Scale.

on the elderly patient's characteristics. Medical comorbidity should be taken into consideration as well as concomitant medication. The starting dose of antipsychotic drugs in older patients should be in the region of 25–50% of that recommended for younger patients (Gregory & McKenna, 1994).

References

ALTAMURA, A. C., MAURI, M. C., COLACURCIO, F., *et al* (1988) Trazodone in late life depressive states: a double-blind multicenter study of amitriptyline and mianserin. *Psychopharmacology Berlin*, **95** (suppl.), S34–S36.
——, ——, RUDAS, N., *et al* (1989) Clinical activity and tolerability of trazodone, mianserin, and amitriptyline in elderly subjects with major depression: a controlled multicenter trial. *Clinical Neuropharmacology*, **12** (suppl. 1), S25–S33.
ATHER, S. A., ANKIER, S. I. & MIDDLETON, R. S. (1985) A double-blind evaluation of trazodone in the treatment of depression in the elderly. *British Journal of Clinical Practice*, **39**, 192–199.
BRAITHWAITE, R. (1982) Pharmacokinetics and age. In *Psychopharmacology of Old Age* (ed. D. Wheatley), pp. 46–54. Oxford: Oxford University Press.
BRANCHEY, M. H., LEE, J. H., AMIN, R. & SIMPSON, G. M. (1978) High- and low-potency neuroleptics in elderly psychiatric patients. *Journal of the American Medical Association*, **239**, 1860–1862.
CASTLEDEN, C. M., GEORGE, C. F., MARCER, D., *et al* (1977) Increased sensitivity to nitrazepam in old age. *British Medical Journal*, i, 10–12.
COHN, J. B., VARGA, L. & LYFORD, A. (1984) A two-center double-blind study of nomifensine, imipramine, and placebo in depressed geriatric outpatients. *Journal of Clinical Psychiatry*, **45**, 68–72.
CRAIG, T. J. & BREGMAN, Z. (1988) Late onset schizophrenia-like illness. *Journal of the American Geriatric Society*, **36**, 104–107.
CROME, P. & DAWLING, S. (1989) Pharmacokinetics of tricyclic and related antidepressants. In *Antidepressants for Elderly People* (ed. K. Ghose), pp. 117–136. London: Chapman and Hall.
DE LEO, D., CEOLA, A. & MAGNI, G. (1984) Viloxazine against placebo in a double-blind study in depressed elderly patients. *Current Therapy Research*, **36**, 234–244.
DE VANNA, M., KUMMER, J., AGNOLI, A., *et al* (1990) Moclobemide compared with second-generation antidepressants in elderly people. *Acta Psychiatrica Scandinavica* (suppl. 360), 64–66.
DUNNER, D. L. (1994) Therapeutic considerations in treating depression in the elderly. *Journal of Clinical Psychiatry*, **55** (suppl.), 48–58.
——, COHN, J. B., WALSHE, T., *et al* (1992) Two combined, multicenter double-blind studies of paroxetine and doxepin in geriatric patients with major depression. *Journal of Clinical Psychiatry*, **53** (suppl.), 57–60.
EKLUND, K., DUNBAR, G. C., PINDER, R. M., *et al* (1985) Mianserin and imipramine in the treatment of elderly depressed patients. *Acta Psychiatrica Scandinavica* (suppl. 320), 55–59.
ERESHEFSKY, L. & RICHARDS, A. L. (1992) Psychoses. In *Applied Therapeutics: The Clinical Use of Drugs* (eds M. A. Koda-Kimble, L. Y. Young, W. A. Kradjan & B. J. Guglielmo), pp. 1–42. Vancouver: Applied Therapeutics.
FAIRBAIRN, A. F., GEORGE, K. & DORMAN, T. (1989) Lofepramine versus dothiepin in the treatment of depression in elderly patients. *British Journal of Clinical Practice*, **43**, 55–60.

FEIGHNER, J. P. & COHN, J. B. (1985) Double-blind comparative trials of fluoxetine and doxepin in geriatric patients with major depressive disorder. *Journal of Clinical Psychiatry*, **46**, 20–25.

——, BOYER, W. F., MEREDITH, C. H., *et al* (1988) An overview of fluoxetine in geriatric depression. *British Journal of Psychiatry*, **153** (suppl. 3), 105–108.

GEORGOTAS, A. & McCUE, R. E. (1989) The additional benefit of extending an antidepressant trial past seven weeks in the depressed elderly. *International Journal of Geriatric Psychiatry*, **4**, 191–195.

——, ——, HAPWORTH, W., *et al* (1986) Comparative efficacy and safety of MAOIs versus TCAs in treating depression in the elderly. *Biological Psychiatry*, **21**, 1155–1166.

GERNER, R., ESTABROOK, W., STEUER, J., *et al* (1980) Treatment of geriatric depression with trazodone, imipramine, and placebo: a double-blind study. *Journal of Clinical Psychiatry*, **41**, 216–220.

GREGORY, C. & McKENNA, P. (1994) Pharmacological management of schizophrenia in older patients. *Drugs and Aging*, **5**, 254–262.

GWIRTSMAN, H. E., AHLES, S., HALARIS, A., *et al* (1983) Therapeutic superiority of maprotiline versus doxepin in geriatric depression. *Journal of Clinical Psychiatry*, **44**, 449–453.

HALIKAS, J. A. (1995) Org 3770 (Mirtazapin) versus trazodone: a placebo controlled trial in depressed elderly patients. *Human Psychopharmacology*, **10**, 125–133.

HAMPEL, H., REITZ, B., BERGER, C., *et al* (1999) A decade of psychopharmacological treatment in elderly psychiatric patients. *Annals of Neurology*, in press.

HARRINGTON, C., TOMPKINS, C., CURTIS, M., *et al* (1992) Psychotropic drug use in long-term care facilities: a review of the literature. *Gerontologist*, **32**, 822–833.

HEGERL, U. & MÖLLER, H. J. (1996) Nortriptylin. *Psychopharmakotherapie*, **1**, 13–27.

HERBERT, M. E. & JACOBSON, S. (1967) Late paraphrenia. *British Journal of Psychiatry*, **113**, 461–469.

HINDMARCH, I. (1992) A review of the psychomotor effects of paroxetine. *International Clinical Psychopharmacology*, **6** (suppl. 4), 65–67.

HONIGFELD, G., ROSENBAUM, M. P., BLUMENTHAL, I. J., *et al* (1965) Behavioral improvement in the older schizophrenic patient: drug and social therapies. *Journal of the American Geriatric Society*, **13**, 57–71.

HOYBERG, O. J., MARAGAKIS, B., MULLIN, J., *et al* (1996) A double-blind multicentre comparison of mirtazapin and amitriptyline in elderly depressed patients. *Acta Psychiatrica Scandinavica*, **93**, 184–190.

HUTCHINSON, D. R., TONG, S., MOON, C. A. L., *et al* (1991) Paroxetine in the treatment of elderly depressed patients in general practice. A double blind comparison with amitriptyline. *British Journal of Clinical Research*, **2**, 43–57.

JANZARIK, W. (1957) Zur Problematik schizophrener Psychosen in hoheren Lebensalter. *Nervenarzt*, **28**, 535–542.

JESTE, D. V., HARRIS, M. J., PEARLSON, G. D., *et al* (1988) Late-onset schizophrenia. Studying clinical validity. *Psychiatric Clinics of North America*, **11**, 1–13.

——, LACRO, J. P., GILBERT, P. L., *et al* (1993) Treatment of late-life schizophrenia with neuroleptics. *Schizophrenia Bulletin*, **19**, 817–830.

——, EASTHAM, J. H., LACRO, J. P., *et al* (1996) Management of late-life psychosis. *Journal of Clinical Psychiatry*, **57** (suppl. 3), 39–45.

KAY, D. W. K. & ROTH, M. (1961) Environmental and hereditary factors in the schizophrenics of old age ("late paraphrenia") and their bearing on the general problem of causation in schizophrenia. *Journal of Mental Science*, **107**, 649–686.

MAKANJUOLA, R. O. (1985) Psychiatric disorders in elderly Nigerians. *Tropical and Geographical Medicine*, **37**, 348–351.

McCUE, R. E. (1992) Using tricyclic antidepressants in the elderly. *Clinics in Geriatric Medicine*, **8**, 323–334.

McGLASHAN, T. H. (1988) A selective review of recent North American long-term follow-up studies of schizophrenia. *Schizophrenia Bulletin*, **14**, 515–542.

174 *Möller*

MERIDETH, C. H., FEIGHNER, J. P. & HENDRICKSON, G. (1984) A double-blind comparative evaluation of the efficacy and safety of nomifensine, imipramine, and placebo in depressed geriatric outpatients. *Journal of Clinical Psychiatry*, **45**, 73–77.

MÖLLER, H. J. & VOLZ, H. P. (1992) Brofaromine in major depressed patients: a controlled clinical trial versus imipramine and open follow-up of up to one year. *Journal of Affective Disorders*, **26**, 163–172.

—— & —— (1993) Brofaromine in elderly major depressed patients – a comparative trial versus imipramine. *European Neuropsychopharmacology*, **3**, 501–510.

NIES, A., ROBINSON, D. S., FRIEDMAN, M. J., *et al* (1977) Relationship between age and tricyclic antidepressant plasma levels. *American Journal of Psychiatry*, **134**, 790–793.

NORMAN, T. R. (1993) Pharmacokinetic aspects of antidepressant treatment in the elderly. *Progress in Neuropsychopharmacology and Biological Psychiatry*, **17**, 329–344.

OBERHOLZER, A. F., HENDRIKSEN, C., MONSCH, A. U., *et al* (1992) Safety and effectiveness of low-dose clozapine in psychogeriatric patients: a preliminary study. *International Psychogeriatrics*, **4**, 187–195.

PHANJOO, A. L., WONNACOTT, S. & HODGSON, A. (1991) Double-blind comparative multicentre study of fluvoxamine and mianserin in the treatment of major depressive episode in elderly people. *Acta Psychiatrica Scandinavica*, **83**, 476–479.

PITNER, J. K., MINTZER, J. E., PENNYPACKER, L. C., *et al* (1995) Efficacy and adverse effects of clozapine in four elderly psychotic patients. *Journal of Clinical Psychiatry*, **56**, 180–185.

PLOTKIN, D. A., GERSON, S. C. & JARVIK, L. F. (1987) Antidepressant drug treatment in the elderly. In *Psychopharmacology: The Third Generation of Progress* (ed. H. Y. Meltzer), pp. 1149–1158. New York: Raven Press.

POST, F. (1966) *Persistent Persecutory States of the Elderly*. London: Pergamon Press.

RABINS, P., PAUKER, S. & THOMAS, J. (1984) Can schizophrenia begin after age 44? *Comprehensive Psychiatry*, **25**, 290–293.

ROOSE, S. P., GLASSMAN, A. H., ATTIA, *et al* (1994) Comparative efficacy of selective serotonin reuptake inhibitors and tricyclics in the treatment of melancholia. *American Journal of Psychiatry*, **151**, 1735–1739.

SALTZ, B. L., WOERNER, M. G., KANE, J. M., *et al* (1991) Prospective study of tardive dyskinesia incidence in the elderly. *Journal of the American Medical Association*, **266**, 2402–2406.

SALZMAN, C. (1987) Treatment of agitation in the elderly. In *Psychopharmacology: The Third Generation in Progress* (ed. H. Meltzer), pp. 1167–1176. New York: Raven Press.

——, SCHNEIDER, L. S. & ALEXOPOULOS, G. (1995) Treatment of depression in the elderly. In *Psychopharmacology: Fourth Generation of Progress* (eds F. Bloom & D. Kupfer), pp. 1471–1477. New York: Raven Press.

SCARDIGLI, G. & JANS, G. (1982) Comparative double-blind study on efficacy and side-effects of trazodone, nomifensine, mianserin in elderly patients. In *Typical and Atypical Antidepressants: Clinical Practice* (eds E. Costa & G. Racagni), pp. 229–236. New York: Raven Press.

SCHNEIDER, L. S. (1993) Efficacy of treatment for geripsychiatric patients with severe mental illness. *Psychopharmacology Bulletin*, **29**, 501–524.

—— & OLIN, J. T. (1995) Efficacy of acute treatment for geriatric depression. *International Psychogeriatrics*, **7** (suppl.), 7–25.

SCHÖNE, W. & LUDWIG, M. (1993) A double-blind study of paroxetine compared with fluoxetine in geriatric patients with major depression. *Journal of Clinical Psychopharmacology*, **13**, 34S–39S.

SHELDON, J. H. (1963) The effect of age on the control sway. *Gerontologia Clinica*, **5**, 129–138.

SIEGFRIED, K. & O'CONNOLLY, M. (1986) Cognitive and psychomotor effects of different antidepressants in the treatment of old age depression. *International Clinical Psychopharmacology*, **1**, 231–243.

STEWART, R. B. (1993) Advances in pharmacotherapy: depression in the elderly – issues and advances in treatment. *Journal of Clinical Pharmacy and Therapeutics*, **18**, 243–253.

SWEET, R. A., MULSANT, B. H., GUPTA, B., *et al* (1995) Duration of neuroleptic treatment and prevalence of tardive dyskinesia in late life. *Archives of General Psychiatry*, **52**, 478–486.

SWIFT, C. G. (1990) Pharmacodynamics: changes in homeostatic mechanisms, receptor and target organ sensitivity in the elderly. *British Medical Bulletin*, **46**, 36–52.

——, SWIFT, M. R., HAMLEY, J., *et al* (1984) Side-effect 'tolerance' in elderly long-term recipients of benzodiazepine hypnotics. *Age and Ageing*, **13**, 335–343.

——, EWEN, J. M., CLARKE, P., *et al* (1985a) Responsiveness to oral diazepam in the elderly: relationship to total and free plasma concentrations. *British Journal of Clinical Pharmacology*, **20**, 111–118.

——, SWIFT, M. R., ANKIER, S. I., *et al* (1985b) Single dose pharmacokinetics and pharmacodynamics of oral loprazolam in the elderly. *British Journal of Clinical Pharmacology*, **20**, 119–128.

TRAN-JOHNSON, T. K., KRULL, A. J. & JESTE, D. V. (1992) Late life schizophrenia and its treatment: pharmacologic issues in older schizophrenic patients. *Clinics in Geriatric Medicine*, **8**, 401–410.

TSUANG, M. M., LU, L. M., STOTSKY, B. A. & COLE, J. O. (1971) Haloperidol versus thioridazine for hospitalized psychogeriatric patients: double-blind study. *Journal of the American Geriatric Society*, **19**, 593–600.

VOLZ, H. P. & MÖLLER, H. J. (1994) Antidepressant drug therapy in the elderly – a critical review of the controlled clinical trials conducted since 1980. *Pharmacopsychiatry*, **27**, 93–100.

——, MÜLLER, H. & MÖLLER, H. J. (1995) Are there any differences in the safety and efficacy of brofaromine and imipramine between non-elderly and elderly patients with major depression? *Neuropsychobiology*, **32**, 23–30.

WAKELIN, J. S. (1986) Fluvoxamine in the treatment of the older depressed patient: double-blind, placebo-controlled data. *International Clinical Psychopharmacology*, **1**, 221–230.

WOERNER, M. G., ALVIR, J. M., KANE, J. M., *et al* (1995) Neuroleptic treatment of elderly patients. *Psychopharmacology Bulletin*, **31**, 333–337.

13 Antidementia drugs

H.-J. GERTZ and H. WOLF

The term 'nootropic drug' was coined by Giurgia in 1976 for when it was found that piracetam had an effect on animal brains. Since then it has been widely used in central Europe as a descriptive term for all drugs which are believed to improve cognitive deficits in aged people, including patients with dementia (Gertz, 1997). However, compounds with a presumably logical background to their development have since appeared, such as calcium antagonists or cholinomimetics, and it has become unclear whether such substances are covered by the term 'nootropics'. The term 'antidementia drugs' has therefore been introduced in Germany as a general term for all drugs which are believed to be useful in the treatment of dementia.

National heterogeneity in the administration of antidementia drugs

Drug therapy of psychiatric patients in the developed countries is supposedly based on results of scientific studies. The demonstration of sufficient therapeutic effects is believed to justify their application. Such studies have been conducted with several antidementia drugs; however, the perception of the results varies considerably between different countries. There is probably no other field in psychopharmacology in which national and cultural influences cause a comparable variability in practice.

Table 13.1 gives an overview of the application of antidementia drugs in selected countries. In 1992 the world market for nootropics and for cerebral vasotherapy amounted to approximately 6.6 billion DM, out of which ginkgo biloba accounted for 500 million DM, prescribed mainly in France and Germany. It appears that in Europe most prescriptions of these compounds are made in France, Germany and Italy, followed by Spain, and Holland. Japan tops the list worldwide.

TABLE 13.1
Sales and geographical breakdown of antidementia drugs (1992)

	DM (millions)
Japan	2315.0
France	985.0
Germany	807.5
Italy	900.0
Spain	265.0
USA	252.5
Canada	17.5
Netherlands	10.0
Australia	0

In Germany several antidementia drugs have been used for many years, some even for decades. At the end of the 1980s, the Bundesgesundheitsamt and the Bundesinstitut für Arzneimittel und Medizinprodukte, respectively, introduced a commission to re-evaluate the existing scientific literature about the efficacy of these drugs. Unfortunately, the commission was discharged before its task had been finished. This is probably the reason why some promising substances have never been officially approved to date; amantadine is an example of such a substance. Table 13.2 shows the nootropic drugs which have received the official approval of the German authorities.

Antidementia drugs approved in Germany

Dihydroergotoxin

Co-Dergocrine-Mesilate contains dihydroergocostrine, dihydro-alpha-ergocryptine, dihydro-beta-ergocryptine, and dihydrocornine in a standardised proportion. Like most secale alkaloids, it displays a wide spectrum of pharmacological effects which cannot be explained by one single basic mechanism on a cellular or molecular level.

In human and animal studies it was shown to block alpha-adreno-receptors (Flückinger & Balthasar, 1967; Berde, 1972). Berde (1972) and Wennmalm (1971) found a positive effect on noradrenaline release in cats and rabbits. It appears to influence the dopaminergic system through its affinity with pre- and postsynaptic dopamine receptors, leading to a long-lasting antagonism of the inhibiting effect of dopamine (Goldstein *et al*, 1978). In the serotonergic system, agonistic effects have been demonstrated (Wright *et al*, 1962). Peripherally, it displays antiserotonergic effects *in vitro*.

TABLE 13.2
Nootropic drugs approved by the Bundesinstitut für Arzneimittel und Medizinprodukte

Substance	Daily dose	Side-effects
Dihydroergotoxin	4–8 mg	Hypotension, vertigo
Piracetam	2.4–4.8 g	Agitation, aggressive behaviour, hypersexuality
Pyritinol	600–800 mg	Loss of appetite, nausea
Nimodipine	90 mg	Hypotension
Nicergoline	15–30 mg	Vertigo, hypotension, sedation
Ginkgo biloba	120 mg	Gastrointestinal upset, headaches, allergic skin reaction
Tetrahydroaminoacridine	160 mg	Elevation of liver enzymes (ALAT), diarrhoea, nausea, vomiting

Although there is no effect on cholinergic receptors (Closse *et al*, 1984), it influences the cholinergic system through cerebral catecholamine increase in old rats (Dravid & Hiestand, 1985) and increases the density of acetylcholine receptors (Le Poncin-Lafitte *et al*, 1985). Bertoni-Freddari *et al* (1987) found positive effects of dihydroergotoxin on synaptic plasticity.

In animal studies, several authors have reported positive effects in states of altered brain metabolism, namely transient ischaemia, hypovolaemic shock and hyperthermia, which are accompanied by improved glucose and oxygen utilisation and absorption (Wiernsperger *et al*, 1978). These findings have been confirmed by clinical positron emission tomography (PET) studies, which showed an improved glucose metabolism in patients suffering from dementia. In animal studies dihydroergotoxin has been shown to improve cerebral microcirculation.

Ginkgo biloba

The usual ginkgo preparations in Western countries contain the extracts Egb 761 or LI 1370, which are standardised on the amount of ginkgo-flavon-glycosides (24% and 25%) and terpinoids (6%). It is not known whether the effects of ginkgo are caused by single active ingredients or by the combined action of several agents. Ginkgo-flavon-glycosides with kaempferol, quercetin and isorhamnetin, and terpinoids with the ginkgolides A, B, C, are considered to be the most important components (Kleijnen & Knipschild, 1992).

Extracts of dried leaves of the ginkgo biloba tree (maidenhair tree) have been known as therapeutic agents for centuries.

Of the several mechanisms of action which could explain its therapeutic role in different stages of the decline of intellectual functions, four shall be mentioned.

First, it increases blood flow through its vasoregulating activity (Költringer *et al*, 1989; Jung *et al*, 1990). This is probably caused by the combined action of several compounds.

Second, the ginkgolides, in particular ginkgolide B, are platelet aggregation factor (PAF) antagonists, thus leading to an inhibition of platelet aggregation, neutrophil degranulation and oxygen-radical production (Braquet & Hosford, 1991).

Third, metabolic changes, in particular changes in neuron metabolism and beneficial influences on neurotransmitter disturbances, have been reported by De Feudis (1991).

Fourth, free-radical scavenging properties – in particular of flavinoids – have been demonstrated by Pincemail *et al* (1989) and others. By prolonging the half-life of endothelium-derived growth factor, this results in a relaxation of contracted blood vessels (Robak & Gryglewski, 1988).

Nicergoline

Nicergoline is a semisynthetic ergoline derivative which was developed in the search for a strong inhibitor of alpha-adrenergic receptors.

It has been assessed in animal and human pharmacological studies and its improvement of the global cerebral blood flow has been demonstrated in both (Le Poncin-Lafitte *et al*, 1984). Its main pharmacological effects (global improvement of altered brain metabolism) must be considered to be independent of vasodilatory mechanisms (Boismare & Lorenzo 1975) – they are rather due to its influences on glucose (Benzi *et al*, 1972; Le Poncine-Lafitte *et al*, 1984), protein and nucleic acid metabolisms (Rossi *et al*, 1988). Maiolo *et al* (1972) found an increased oxygen utilisation, and Shintomi *et al* (1987) an increased activity of the cerebral cytochromoxidase. It also seems to affect neuronal membrane metabolism (Benzi *et al*, 1979).

Nimodipine

Like all calcium antagonists, nimodipine inhibits calcium transport through receptor-activated channels and membranes, and leads to relaxation of smooth-muscle cells (Van Zwieten, 1986). It has been suggested that excessive calcium influx represents the final common pathway of neuronal death after various insults, such as hypoglycaemia, excitotoxin release and hypoxia. Furthermore, tangle-like changes in tau have been associated with calcium influx (Cheng & Mattson, 1992).

In most species, nimodipine seems to display selectively enhanced effects on cerebral vessels. It antagonises the vasoconstrictory effects of vasoactive substances such as potassium chloride, thromboxan A2, and serotonin (Towart & Kazda, 1985), and has been shown to display direct cerebrovascular effects, preferentially on arterioles, in animal experiments and a few human experimental studies (Schmidli *et al*, 1985; Takayasu *et al*, 1988). In human stroke, nimodipine improves functional impairment of morphologically intact tissue surrounding an ischaemic focus and the metabolic deactivation of remote brain regions (Hakim *et al*, 1989). Neuroprotective (Hoffmeister *et al*, 1982), anticonvulsive (Meyer *et al*, 1986), and antiamnestic (Zhang & Cheng, 1986) effects have been studied and discussed by several authors. In animal models, studies indicate that altered calcium homeostasis in ageing hippocampal neurons may be the basis for age-associated memory loss and that the use of nimodipine may facilitate learning (Deyo *et al*, 1989).

Piracetam

Piracetam is the prototypic nootropic, a cyclic relative of gamma-aminobutyric acid (GABA). Its pharmacological effects have been extensively assessed in experimental animals. Different enzymes involved in glucose metabolism have been found to be influenced by piracetam. It is believed to protect rabbits and other rodents from hypoxia-induced amnesia and electroconvulsive-shock-induced amnesia, and to reverse scopolamine-induced amnesia in mice. Moreover, Nybäck *et al* (1979) found an increase in dopamine release, and Wurtmann *et al* (1981) described an increased release of acetylcholine in the hippocampus and striatum. Müller (1988) reported an increased density of cholinergic receptors.

Pyritinol

The main pharmacological effect of pyritinol is the improvement of brain metabolic alterations in states of hypoxia, ischaemia and intoxication. In animal studies, an increase in glucose uptake and utilisation (Greiner *et al*, 1988) has been found. Furthermore, it affects the metabolisation of nucleic acids (Kanig, 1974) and neuronal membranes by significantly increasing phospholipid levels (Martin & Widdowson, 1989). It also influences cortical acetylcholine release and cholinergic transmission (Greiner *et al*, 1988), stabilises damaged membranes by inhibiting lysosomal enzymes, and prevents the formation of free radicals (Benesova *et al*, 1982; Pavlik & Pilar, 1989).

In experimental animals it had positive effects on locomotor activity, coordination and cognitive functions (Marston *et al*, 1987). In human pharmacological and clinical studies, electroencephalography changes typical of increased vigilance have been demonstrated (Ihl *et al*, 1988).

Herrschaft (1978) found positive effects on the regional cerebral blood flow of patients with vascular dementia, Mubrin *et al* (1989) described an improvement of cerebral blood flow, in particular in ischaemic areas in patients with Alzheimer's disease. Wieding *et al* (1987) demonstrated positive haemodynamic effects of pyritinol which are believed to be due to an increased concentration of adenosine triphosphate in red blood cells.

Tacrine

Tacrine, 9-amino-1,2,3,4-tetrahydroaminoacridine (THA), is a synthetic acetylcholinesterase inhibitor. It has been shown to increase pre-synaptic acetylcholine release by blocking slow potassium channels, and to increase postsynaptic monoaminergic stimulation by interfering with noradrenaline and serotonin uptake. These latter characteristics occur at concentrations higher than those required to achieve acetylcholinesterase inhibition, and therefore probably do not con-tribute to the drug's clinical effects.

Clinical studies

Short-term effects

Given the immense diversity in prescribing practice in different countries, it would be useful to obtain objective comparative data on the efficacy of the various drugs. Such data would help to resolve issues such as the use of tacrine in the USA as the only accepted pharma-cological therapy for Alzheimer's disease, whereas other nootropics which are approved in European countries are not approved in the USA. Nimodipine, for instance, was not found to be sufficiently effective in the treatment of dementia by the US Food and Drug Administration (FDA). It received the FDA approval only for the treatment of intracerebral haemorrhage. On the other hand, tacrine was not approved as an antidementia drug in the UK.

Most of the compounds discussed here have been tested extensively in several independent studies for their clinical efficacy. However, older studies in particular often had vague diagnostic inclusion criteria. Most studies with nicergoline and hydergine have been performed in Italy. The methods used remain unclear in many instances. In recent years, some sound studies have been conducted with piracetam, nimodipine and tacrine. Those with tacrine, in particular, have initiated a more sophisticated discussion about methodological issues.

Double-blind, placebo-controlled studies have assessed the efficacy of tacrine in large samples of patients with Alzheimer's disease (Chatellier *et al*, 1990; Gauthier *et al*, 1990; Cheng & Mattson, 1992; Davis *et al*, 1992; Farlow *et al*, 1992). Tacrine and lecithin produced statistically significant improvements in score on the Mini-Mental State Examination in two investigations of Alzheimer's disease (Gauthier *et al*, 1990; Eagger *et al*, 1992). A six-week crossover trial using an enriched population design with 215 patients (Davis *et al*, 1992) demonstrated that patients treated with tacrine showed significantly less decline in cognitive function than did the placebo-treated group, as assessed by the Alzheimer's Disease Assessment Scale cognitive subscale. A 12-week parallel group design that included 273 patients demonstrated a significant cognitive improvement with tacrine (Farlow *et al*, 1992).

The side-effects of tacrine include nausea, abdominal distress, tachycardia, and liver toxicity. The liver damage noted with this agent is dose dependent and reversible upon discontinuation.

The tacrine data indicate that anticholinesterase therapy is likely to benefit a subgroup of patients with Alzheimer's disease. The lack of efficacy in some patients in these investigations may be due to underdosing. Improvement with tacrine appears to be dose dependent, with over 50% of patients improving at the highest doses (Farlow *et al*, 1992). The results from these large-scale studies contributed to tacrine being the first FDA-approved drug for the treatment of Alzheimer's disease.

At present, it is not possible to compare the various substances directly. Systematic comparative studies are rare. Understandably, methodological approaches, age of the patients and severity of symptoms differ between the studies. In particular, criteria regarding the inclusion of coincidental vascular pathology differ significantly between the USA and Germany. In many of the European studies, cases with vascular pathology were included.

One example of a study comparing two compounds and placebo is the nimodipine study by Kanowski *et al* (1988). Nimodipine (90 mg) as well as hydergine (4 mg) turned out to be more effective than placebo. Nimodipine was more effective than hydergine. All these differences were statistically significant. Total duration of the study was 12 weeks. Similar results have been reported by Fischhof *et al* (1990).

Nevertheless, scrutinising recent studies on piracetam, nimodipine and tacrine, the similarity of the results is striking. Most of these studies have been conducted with mild or moderate dementia. Mostly, the verum group improved by around 20%, regardless of the measures used (Kanowski *et al*, 1988; Farlow *et al*, 1992; Knapp *et al*, 1994).

Slowing of progression

Other studies have tried to slow the progression of dementia in long-term approaches. Such a study was conducted by Croisile *et al* (1993) with piracetam. The authors performed a one-year, double-blind, placebo-controlled, parallel-group study with a high dose of piracetam (8 g/day) in 33 out-patients with early probable Alzheimer's disease. Thirty subjects completed the one-year study. No improvement occurred in either group, but the study confirmed a significant slowing of the progression after high-dose and long-term treatment with piracetam. It appeared that piracetam had its main effect on memory performance. Semantic and implicit memory seemed better preserved than episodic memory.

Similar studies with similar results have been performed with tacrine. Knopman *et al* (1996) reported that tacrine in doses of over 80 mg/day was associated with a reduced likelihood of living in nursing homes after two years. At baseline, the out-patients were at least 50 years of age, and met the criteria for probable Alzheimer's disease, with MMSE scores between 10 and 26.

A methodologically weaker study with hydergine given over 15 months in patients suffering from an organic brain syndrome has also shown a slowing of disease progression (Kugler *et al*, 1978).

The idea of merely stabilising, not improving, a patient's psycho-pathology at a certain level has implications which have not yet been resolved. How can one prove therapeutic effects in a single patient and when should pharmacological therapy be started?

The slowing of disease progression with antidementia drugs seems to be convincing in studies involving group comparisons between verum and placebo. However, in clinical practice the criterion of slowing of disease progression is hardly applicable, in particular in the treatment of a single patient, since it cannot reliably be distinguished from non-response. For all antidementia drugs which are approved in Germany, improvement of symptoms has been demonstrated in short-term studies. Thus, *improvement* should be the pivotal point for the judgement of therapeutic efficacy in clinical practice. In view of the fact that antidementia drugs only slow disease progression, it is necessary to initiate therapy before full-blown dementia has developed. At present, this approach is of limited practicability, since there are unresolved diagnostic problems regarding the detection of the preclinical stages of dementia.

General therapeutic considerations

At present a number of pathogenetic models and hypotheses are discussed in Alzheimer's research:

 (a) amyloid (beta-A4) pathology;
 (b) tau pathology;
 (c) nerve cell and synaptic loss;
 (d) cholinergic deficit.

All these have somewhat different implications for the development of therapeutic strategies and the application of antidementia drugs.

Amyloid

Simplified, the histologically stainable and visible manifestations of beta-A4 deposits can be regarded as the so-called plaques. These lesions have been called senile plaques for decades, but are found in the presenium as well, although usually in small numbers. They consist of formed filamentous amyloid and – particularly in the early stages of their development – of non-structured beta-amyloid. Neurites within the plaques are of two major types. First, there are fusiform neurites that mainly contain paired helical filaments and some dense laminated bodies. The neurites of the second type are enlarged bulbous struc-tures that contain neurofilaments, laminated bodies, synaptic vesicles, mitochondria and lysosomes (Hansen *et al*, 1987; Terry *et al*, 1987). In addition, the abnormal plaques contain amyloid precurser protein, growth-associated protein (GAP 43), protein kinase C (Masliah *et al*, 1990), tau (Joachim *et al*, 1987), ubiquitin, brain spectrin, synaptophysin (Masliah *et al*, 1991), as well as a wide variety of neurotransmitters (e.g. substance P, acetylcholine) (Armstrong *et al*, 1989; Munoz, 1991). The presence of GAP 43 implies that at least some of the neurites are regenerative sprouts rather than degenerative swellings. The amyloid fibrils are immunoreactive with antibodies against beta-amyloid. Beta-amyloid is a cleavage product of a large amyloid precursor protein (APP). Beta-A4 is probably also deposited in the brain in a soluble, non-aggregated form.

In the neocortex, the soluble form 'matures' into amyloid fibres, eventually becoming fully fledged plaques. The transition of beta-A4 from a soluble to an aggregated form affects its bioactivity. Beta-A4 appears to increase the vulnerability of neurons to secondary challenges. In an aggregated state, beta-A4 induces direct apoptotic cell death (*in vitro*) (Cotman & Pike, 1994).

Beta-A4 is derived from processing of APP (Robakis *et al*, 1991). Amyloid precursor protein can undergo secretory processing that occurs within the domain of beta-A4, thereby precluding amyloid genesis. In contrast, lysosomal processing of APP can produce amyloidogenic fragments (Estus *et al*, 1992a,b).

Agents that interfere with beta-A4 production or deposition offer potential therapeutic strategies to alter the course of Alzheimer's dementia. A study using cell cultures suggested that the lysosomal inhibitor chloroquine may shunt APP to the secretase pathway, thereby leading to the release of non-amyloidogenic fragments (Caporaso *et al*, 1992). Numerous pharmaceutical companies have active drug-discovery programmes directed at inhibiting amyloidogenesis through specific protease inhibitors.

However, in the course of the disease, plaque pathology is well established before the full-blown picture of dementia is apparent (Gertz *et al*, unpublished; Bancher *et al*, 1996). Mann *et al* (1988) have shown that there is no increase in plaque numbers during the course of dementia. These results suggest that therapeutic interventions directed at the inhibition of beta-A4 assembly have to be started before clinical symptoms are present.

Tau

There can be little doubt that neurofibrillary tangles (NFTs) are critical lesions in Alzheimer's disease. In normal ageing there are often a few tangles in layer II of the entorhinal cortex and in the pyramidal cells of area CA1 of the hippocampus. They are, however, rare in the neocortex of normal elderly persons. Most cases of Alzheimer's disease have large numbers of tangles in the entorhinal and hippocampal areas and significant numbers in the neocortex as well (Gertz *et al*, 1996).

The tangle involves the cytoplasm of the larger neurons and only rarely affects small or medium ones. The lesions are made up of masses of intracellular argentophilic fibres. These bundles are flame shaped or globoid. Particularly in the entorhinal cortex and hippocampus, ghost tangles occur from neurons that have died. There is no doubt that tangle-bearing neurons die, but whether the tangles cause cell death is still an open question. Cell death in the neocortex occurs in significant degrees even in the absence of NFTs. Nevertheless, tangles are a suitable marker for regions affected by neuron loss in brain affected by Alzheimer's disease (Bondareff *et al*, 1989).

The principal biochemical component of the paired helical filaments (PHF) is assumed to be an abnormal phosphorylated tau protein. Some regard normal unaltered tau to constitute PHF. Tau protein accumulates to PHF. Because of the significant correlation between the amount of PHF in the neocortex and cognitive function, some believe that the inhibition of tau accumulation would be a crucial step in the development of an anti-Alzheimer drug.

The dynamics of tau accumulation seem to be different from that of beta-A4. Tangle accumulation seems to go along with cognitive disturbances. Cases with minimal dementia according to CAMDEX criteria (Roth *et al*, 1986) show a relative increase of tangle pathology compared with normal subjects. There is a further increase from minimal dementia to dementia (Gertz *et al*, unpublished; Bancher *et al*, 1996).

With regard to tau pathology, an intervention could be promising in very early stages of the disease.

Nerve cell loss and synaptic alterations

Diminished concentration of larger neurons is apparent in the neocortex of patients with Alzheimer's disease, even with superficial examination using oversight stains such as Nissl or haematoxylin and eosin. Studies by Hansen *et al* (1988) reveal a neocortical decrease of about 30% of large neurons.

Ball (1977) has shown severe loss of hippocampal pyramidal cells in Alzheimer's disease. Hyman *et al* enumerated a great loss of neurons from layer II of the entorhinal cortex. Several independent groups have shown a neuronal loss within the nucleus basalis of Meynert (Arendt *et al*, 1983, 1985; Gertz, 1995). The accompanying loss of synapses has been demonstrated by early electromicroscope and Golgi studies (Mehraein *et al*, 1975). The development of antibodies against synaptic proteins has made it possible to explore certain molecular alterations of the synapses in Alzheimer's disease. Work with the presynaptic marker synaptophysin and with brain spectrin has shown an average decrease of 45% in presynaptic terminals (Masliah *et al*, 1989; Brion *et al*, 1991).

The relation between cell death, and tau and beta-A4 accumulation is still unclear. Besides beta-A4 and tau pathology, other hypotheses have been discussed as potential causes of cell death in Alzheimer's disease, such as a lack of neurotrophic factor (NGF), glutamate-receptor-mediated excitotoxity, free radicals and others.

The therapeutic hypotheses for several nootropics, such as nimo-dipine, piracetam, and ginkgo are directed at inhibiting cell death. Theoretically, it is likely that however potent a compound is as a neuroprotective substance or in preventing cell death, recovery from symptoms can never be expected once dementia has become established.

Cholinergic deficit

Cortical cholinergic innervation is derived almost exclusively from the nucleus basalis of Meynert (Ch 1–Ch 4 cell group). Ch 1 and Ch 2 are suppliers of the hippocampus and constitute the so-called septo-hippocampal pathway. No local cholinergic neurons have been observed in the adult human cortex. Cholinergic axons exert their neurotransmitter effects through the mediation of nicotinic and muscarinic receptors. Molecular biological studies have identified five distinct nicotinic receptor subunits, which are thought to be combined in various configurations. Two or three different pharmacological types of nicotinic receptors seem to exist (Lindstrom *et al*, 1987; Giacobini, 1990). Their regional distribution in the brain is unclear. In addition, acetylcholine acts through five subtypes of muscarinic receptors. The subtypes M1 and M2 have received the greatest attention.

In 1976 Bowen *et al*, as well as Davis and Moloney, reported a major depletion of cortical cholinergic innervation. Their observation provided the foundation for what has come to be known as the cholinergic theory of Alzheimer's disease. It has been suggested that Alzheimer's is a disease of the cholinergic system, in the same way that Parkinson's disease is one of the dopaminergic system.

Nerve cell loss in the nucleus basalis of Meynert (NbM) amounted to more than 75% in one study (Whitehouse *et al*, 1982). Most groups found reductions of 40–60% (Arendt *et al*, 1983, 1985; Mann *et al*, 1984; Gertz *et al*, 1987). Studies using acetylcholinesterase (AchE) histochemistry or choline acetyltransferase immunohistochemistry have demonstrated a widespread loss of cortical cholinergic innervation. It has to be kept in mind that AchE is an enzyme of cholinoceptive neurons as well as of cholinergic axons.

Several studies reported no change in the density or affinity of the total population of cortical muscarinic receptors (e.g. Kellar *et al*, 1987). Others have shown a 20–30% reduction in receptor density, mainly in the hippocampus (e.g. Weinberger *et al*, 1991). Immuno-histochemical studies have confirmed the existence of a differential loss of nicotinic and muscarinic receptors in Alzheimer's disease. Studies comparing muscarinic and nicotinic receptors show no loss or only a small loss of muscarinic receptors and a significant loss of nicotinic receptors. Within the muscarinic receptor population, there seems to be little or no change in the total number of M1 receptors but a consistent decrease in M2 receptors (Jansen *et al*, 1990; Schroeder,

1991). M1 receptors are placed postsynaptically, M2 receptors mainly presynaptically.

The shining example of transmitter substitution in diseases of the central nervous system is Parkinson's disease. Treatment with direct or indirect dopaminergic agents leads to convincing therapeutic results. The pathological anatomy of Parkinson's disease has many similarities with Alzheimer's disease.

In general, transmitter substitution seems to be very promising as long as postsynaptic structures are available. In Alzheimer's disease, this seems to be the case. With regard to the course of the disease, transmitter substitution even seems to work when applied very late, and until then it should work whenever it is applied. Its effects should be more or less independent of the stage of the disease.

Given the consistency of the predominantly presynaptic cholinergic deficit it is surprising that cholinergic therapy does not do better. Its efficacy must be regarded as similar to that of non-specific empirical treatment schemes. It is difficult to understand why – with the cholinergic deficit being so obvious in Alzheimer's disease – cholinergic substitution has so little effect.

Several reasons can be discussed. The cholinergic system of cortical innervation is probably a very complicated one. The nigrostriatal system, for example, consists at least partly of free axonal endings which release dopamine into the extracellular space to its receptors. This may be the reason why the nigrostriatal dopaminergic system is so effectively accessible for L-dopa substitution in Parkinson's disease. On the other hand, cholinergic transmission acts via synapses. It has been shown that single hippocampal neurons have symmetric and asymmetric cholinergic synapses. Thus, acetylcholine seems to have inhibiting and excitatory properties on one single neuron.

Synaptic plasticity, which has been extensively examined in experimental animals, could be another explanation. Within the molecular layer of the fascia dentata the principal afferent systems terminate within adjacent but non-overlapping laminae (Cotman *et al*, 1981). The cholinergic septo-hippocampal fibres form a dense supragranular innervation immediately above the granular cell layer (Mosko *et al*, 1973). There is evidence that granular cells are excited by cholinergic boutons mainly located on apical dendrites near the soma (Fonnum, 1970).

Disappearance of dendritic spines is shown to follow presynaptic interruption. In cases of specific afferents, spines along only a portion of the dendrites are affected. One might therefore have expected that the reduction of nerve cells in CA_1 and CA_2 which occurs in Alzheimer's disease would lead to a pronounced reduction of spines in that part of the dendrites where cholinergic afferents form synapses, that is, in the most proximal part (Gertz *et al*, 1987). But in this dendritic region, spine density actually remains unchanged.

A possible explanation for these findings might be found in compensatory sprouting of surviving axons. It is known that terminals lost through injury to one of its afferents are replaced in part or wholly by sprouting of undamaged input (Cotman *et al*, 1981). Thus, in Alzheimer's disease replacement of the lost cholinergic afferents could be possible. Two possible mechanisms are suggested.

First, the remaining cholinergic neurons of CA_1 and CA_2 sprout collaterally to maintain the number of synapses with the granular cells to the fascia dentata. This is in agreement with the findings that cholinergic muscarinic receptors do not change in number in Alzheimer's disease (Lang & Henke, 1983). On the other hand, the loss of the presynaptic marker ChAT in Alzheimer's disease may indicate a qualitative change in the axon terminals rather than a loss of synapses.

Second, decreased cholinergic input to the hippocampus may be substituted by a monoaminergic one, as in experimental animals (Crutcher *et al*, 1981). This suggestion is supported by the finding that in Alzheimer's disease, monoamine oxidase-B activity is significantly increased in the hippocampus (Adolfson *et al*, 1980). A take-over of cholinergic synapses by other transmitter systems could explain the limited efficacy of cholinomimetics in Alzheimer's disease.

Conclusion

It can be concluded that our knowledge of the aetiology and the pathogenesis of dementing disorders in later life has important implications for therapeutic intervention in these diseases.

References

ADOLFSON, R., GOTTFRIES, C. G., ORLAND, L., *et al* (1980) Increased activity of brain and platelet monoamine oxidase in dementia of Alzheimer type. *Life Sciences*, **27**, 1029–1034.

ARENDT, T., BIGL, V., ARENDT, A., *et al* (1983) Loss of neurons in the nucleus basalis of Meynert in Alzheimer's disease, paralysis agitans and Korsakoff's disease. *Acta Neuropathologica*, **61**, 101–108.

——, ——, TENNSTEDT, A., *et al* (1985) Neuronal loss in different parts of the nucleus basalis is related to neuritic plaque formation in cortical target areas in Alzheimer's disease. *Neuroscience*, **14**, 1–14.

ARMSTRONG, D. M., BENZING, W. C., EVANS, J., *et al* (1989) Substance P and somatostatin coexist within neuritic plaques: implication for the pathogenesis of Alzheimer's disease. *Neuroscience*, **31**, 663–671.

BALL, M. J. (1977) Neuronal loss, neurofibrillary tangles and granulovacuolar degeneration in the hippocampus with aging and dementia. A quantitative study. *Acta Neuropathologica*, **37**, 111–118.

BANCHER, C., JELLINGER, K., LASSMAN, H., *et al* (1996) Correlations between mental state and quantitative neuropathology in the Vienna Longitudinal Study on Dementia. *European Archives of Psychiatry and Clinical Neurosciences*, **246**, 137–146.

BENESOVA, O., PAVLIK, A., YOSHIDA, H., *et al* (1982) *Advances in Pharmacology and Therapeutics. Vol. 5. Toxicology and Experimental Models*, pp. 199–210. Oxford: Pergamon Press.

BENZI, G., DE BERNADI, M., MANZO, L., *et al* (1972) Effect of lysergide and nicergoline on glucose metabolism investigated on the dog brain isolated in situ. *Journal of Pharmaceutical Sciences*, **61**, 348–352.

——, ARRIGONI, E., PASTORIS, O., *et al* (1979) Effect of some drugs on cerebral energy state during and after hypoxia and complete or incomplete ischemia. *Biochemical Pharmacology*, **28**, 435–439.

BERDE, B. (1972) Some new vascular and biochemical aspects of the mechanism of action of ergot compounds. *Headache*, **11**, 139–147.

BERTONI-FREDDARI, C., GIULI, C., PIERI, C., *et al* (1987) The effect of chronic hydergine treatment on the plasticity of synaptic junctions in the dentate gyrus of aged rats. *Journal of Gerontology*, **42**, 482–486.

BOISMARE, F. & LORENZO, J. (1975) Study of the protection afforded by nicergoline against the effects of cerebral ischemia in the cat. *Arzneimittelforschung*, **25**, 410–413.

BONDAREFF, W., MOUNTJOY, C. Q., ROTH, M. & HAUSER, D. L. (1989) Neurofibrillary degeneration and neuronal loss in Alzheimer´s disease. *Neurobiology of Aging*, **10**, 709–715.

BOWEN, D. M., SMITH, C. B., WHITE, P. & DAVISON, A. N. (1976) Neurotransmitter-related enzymes and indices of hypoxia in senile dementia and other abiotrophies. *Brain*, **99**, 459–496.

BRAQUET, P. & HOSFORD, D. (1991) Ethnopharmacology and development of natural PAF antagonists as therapeutic agents. *Journal of Ethnopharmacology*, **32**, 135–139.

BRION, J. P., COUCK, A. M., BRUCE, M., *et al* (1991) Synaptophysin and chromogranin A immunoreactivities in senile plaques of Alzheimer's disease. *Brain Research*, **539**, 143–150.

CAPORASO, G. L., GANCY, S. E., BUXBAUM, J. D., *et al* (1992) Chloroquine inhibits intracellular degradation but not secretion of Alzheimer B/A4 amyloid precursor protein. *Proceedings of the National Academy of Sciences, USA*, **89**, 2252–2256.

CHATELLIER, G. & LACOMBLEZ, L., ON BEHALF OF GROUPE FRANCAIS D'ETUDE DE LA TETRAHYDRO-AMINOACRIDINE (1990) Tacrine (tetrahydroaminoacridine; THA) and lecithin in senile dementia of the Alzheimer's type: a multi-center trial. *British Medical Journal*, **300**, 495–499.

CHENG, B. & MATTSON, M. P. (1992) Glucose deprivation elicits neurofibrillary tangle-like antigenic changes in hippocampal neurons: prevention by NGF and bFGF. *Experimental Neurology*, **117**, 114–123.

CHUNG, K. F., DENT, G., MCCUSKER, M., *et al* (1987) Effect of a ginkgolide mixture (BN 52063) in antagonising skin and platelet responses to platelet activating factor in man. *Lancet*, **i**, 248–251.

CLOSSE, A., FRICK, W., DRAVID, A., *et al* (1984) Classification of drugs according to receptor profiles. *Naunyn Schmiedebergs Archives of Pharmacology*, **237**, 95–101.

COTMAN, C. W. & PIKE, C. J. (1994) ß-Amyloid and its contributions to neurodegeneration in Alzheimer's disease. In *Alzheimer Disease* (eds R. D. Terry, R. Katzmann & K. L. Bick), pp. 305–315. New York: Raven Press.

——, LEWIS, E. R. & HAND, D. (1981) The critical afferent theory: a mechanism to account for septohippocampal development and plasticity. In *Lesion-Induced Neuronal Plasticity in Sensorimotor Systems* (eds H. Flohr & W. Precht), pp. 13–26. Berlin: Springer.

CROISILE, B., TRILLET, M., FONDARAI, J., *et al* (1993) Long-term and high-dose piracetam treatment of Alzheimer's disease. *Neurology*, **43**, 301–305.

CRUTCHER, K. A., BROTHERS, L. & DAVIS, J. N. (1981) Sympathetic noradrenergic sprouting in response to central cholinergic denervation: a histochemical study of neuronal sprouting in the rat hippocampal formation. *Brain Research*, **210**, 115–128.

DAVIS, P. & MALONEY, A. J. F. (1976) Selective loss of central cholinergic neurons in Alzheimer's disease. *Lancet*, *ii*, 1403.

DAVIS, K. L., THAL, L. J., GAMZU, E., *et al* (1992) Tacrine in patients with Alzheimer's disease: a double blind placebo controlled multicenter study. *New England Journal of Medicine*, **327**, 1374–1379.

DE FEUDIS, F. G. (1991) *Ginkgo Biloba Extract (Egb 761): Pharmacological Activities and Clinical Applications*, pp. 79–84. Paris: Editions Scientifiques Elsevier.

DEYO, R. A., STRAUBE, K. T. & DISTERHOFT, J. F. (1989) Nimodipine facilitates associated learning in aging rabbits. *Science*, **243**, 809–811.

DRAVID, A. R. & HIESTAND, P. (1985) Deficit des activites enzymatiques cholinergiques dans les zones septo-temporales de l´hyppocampe de rat ageet dans le cerveau anterieur de souris agée. Action du traitment par l´hydergine. *Journal of Pharmacology*, **16** (suppl. 3), 29–37.

EAGGER, S., MORANT, N., LEVY, R. & SAHAKIAN, B. (1992) Tacrine in Alzheimer's disease: time course of changes in cognitive function and practice effects. *British Journal of Psychiatry*, **160**, 36–40.

ESTUS, S., GOLDE, T. & KUNISHITA, T., *et al* (1992a) Potentially amyloidogenic, carboxyl-terminal derivatives of the amyloid protein precursor. *Science*, **155**, 726–730.

——, & YOUNKIN, S. G., *et al* (1992b) Normal processing of the Alzheimer's disease amyloid beta protein presursor generates potentially amyloidogenic carboxyl-terminal derivatives. *Annals of the New York Academy of Sciences*, **31**, 138–148.

FARLOW, M., GRACON, S. I., HERSHEY, L. A., *et al* (1992) A controlled trial of tacrine in Alzheimer's disease. *Journal of the American Medical Association*, **268**, 2523–2529.

FISCHHOF, P. K., RÜTHER, E., WAGNER, G. & LITSCHAUER, G. (1990) Therapieergebnisse mit Nimodipin bei primär degenerativer Demenz und Multiinfarktdemenz. *Zeitschrift für Geriatrie*, **3**, 320–327.

FLÜCKINGER, E. & BALTHASAR, H. U. (1967) Dihydroergocristin: Unterschiedliche Wirkungen an venösem und arteriellem Gewebe. *Arzneimittelforschung*, **17**, 6–9.

FONNUM, F. (1970) Topographical and subcellular localization of choline acetyltransferase in rat hippocampal region. *Journal of Neurochemistry*, **17**, 1029–1037.

GAUTHIER, S., BOUCHARD, R., LAMONTAGNE, A., *et al* (1990) Tetrahydroaminoacridine–lecithin combination treatment in patients with intermediate stage Alzheimer's disease. *New England Journal of Medicine*, **322**, 1272–1276.

GERTZ, H. J. (1995) Nucleus basalis of Meynert nerve cell number in human fetal brains, in adults, and in patients suffering from dementia of Alzheimer's type. In *Treating Alzheimer's and Other Dementias* (eds M. Bergener & S. I. Finkel), pp. 3–11. Berlin: Springer.

—— (1997) Nootropika. In *Lehrbuch der Gerontopsychiatrie* (ed. H. Förstl), pp. 163–171. Stuttgart: Enke Verlag.

——, CERVOS-NAVARRO, J. & EWALD, V. (1987) The septo-hippocampal pathway in patients suffering from senile dementia of Alzheimer's type. Evidence for neuronal plasticity? *Neuroscience Letters*, **76**, 228–232.

——, XUEREB, J. H., HUPPERT, F. A., *et al* (1996) The relationship between clinical dementia and neuropathological staging (Braak) in a very elderly community sample. *European Archives of Psychiatry and Clinical Neurosciences*, **246**, 132–136.

GIACOBINE, E. (1990) Cholinergic receptors in human brain: effects of aging in Alzheimer's disease. *Journal of Neuroscience*, **27**, 548–560.

GIURGIA, C. (1976) Piracetam: nootropic pharmacology of neurointegrative activity. *Current Developments in Psychopharmacology*, **3**, 223–273.

GOLDSTEIN, M., LEW, J. Y., HATA, F. & LIEBERMAN, A. (1978) Binding interactions of ergot alkaloids with monoaminergic receptors in the brain. *Gerontology*, **24** (suppl. 1), 76–85.

GREINER, H. E., HAASE, A. F. & SEYFRIED, C. A. (1988) Neurochemical studies on the mechanism of action of pyritinol. *Pharmacopsychiatry*, **21**, 26–32 (special issue).

HAKIM, A. M., EVANS, A. C., BERGER, L., et al (1989) The effect of nimodipine on the evolution of human cerebral infarction studied by PET. *Journal of Cerebral Blood Flow and Metabolism*, **9**, 523–534.

HANSEN, L. A., ARMSTRONG, D. M. & TERRY, R. D. (1987) An immunohistochemical quantification of fibrous astrocytes in the aging human cerebral cortex. *Neurology of Aging*, **8**, 1–6.

——, DE THERESA, R., DAVIES, P. & TERRY R. D. (1988) Neocortical morphometry, lesion counts, and choline acetyltransferase levels in the age spectrum of Alzheimer's disease. *Neurology*, **38**, 48–54.

HERRSCHAFT, H. (1978) Die Wirkung von Pyritinol auf die Gehirndurchblutung des Menschen. *Münch Medizin Wochenschrift*, **120**, 1263–1268.

HOFFMEISTER, F., BENZ, U., HEISE, A., et al (1982) Behavioral effects of nimodipine in animals. *Arzneimittelforschung/Drug Research*, **32**, 347–360.

IHL, R., MAURER, K., DIERKS, T. & WANNENMACHER, W. (1988) Effects of pyritinol on the distributation of electrical brain activity. *Pharmacopsychiatry*, **21**, 343–345.

JANSEN, K. L., FAULL, R. L. DRAGUNOW, M., et al (1990) Alzheimer's disease: changes in hippocampal N-methyl-D-aspartate, quisqualte, neurotensin, adenosine, benzodiazepine, serotonin and opioid receptors – an autoradiographic study. *Neuroscience*, **39**, 613–627.

JOACHIM, C. L., MORRIS, J. H., SELKOE, D. J. & KOSIK, K. S. (1987) Tau epitopes are incorporated into a range of lesions in Alzheimer's disease. *Journal of Neuropathology and Experimental Neurology*, **46**, 611–622.

JUNG, F., MROWIETZ, C., KIESEWETTER, H. & WENZEL, E. (1990) Effect of Ginkgo biloba on fluidity of blood and peripheral microcirculation in volunteers. *Arzneimittelforschung*, **40**, 589–593.

KANIG, K. (1974) Zum Einfluß enzephalotroper Pharmaka auf die Nukleinsäurestoffwechsel des Gehirns. *Arzneimittelforschung*, **24**, 1093–1095.

KANOWSKI, S., FISCHHOF, P., HIERSEMENZEL, H., et al (1988) Wirksam-keitsnachweis von Nootropika am Beispiel von Nimodipin – ein Beitrag zur Entwicklung geeigneter klinischer Prüfmodelle. *Zeitschrift für Gerontopsychologie und -psychiatrie*, **1**, 35–44.

KELLAR, K. J., WHITEHOUSE, P. J., MARTINO-BARROWS, A. M., et al (1987) Muscarinic and nicotinic cholinergic binding sites in Alzheimer's disease cerebral cortex. *Brain Research*, **436**, 62–68.

KLEIJNEN, J. & KNIPSCHILD, P. (1992) Ginkgo biloba. *Lancet*, **340**, 1136–1139.

KNAPP, M. J., KNOPMAN, D. S. SOLOMON, P. R., et al, FOR THE TACRINE STUDY GROUP (1994) A 30-week randomized controlled trial of high-dose tacrine in patients with Alzheimer's disease. *Journal of the American Medical Association*, **271**, 985–991.

KNOPMAN, D., SCHNEIDER, L., DAVIS, K., et al (1996) Effects on nursing home placement and mortality. *Neurology*, **47**, 166–177.

KÖLTRINGER, P., EBER, O., LIND, P., et al (1989) Mikrozirkulation und Viskoelastizität des Vollblutes unter Ginko-biloba-extrakt. Eine plazebokontrollierte, randomisierte Doppelblind-Studie. *Perfusion*, **1**, 28–30.

KUGLER, J., OSWALD, W. D., HERZFELD, U., et al (1978) Langzeit-therapie altersbedingter Insuffizienzerscheinungen des Gehirns. *Medizin Wochenschrift*, **103**, 456–462.

LANG, W. & HENKE, H. (1983) Cholinergic receptor binding and autoradiography in brains of non-neurological and senile dementia of Alzheimer-type patients. *Brain Research*, **267**, 271–280.

LE PONCIN-LAFITTE, M., GROSDEMOUGE, G., DUTERTE, D. & RAPIN, J. R. (1984) Simultaneous study of haemodynamic, metabolic and behavioural sequelae in a model of cerebral ischaemia in aged rats: effects of nicergoline. *Gerontology*, **30**, 109–119.

——, RAPIN, J. R. & DUTERTE, D. (1985) Learning and cholinergic neurotransmission in old animals: the effect of hydergine. *Journal of Pharmacology, Paris*, **16** (suppl. 3), 57–63.

LINDSTROM, J., SCHOEPFER, R. & WHITING, P. (1987) Molecular studies of the neuronal nicotinic acetylcholine receptor family. *Molecular Neurobiology*, **1**, 281–337.

MAIOLO, A. T., BIANCHI PORRO, G., *et al* (1972) Effects de la nicergoline sur l'thémodynamique cérébrale et la metabolisme cérébral dans l'hypertension artérielle essentielle et l'arteriosclerose. *Clinical Thérapie*, **62**, 239–252.

MANN, D. M. A., YATES, P. O. & MARCYNIUK, B. (1984) Changes in nerve cells of the nucleus basalis of Meynert in Alzheimer's disease and their relationship to ageing and to accumulation of lipofuscin pigment. *Mechanical Ageing Devices*, **25**, 189–204.

——, MARCYNIUK, B., YATES, P. O., *et al* (1988) The progression of the pathological changes of Alzheimer's disease in frontal and temporal neocortex examined both at biopsy and at autopsy. *Neuropathology and Applied Neurobiology*, **14**, 177–195.

MARSTON, H. M., MARTIN, K. J. & ROBBINS, T. W. (1987) Effects of the chronic administration of pyrithioxine on behaviour and cholinergic function of young and aged rats. *Journal of Psychopharmacology*, **1**, 237–243.

MARTIN, K. J. & WIDDOWSON, L. (1989) The role of membrane phospholipids in acetylcholine synthesis: observations with pyritinol. In *Pharmacological Interventions of Central Cholinergic Mechanisms in Senile Dementia (Alzheimer's Disease)* (eds H. Kewitz, T. Thomsen & H. Bickel), pp. 129–132. München: Zuckschwerdt.

MASLIAH, E., TERRY, R. D., DE TERESA, R. M. & HANSEN, L. A. (1989) Immunohistochemical quantification of the synapse-related protein synaptophysin in Alzheimer disease. *Neuroscience Letters*, **103**, 234–239.

——, COLE, G., SHIMOHAMA, S., *et al* (1990) Differential involvement of protein kinase C isozymes in Alzheimer's disease. *Journal of Neuroscience*, **10**, 2113–2124.

——, TERRY, R. D., ALFORD, M., *et al* (1991) Cortical and subcortical patterns of synaptophysin-like immunoreactivity in Alzheimer disease. *American Journal of Pathology*, **138**, 235–246.

MEHRAEIN, P., YAMADA, M. & TARNOWSKA-DZIDUSZKO, E. (1975) Quantitative study on dendrites and dendritic spines in Alzheimer's disease and senile dementia. *Advances in Neurology*, **12**, 453–458.

MEYER, F. B., ANDERSON, R. E., YAKSCH, T. L. & SUNDT, T. M. (1986) Effect of nimodipine on intracellular brain pH, cortical blood flow and EEG in experimental focal cerebral ischemia. *Journal of Neurosurgery*, **64**, 617–626.

MOSKO, S., LYNCH, G. & COTMAN, C. W. (1973) The distribution of septal projections to the hippocampus of the rat. *Journal of Comparative Neurology*, **152**, 163–174.

MUBRIN, Z., KNEZEVIC, S., SPILICH, G., *et al* (1989) Normalization of rCBF pattern in senile dementia of Alzheimer's type. *Psychiatry Research*, **29**, 303–306.

MÜLLER, W. E. (1988) Veränderung zentraler Neurorezeptoren unter besonderer Berücksichtigung der m-Cholinrezeptoren, ein Aspekt des biologischen Alterns. In *Wirkungen und Wirksamkeit von Nootropika* (ed. H. Helmchen), pp. 42–61. Berlin: Springer.

MUNOZ, D. G. (1991) Chromogranin A-like immunoreactive neurites are major constituents of senile plaques. *Laboratory Investigations*, **64**, 826–832.

NYBÄCK, H., WIESEL, F.-A. & SKETT, P. (1979) Effects of piracetam on brain monoamine metabolism and serum prolactin levels in the rat. *Psychopharmacology*, **61**, 235–238.

PAVLIK, A. & PILAR, J. (1989) Protection of cell proteins against free radical attack by nootropic drugs: scavenger effect of pyritinol confirmed by electron spin resonance spectroscopy. *Neuropharmacology*, **28**, 557–561.

PINCEMAIL, J., DUPUIS, M., NASR, C., *et al* (1989) Superoxide anion scavenging effect and superoxide dismutase activity of Ginkgo biloba extract. *Experientia*, **45**, 708–712.

ROBAK, J. & GRYGLEWSKI, R. J. (1988) Flavonoids are scavengers of superoxide anions. *Biochemical Pharmacology*, **37**, 837–841.

ROBAKIS, N. K. (1994) ß-Amyloid and amyloid precursor protein. In *Alzheimer Disease* (eds R. D. Terry, R. Katzmann & K. L. Bick), pp. 317–326. New York: Raven Press.

——, ANDERSON, J. P., REFOLO, L. M., *et al* (1991) Expression of the Alzheimer amyloid precursor in brain tissue and effects of NGF and EGF on its metabolism. *Clinical Neuropharmacology*, **14** (suppl.), S15–S23.

ROSSI, A. C., CARFAGNA, N., CACCIA, C., *et al* (1988) Neurochemical effects of ergoline derivatives. In *Ergot Alkaloids and Aging Brain: An Update on Nicergoline. Proceedings from an International Symposium, Rome, 1987* (eds J. Kugler & A. Agnoli) pp. 16–24. Rome: Excerpta Medica.

ROTH, M., TYM, E., MOUNTJOY, C. Q., *et al* (1986) CAMDEX: a standardised instrument for the diagnosis of mental disorder in the elderly with special reference to the early detection of dementia. *British Journal of Psychiatry*, **149**, 698–709.

SCHMIDLI, J., SANTILLAN, G. G., SAEED, M., *et al* (1985) The effect of nimodipine, a calcium antagonist, on intracortical arterioles in the cat brain. *Current Therapy Research*, **38**, 94–103.

SCHROEDER, H. (1991) Cellular distribution and expression of cortical acetylcholine receptors in aging and Alzheimer´s disease. *Annals of the New York Academy of Science*, **640**, 189–192.

SHINTOMI, K., YOSHIMOTO, K., OGWA, Y., *et al* (1987) Pharmacological effects of nicergoline and its metabolites, decomposition products and impurities in animals. *Journal of Pharmacobiodynamics*, **10**, 35–48.

TAKAYASU, I. M., BASETT, J. E. & DACEY, R. G. (1988) Effects of calcium antagonists on intracerebral penetrating arterioles in the rat. *Journal of Neurosurgery*, **69**, 104–109.

TERRY, R. D., DE TERESA, R. & HANSEN, L. A. (1987) Neocortical cell counts in normal human adult aging. *Annals of Neurology*, **21**, 530–539.

TOWART, R. & KAZDA, S. (1985) Effects of calcium antagonist nimodipine on isolated cerebral vessels. In *Nimodipine: pharmacological and clinical properties* (eds E. Betz, K. Deck & F. Hoffmeister) pp. 147–161. New York/Stuttgart: Schattauer.

VAN ZWIETEN, P. A. (1986) Differentiation of calcium entry blockers into calcium channel blockers and calcium overload blockers. *European Neurology*, **25** (suppl. 1), 57–67.

WEIL, C. (1988) *Hydergine: Pharmacologic and Clinic Facts.* New York: Springer.

WEINBERGER, D. R., GIBSON, R., COPPOLA, R., *et al* (1991) The distribution of cerebral muscarinic acetylcholine in vivo in patients with dementia. A controlled study with 123IQNB and single proton emission computed tomography. *Archives of Neurology*, **48**, 169–176.

WENNMALM, A. (1971) Quantitative evaluation of release and reuptake of adrenergic transmitter in the rabbit heart. *Acta Physiologica Scandinavica*, **82**, 532–538.

WHITEHOUSE, P. J., PRICE, D. L., STRUBLE, R. G., *et al* (1982) Alzheimer's disease and senile dementia: loss of neurons in the basal forebrain. *Science*, **215**, 1237–1239.

WIEDING, J. U., ARGYRAKIS, A. & SCHÖNLE, P. (1987) Erythrozytenverformbarkeit und -aggregation. Beeinflussung durch Pyritinol bei Patienten mit akuter zerebraler Ischämie. *Forschrift für Medizin*, **105**, 157–158.

WIERNSPERGER, N., GYGAX, P. & DANZEISEN, M. (1978) Cortical pO distribution during oligemic hypotension and its pharmacological modifications. *Arzneimittelforschung*, **28**, 768–770.

WRIGHT, A. M., MORREHEAD, M., & WELSH, J. H. (1962) Vasodilators in senile dementias. *British Journal of Pharmacology*, **18**, 440–450.

WURTMANN, R. J., MAGIL, D. C. & REINSTEIN, D. K. (1981) Piracetam diminishes hippocampal acetylcholine levels in rats. *Life Sciences*, **28**, 1091–1093.

ZANG, J. & CHENG, X. (1986) Effects of three cerebral vasodilators – nimodipine, nifedipine and vincamine on chemical-induced amnesia in rodents. *Acta Pharmalogica Sinica*, **21**, 731–735.

Index

Compiled by LINDA M. ENGLISH